SINGERS, HEROES, AND
GODS IN THE *ODYSSEY*

A volume in the series

MYTH AND POETICS

edited by GREGORY NAGY

A full list of titles in the series appears at the end of the book.

SINGERS, HEROES, AND GODS IN THE *ODYSSEY*

CHARLES SEGAL

CORNELL UNIVERSITY PRESS

ITHACA AND LONDON

First published 1994 by Cornell University Press
First printing, Cornell Paperbacks, 2001

Printed in the United States of America

Library of Congress Cataloging-in-Publication Data
Segal, Charles, 1936–
    Singers, heroes, and gods in the Odyssey / Charles Segal.
      p.   cm. — (Myth and poetics)
    Includes bibliographical references (p.   ) and index.
    ISBN 0–8014–3041–0 (cloth : alk. paper)
    ISBN 0–8014–8726–9 (pbk. : alk. paper)
    1. Homer. Odyssey.   2. Epic poetry, Greek—History and criticism.
  3. Odysseus (Greek mythology) in literature.   4. Bards and bardism
in literature.   5. Gods, Greek, in literature.   6. Heroes in
literature. I. Title. II. Series.
PA4167.S44   1994
883'.01—dc20   94-25437

Cloth printing   10 9 8 7 6 5 4 3 2 1
Paperback printing   10 9 8 7 6 5 4 3 2 1

For Nancy
ὁμοφρονεούσῃ νοήμασιν

and for Cora
τυτθῇ ἐούσῃ

Contents

Foreword

GREGORY NAGY

There are many books about the myths and many about the poetics of the Homeric *Odyssey* but few that successfully treat both topics together. Such a book is Charles Segal's *Singers, Heroes, and Gods in the "Odyssey,"* a particularly distinguished entry in the Myth and Poetics series. Segal shows how myth and poetics are interwoven in the very fabric of this epic, and how these interweavings help us to appreciate the *Odyssey* as an epic in its own rights, defining itself through its distinctness from the *Iliad*.

Anyone who tries to arrive at a universalizing definition of epic finds it easy to forget altogether about the *Odyssey* and to think only of the *Iliad*. A celebrated essay by Mikhail Bakhtin, "Epic and Novel," provides a construct of "epic" that may indeed fit the *Iliad* admirably—but it fits *only* the *Iliad*. The *Odyssey* comes closer to Bakhtin's construct of the "novel." And yet, the *Odyssey* is epic as well, and its essence as epic depends on its opposition to the *Iliad*—much as Bakhtin's model of the novel depends on its opposition to his model of epic.

If it is the poetic destiny of Achilles to become the main hero of "the tale of Troy"—which is, after all, the literal meaning of the *Iliad*—then the destiny of Odysseus as the main hero of his own epic must go beyond the *Iliad*, beyond the tale of Troy. There are ironies here, since myth insists that Troy was destroyed not by the might of Achilles but by the guile of Odysseus, inventor of the Wooden Horse. Still, the tale of Troy, as the epic of the *Iliad*, belongs not to Odysseus but to Achilles. This is a matter of poetics as well as myth. Thus the *kleos* or "epic glory" reserved for Achilles in the *Iliad* cannot be the same song as the *kleos* Odysseus must achieve in his own epic. Odysseus must bypass the Sirens, who are quoted by the epic as saying (or singing) explicitly that

ix

their repertoire includes all the tales to be told about Troy. If Odysseus gives in to the temptation to dwell on his glory days in the old tales of Troy, he will fail to achieve his own new tale in the making, his own *Odyssey*. This too is a matter of poetics as well as myth.

To be the hero of the *Odyssey* is to *become* a hero of a different kind of epic, an odyssey—in the mythical sense of a vision quest, a journey of a soul, a search for the self. The process of becoming is the central concern of the first part of Segal's book. The poetics of such an odyssey are also interwoven with myths of the seer, the shaman, the trickster. In this different kind of epic, we are invited to discover complexities not made explicit in the *Iliad*. No longer is the essence of the hero fatalistically bound to his status as warrior. No longer is it possible to assume that the will of the gods is actually the same thing as the plot of epic, as the *Iliad* seems to claim. No longer can we view the poet himself as the monolithic spokesman of epic truths. Suddenly our vision is refracted, as the *Odyssey* begins to reveal to us through its own storytelling a variety of different poets belonging to different social categories. We can find striking analogies in other cultures: medieval Ireland, for example, had a highly sophisticated system of gradation, categorizing poets—who were legally artisans—by rank, function, training, artform. In the *Odyssey* as well, poets run the gamut in social status: they can be rivals of master artisans, of beggars, even of kings. And they all, including the would-be poet of his own adventures, Odysseus himself, seem to be saying different things in different situations.

The ambiguities of the Homeric *Odyssey*—especially the moral ones—must be understood in their literary, cultural, and even economic contexts. Only in this way can we learn to appreciate the design of this epic as epic. As Segal makes clear, this design is no accident, no spontaneous combustion of primitive genius. The poetics of the *Odyssey* are not the retrospective formulations of later ages that somehow finally succeeded in systematizing the creative instincts of a prototypical poetic soul whom we must imagine was as yet unaware of poetics. Rather, they are the living and working poetics of an art form realized in the epic itself.

The *Odyssey* is left open-ended as its narrative draws to a close, but even this open-endedness has its purpose. The gap between humankind and the gods, so keenly felt in the *Iliad*, may have become even more vast in the *Odyssey*, but this vastness too has its purpose. In this way, the *Odyssey* makes room for the ever-expanding horizons of what Segal calls its "landscape of imagination." It makes room for a world of myths that will test the very limits of epic.

Preface

This volume represents some thirty years of teaching and writing about the *Odyssey*. Seven of the ten chapters have been previously published, but all of them have been revised for this volume. Although I have not changed the substance of the original publications, I have recast, abbreviated, or expanded some sections and added some new points of detail. I have divided the study of the Phaeacians, originally published as a single article, into two parts (Chapters 2–3) to bring it closer to the scale of the other chapters. I originally wrote the fourth chapter as a sequel to my study of the Phaeacians, and I am happy to have its thematic affinities here restored. Chapter 7 was originally delivered at the annual meeting of the American Philological Association in December 1992 and is here published for the first time. Chapter 8 is also previously unpublished, although an earlier version of the last section will appear in a Festschrift for Giovanni Tarditi.

While I have tried to make these studies more accessible to a general audience, I have not attempted to disguise the differences in approach between essays that were written, in some cases, thirty years apart. Readers will doubtless be struck by the shift from the more individual-centered psychological orientation of Chapters 2–4 to the social and anthropological approaches of Chapters 6–8 and may find it interesting to observe how a single interpreter's work may undergo changes in method and emphasis over a period of scholarly activity that moves from New Criticism to structuralism and poststructuralism. There are continuities too, however, as the relation between Chapter 10 and Chapters 2–4 will show.

It is a testimony to the popularity and importance of the *Odyssey* that the secondary literature continues to increase at an extraordinary rate. In the case of the older essays (Chapters 2–5), I have added a few references to major more recent discussions and some cross-references to the later chapters, but neither here nor in the later essays do I attempt bibliographical completeness. To make the book accessible to the wide readership that the *Odyssey* has always had and deserved, I have translated all the Greek (in two instances borrowing from the fine poetic versions of Robert Fitzgerald and Richmond Lattimore respectively) and transliterated individual words. Translations from other languages are also my own unless otherwise noted. In my translations I try to stay reasonably close to the original; I make no claim to literary merit.

These essays could not have been written without the opportunities for study and research made possible, at different times, by the American Academy in Rome, the National Endowment for the Humanities, the Center for Advanced Study in Behavioral Sciences, and the National Humanities Center, where the volume received its final form during my fellowship in 1993–94. To all these institutions I express my deep thanks. I would like to recall the original dedication of Chapter 5 to the memory of Gabriel Germain, whom I had the pleasure of meeting a few years before his death, and the influential work of Bruno Gentili (for whose Festschrift Chapter 9 was originally written) on oral poetics, performance, and the continuities between epic and later folk traditions. I thank the many students and colleagues from whom I have learned about the *Odyssey* over the years and also the friends and colleagues who have given advice, comments, and copies of their publications. I particularly thank Joseph Russo of Haverford College, Stephen Scully of Boston University, and William F. Wyatt, Jr., of Brown University for memorable Homeric conversations. To Gregory Nagy I owe a particular debt of gratitude for steady, expert, and enthusiastic guidance in the shaping of the volume. It has been a pleasure, once again, to work with Bernhard Kendler of Cornell University Press, whom I thank for useful and timely suggestions. I am indebted to the Press's anonymous reader for helpful comments and to Nancy Malone for meticulous copyediting. I thank P. Lowell Bowditch and Jessica Eichelburg for help in the preparation of the manuscript.

I thank the following editors and journals for permission to use, in revised form, material that originally appeared in their publications:

Chapter 1, Introduction: Pages 12–14 of my essay "Classics and Comparative Literature," *Materiali e Discussioni per l'Analisi dei Testi Classici* 13 (1985): 9–21.

Chapters 2 and 3: "The Phaeacians and the Symbolism of Odysseus' Return," *Arion* 1, no. 4 (1962): 17–64.

Chapter 4: "Transition and Ritual in Odysseus' Return." *La Parola del Passato* 116 (1967): 321–42.

Chapter 5: "*Kleos* and Its Ironies in the *Odyssey*," *Antiquité Classique* 52 (1983): 22–47.

Chapter 6: "Bard and Audience in Homer," in Robert Lamberton and John J. Keaney, eds., *Homer's Ancient Readers* (Princeton: Princeton University Press, 1992), pp. 3–29.

Chapter 9: "Teiresias in the Yukon: A Note on Folktale and Epic (*Odyssey* 11, 100–144 and 23, 248–87)," in Roberto Pretagostini, ed., *Tradizione e innovazione nella cultura greca da Omero all' età ellenistica: Scritti in onore di Bruno Gentili* (Rome: Gruppo Editoriale Internazionale, 1993), 1: 61–68.

Chapter 10: "Divine Justice in the *Odyssey:* Cyclops, Helios, and Poseidon," *American Journal of Philology* 113 (1992): 489–518.

I cite the Greek text of the *Odyssey* from Peter Von der Mühll's third Teubner edition, *Homeri Odyssea* (1945; reprint, Stuttgart, 1984), although I do not always accept his excisions. The text of the *Iliad* is cited from David B. Monro and T. W. Allen's Oxford Classical Text, *Homeri Opera*, volumes 1 and 2, *Ilias*, 3d edition (Oxford, 1920). Other authors are cited from the standard Oxford or Teubner editions. The transliterations of Greek aim at clarity for Anglophone readers rather than at any particular system. I use a macron to mark a long vowel where this seems helpful or necessary. To avoid confusion in matters of prosody, I transliterate Greek upsilon as *u*. I use the "equals" sign to indicate verses that are repeated in different parts of the poem. Because of the *Odyssey*'s place in the mainstream of European culture, I have preferred the Latinate form of its more familiar proper names (e.g., Circe and Alcinous rather than Kirkē and Alkinoos).

My dedication (ὀλίγον τε φίλον τε) expresses my constant gratitude to my wife, Nancy Jones, for much sage advice and for her ever present and loving support.

C<small>HARLES</small> S<small>EGAL</small>

Cambridge, Massachusetts

PART ONE

THE MYTHICAL JOURNEY
AND THE HERO

CHAPTER I

Introduction:
The Landscape of Imagination

Around the time that Friedrich August Wolf was excogitating his *Prolegomena ad Homerum,* published in 1795, the young Goethe, sitting in the botanical gardens of Palermo, was musing on Nausicaa and "das Land wo die Zitronen blühen" ("the land where the lemon trees blossom"). Untroubled by the problem of multiple authorship, awkward transitions, doublets, redactors, or *Bearbeiter* (editors), he responded to the *Odyssey*'s imaginative world. And rightly so, for the special charm of this poem is the way it transports us to places that fascinate. Many centuries after the time when the poem was first sung, these places haunt our imagination still. This is in part because the *Odyssey* creates an imaginative landscape, a landscape of the imagination. Its world is populated, of course, by fabulous monsters, but its cities, harbors, oceans, and islands are also the setting for the familiar ways of men and women, as the opening lines tell us. The fact that scholars from antiquity to the present have tried to locate these settings in real places that they can visit and photograph is perhaps the finest tribute to Homer's art. Although it is by no means children's literature, the *Odyssey* is often the first work of antiquity that children encounter, and it still appeals to the child in adults, our eagerness and curiosity to learn about the world.

In contrast to the varied, ever-changing world of the *Odyssey,* the *Iliad* creates essentially one landscape, the austere war-world of Troy. The gods on Olympus, the evocations of the Greek homeland, and the similes provide relief and variety, of course, but ultimately they only intensify the concentration on a single place, the all-absorbing struggle around the walls, in the narrow plain between the city and the ships, the

3

towers and the sea. The *Odyssey* operates with almost the opposite technique. Instead of concentration and exclusion, it uses expansiveness and exploration. It begins not in the primary setting of the action, as does the *Iliad,* but in the remote, divine realm of Olympus. Then, with a brief glance at Calypso's mysterious island, the navel of the sea, it moves to Ithaca and from there follows Telemachus on his travels to Pylos and Sparta as he goes in search of his father. With Nestor and Menelaus, the poem reaches outward once more, back to Troy during the war years and to the dangerous places of the return journey. Only then does it come to Odysseus, to follow him back and forth through his fabulous adventures, from Calypso to the Phaeacians, and to the fairyland that holds Cyclops and Circe, Scylla and Charybdis, and the losses that each of these adventures brings.

In the *Iliad* the surrounding world seems almost incidental to the terrible events. The heroes' eyes are fixed on the life-and-death struggle against their enemies, not on the sky or the hills or the trees and their fruit. The view from Olympus takes in the vast sweep of sky or mountain; but when we mortal viewers glimpse the natural world or some intimate scene of daily life, generally in the similes, we seem to be looking out through the prison bars of a tragic world of war and death. This doomed perspective enormously enhances the grandeur or sweetness of a setting that is wholly or in part threatened with destruction at every moment. In the *Odyssey,* however, everyone notices his or her surroundings and dwells on them with fascinated wonder and with loving detail. Even the god Hermes, frequent flyer though he is, lingers admiringly over the landscape of Calypso's remote island (5.73–77). The poem also gives us multiple perspectives on the same setting. We see Calypso's cave, Circe's dwelling, or even Odysseus' palace both from a distance and from within. We approach the Phaeacian land like a new settler or a shipwrecked sailor desperately seeking safety, but we also see it with the proud familiarity of the inhabitants.

The *Odyssey* narrows our view of Olympus, whose bickerings often provide comic relief to the *Iliad*'s tragic human world. As we shall see in Chapter 10, the *Odyssey*'s gods are remoter and more serious (though not always more intelligible) than the *Iliad*'s. Yet its ability to create a convincing world, or worlds, is the gift of true poetry, which opens our minds to worlds other than that we ordinarily live in. Nothing expands or enlivens the imagination so much as visiting new places, and we never seem to tire of imaginary travels, be they Gulliver's or those of Italo Calvino's delightful modern odyssey, *Invisible Cities.* The worlds of the *Odyssey* are not only those of anthropophagous ogres, nubile princesses in magical gardens, and sexy enchantresses but also include the prosaic, workaday life of eighth-century B.C. rural Greece, as we see it, for example, in Eumaeus' pig farm or Laertes' carefully planted orchards.

The sharp differences between the shifting realm of the sea and its trials in the first half of the *Odyssey* and the more prosaic life of the palace and its troubles in the second have led some scholars to posit the poem's seriatim origins, so that the poem we have is the result of a later stitching together of a sailor's yarn and a plot of revenge. But the connections between the two halves are too close to be the result of mechanical editing. The very heart of this poem is in fact the linking of the near and the distant. It explores the way in which the traveler's far-flung experiences turn back upon themselves in redefining and recreating a whole life cycle.[1]

To be sure, the self that this process implies differs from a modern self. The Homeric self (or, to be more precise, the literary representation of the self in the Homeric poems) has less autonomy or individuality than the modern self, is more bound to social categories such as king, warrior, or merchant, is more strongly defined by one's position in city, family, clan, or generation, and is expressed in situations of face-to-face exchange rather than in solitude or introspection.[2] The very notion of selfhood, as postmodern critics untiringly remind us, is a social construction and in the case of Homer probably the construction of a privileged social class, the warrior-aristocrats who in some form or other "paid for" the composition of the *Iliad* and the *Odyssey* (see below, Chapters 6 and 7). Nevertheless, as contemporary film and fiction continue to show, storytelling, with its mythical undercurrents, remains one of humankind's most valuable resources for understanding our own and others' selves. Poets over the centuries have used the imaginative coordinates of place to evoke and explore states of mind and feeling, and we moderns still use and respond to the technique.

The interpretations of classical literature tend to vacillate between assumptions of sameness and difference. To some, Homer, Sophocles, Catullus, Virgil, Horace, and Ovid are inspiring because they show a remote people who illustrate our own concerns, foibles, strengths, and deficiencies. To others, the ancients are illuminating for their otherness,

[1] See Chapters 2–4 below.
[2] See Russo and Simon (1968) passim.

their contrasts with modern postindustrial society. Both points of view have validity, and it is not my concern to negotiate the polarities here. Notions of primitive simplicity and directness, however, do sometimes get in the way of appreciating the literary sophistication that these extraordinary epics in fact exhibit. Homeric "simplicity" is a heritage from the Romantic idealization of the epics as the voice of a "naïve" folk tradition or (as in Matthew Arnold's *On Translating Homer* and John Ruskin's "Of the Pathetic Fallacy") as an antidote to modern complexity and sentimentality.

The tendency to concentrate on Homer's surface clarity also dominates what is probably the single most influential interpretative essay on the *Odyssey* in our time, Erich Auerbach's "Odysseus' Scar," the opening chapter of *Mimesis*. [3] I do not wish to diminish the value of Auerbach's observations on what he calls the "vertical" dimension of the biblical narrative, or on the pervasiveness of a divinely appointed historical destiny, or on the biblical development of a personality over a whole lifetime, or on the intense emotionality of domestic situations, or his basic contrast between Homer's precise foregrounding of details and the more elliptical biblical narrative of the sacrifice of Isaac. Yet every close reader of Homer knows how many elliptical moments there are in the *Iliad* and *Odyssey,* how many shadowy details or sudden leaps or famous "silences." One of the most suggestive of these last in fact occurs in the very passage that Auerbach studies, the mysterious inattentiveness of Penelope to the loud clang of the falling basin: "[Eurycleia] looked toward her [Penelope] with her eyes, wishing to tell her of her dear husband who was within; but Penelope could not turn her look to meet hers or perceive her, for Athena distracted her mind" (19.478–80). Penelope's inattention is essential to the suspense of the narrative, but it is not a feature of self-sufficient surface lucidity.

Viewed in a perspective different from Auerbach's, the episode of the scar is revealing for the ways in which formulaic language and mythical patterns taken together give Odysseus' journey its significance as an implicit definition of what we would call identity. As a number of scholars have shown, the episode of the scar draws on the initiatory function of hunting in Greek myths of adolescent passage to adulthood. Looking at the account of the scar in this light, we see how clearly it functions as a microcosm of the life cycle of Odysseus, here recaptured and condensed into a single emblematic moment.

[3] Auerbach (1957) 1–20.

The episode takes us from the time when Odysseus' mother first "gave him birth" (19.355) to his "nurture" by Eurycleia, his naming by his grandfather, and then his bloom of early manhood, or *hēbē*. And of course in the present situation he appears in the guise of an old man. The episode thus surveys the entire course of a mortal life. Eurycleia's brief and touching remark on how "mortals age quickly in adversity," then, is more than just local pathos (19.360). The rapidity of the narrative underlines these paradigmatic connections. From Eurycleia's recognition of the scar in 19.392f., Homer moves at once to a brief mention of the boar hunt on Parnassus in 393f. He then shifts abruptly to a point further back in time to the earlier scene when this nurse again handled Odysseus, putting the infant into his grandfather's arms to be named. The grandfather has journeyed from Parnassus to Ithaca specifically for the occasion (399–402).[4] The hunt immediately follows the naming episode (τῶν ἔνεκ' ἦλθ' 'Οδυσεύς, "For the sake of this Odysseus came," 413). It serves as the trial or test marking the hero's successful passage to maturity, and it validates the heroic inheritance that the grandfather confers in the act of naming. In early Greek myth the hunt regularly attends the male generational passage from adolescence to manhood.[5]

This analogical function of the mythical pattern operates at a still deeper level of the narrative, for in the story of the scar Odysseus had returned home with glorious gifts (19.413f. = 459f.), as he has just now done in coming back from the Phaeacians in book 13. In fact, in telling his false story about himself to Penelope earlier in book 19, Odysseus transformed those mysterious gifts into guest-gifts left by his fictitious Odysseus at a cave of Eileithyia, goddess of *birth*, on Crete at Amnisus (19.185–89). The goddess of birth is relevant at this point of renewal.

Darkening with further complications Auerbach's limpid and well-illuminated foreground are the important links that exist between the scar and Odysseus' real and metaphorical journeys earlier into and out of his past. The boar that lunges at the adolescent Odysseus to inflict the

[4] Note too how the movements between Ithaca and Parnassus reinforce the temporal recessiveness of the story and bring us back from the past to the present: 19.394, 399, 411, 413, 461f., 466. Note especially 394 = 466, Παρνησόνδ' ἐλθόντα ("going to Parnassus"), and the connection of Odysseus' attainment of early manhood, or ἥβη, with his trip to Parnassus in 410f., where Autolycus gives instructions, on naming Odysseus, that "on reaching manhood he should come to Parnassus to the great house of [his] mother's family" (ἡβήσας . . . ἔλθη Παρνησόνδ '). The temporal and spatial movements are closely correlated.

[5] See Rubin and Sale (1983) 141ff., with the bibliography on 165–66n.6.

scar on his thigh lurks in a thicket that is almost identical to the thicket from which the grizzled, sea-battered Odysseus emerged among Nausicaa's Phaeacian maidens at the end of book 5.[6] That is the moment when Odysseus escapes from Poseidon's angry sea and crosses from the dangerous fairy-tale world of his adventures to civilized life among the Phaeacians. The repetition helps link the three trials of this exemplary hero in his passage through life. The first test (moving in chronological order) is the hunt that makes him a man. The second is his journey back through the unknown via the Phaeacians after the peak of his mature success at Troy. The third and last trial is the present situation, the reclaiming of his house in its multiple aspects and demands as his life looks toward its close. The earlier crossing between life and death in the perilous seas between Troy and Greece parallels both the confrontation with the boar on a famous mountain in Greece and the present dangerous passage in an interior setting and indeed by his own hearth on Ithaca. The hero's challenges become both more familiar and more inward as they move from a mysterious ocean to the wild (if well-known) rocks and forests of Parnassus and then to the palace on Ithaca.

The analogies between these transitional moments become even stronger on a closer examination of Homer's language. The description of the confrontation with the boar evokes a battle between heroic warriors (e.g., 19.437f. and 447–49). It thus foreshadows Odysseus' prowess as a wielder of the spear both at Troy and, near at hand, in the contest soon to come with his human enemies. To dig deeper still, the phrase κραδάων δολιχόσκιον ἔγχος, "brandishing the long-shadowing spear" (19.438; cf. 448), though common in the battle scenes of the *Iliad,* is rare in the *Odyssey.* It recurs on only two other occasions in the poem. It appears in Telemachus' first deed of martial valor when he stands beside his father against the suitors (22.95 and 97); and it is used of Laertes' cast against Eupeithes, father of Antinous, worst of the suitors, in the final battle (24.519 and 522). Thus this first test of Odysseus' manhood reaches out in widening ripples through the narrative to confirm the survival power of the patriarchal line at points of crisis and the toughness of the inherited martial valor that passes from father Laertes to son to grandson. The story of the scar thus complements the reinvigoration of Laertes, who "takes joy" when "son and grandson strive for martial valor" (24.514f.). For good measure, it reaffirms

[6] The verses describing the two thickets are virtually the same: cf. *Od.* 19.440–43 and 5.478–81.

patriarchal inheritance a generation further back and on the other, guileful side of Odysseus' heroism, embodied in his maternal grand-father, Autolycus.

Auerbach's essay remains a superb introduction to the modes of Homeric narration. Nevertheless, it illustrates the price paid for stand-ing so far back from the whole context, particularly the loss of cultural depth and specificity. Despite its charm, lucidity, and love of sheer storytelling, the *Odyssey* is not a simple poem. Even its much admired limpidity of narrative has depths that become fully visible only when style, narrative design, and mythical patterns are studied together.

That study is the aim of this volume. The three sections of the book and the three terms of the title—singer, hero, and god—correspond to the three major perspectives on the poem that I develop (although not in that order). The first section concentrates on the poem's uses and trans-formations of mythical patterns and on the hero's journey as a reflection on the mortal condition. The second focuses on the *Odyssey*'s insistent self-consciousness about what we may generalize as poetics. And in the third I examine the poem's presentation of moral action both in human behavior and in the ways of the gods.

The first section approaches the poem through the mythical journey and the uses and transformations of mythic patterns. Beginning with the place of Odysseus' long Phaeacian narrative in the epic as a whole, Chapters 2 and 3 view the action of the poem as a journey through mortal time as the aging and much-enduring hero experiences the losses and recuperations of human life. The fourth chapter considers how a few recurrent ritual actions and motifs articulate the theme of transition. Chapter 5 shifts the emphasis from mythical themes to issues of poetics and the epic tradition and thus forms a bridge to the book's second section. In it I discuss the *Odyssey*'s special version of heroic fame and so deal with the poem as a journey away from the world of the *Iliad* and as a reflection on heroic poetry.

Chapters 6 and 7 focus more specifically on poetics and the bard's place in heroic society, but from somewhat different perspectives. Chapter 6 offers a broad survey of Homer's views of the singer and his song, with special attention to audience-bard situations in the *Odyssey*. Chapter 7 examines the ambiguous status in which the *Odyssey* places the bard by associating him with the heroic guest on the one hand and with the needy and mendacious beggar on the other. Drawing on the anthropological approaches of scholars such as Moses Finley, Louis Gernet, James Redfield, and Jean-Pierre Vernant, I explore how the poet ennobles his status through situations of heroic hospitality and exchange and through comparisons between bardic and warrior roles but also deftly manages to keep the bard in his place as a subordinate. The bardic performance as a situation of exchange is interestingly illuminated by comparing the palace-centered, heroic exchanges of Homer with the civic-centered settings of the so-called Herodotean Life of Homer.

Focusing on the scenes of Odysseus' disguise in the house of his loyal swineherd Eumaeus, in Chapter 8 I explore the ambiguities surrounding disguise, the beggar, and the telling (singing) of false stories. I continue the discussion of the implicit economics of the poem and of distinctions in social roles and positions but pay particular attention to books 14 and 15. These rather neglected books emphasize the vicissitudes of life in an unpredictable world where the status boundaries and firm values of the *Iliad* have become fluid and unstable. The second part of the essay returns to the themes of poetics in the paradoxical truth-in-lies of the beggar's narratives. Wrapped in the rags of the mortal contingency and ephemerality that drive him to seize the earthy opportunities of the moment, the king who is disguised as a beggar and talks like a bard embodies the poem's power of mimetic representation, its ability to render the multiple guises and disguises of reality in the changing, precarious world that the *Odyssey* depicts.

The third and last section of the book returns to myth and the gods. Chapter 9 begins with a recent folklore parallel to Teiresias' prophecy of Odysseus' calm death and shows how the poem transforms this motif into its characteristic mood of personal interaction as Odysseus shares his prophecy with Penelope on the night of their long-postponed reunion. The last chapter again takes a broad view of the poem. It deals with a central issue, the gods' place in the *Odyssey*'s moral vision. Beginning with what has long been regarded as a major interpretive problem, namely, the discrepancy between the developed morality of Zeus and the primitive anthropomorphism of gods such as Poseidon and Helios, I offer a radically unitary reading of the poem's mythical chronology and theology. In looking again at the episodes of Polyphemus and the Cattle of the Sun, I return to some of the issues raised in the essays on the Phaeacians in Chapters 2 and 3, but in a different and complementary perspective. The *Odyssey*'s action, like the *Iliad*'s, could be described as "the will of Zeus," but it is a rather different Zeus. Understanding the gods' place in human life turns out to be one of the chief objects of the hero's quest, but to what extent he succeeds is left open at the end. This closing scene reminds us how far Odysseus has come, but it also reveals the gap between human impulses and the vision of the gods. Homer's narrative voice identifies with that larger vision. Like the tragedians after him, therefore, he uses myth not to idealize but to depict a human reality that in this case includes violence and bloodthirsty vengefulness even in the hero famed for his wiliness, restraint, and prudence.

CHAPTER 2

The Phaeacians and Odysseus' Return: Part 1, Suspension and Reintegration

The Role of the Phaeacians

The *Odyssey,* says Eustathius, is "more pungent" or "sharper" than the *Iliad* because of the depths of its thoughts in an appearance of surface simplicity.[1] The poem impresses at once by the complexity of its structure and the seriousness of its treatment. Comic episodes there are, but on the whole, determination, suffering, and a sense of inevitability underlie the imaginative elaborateness of the narrative. There persists throughout the unquenchable desire of the long-absent warrior and wanderer to return, against obstacles on either side of "reality": the monsters of the strange world between Calypso and the Phaeacians described in Odysseus' recollected narrative in Alcinous' palace and the more familiar, indeed almost prosaic, dangers of Ithaca. And between the two worlds lies Scheria, the land of the Phaeacians, a favored race, but mortal.

At several points Odysseus comes close to reaching his goal, only to be delayed again, as if compelled to go through a succession of adventures and difficulties that have been likened to patterns of initiation or ritual performance.[2] Yet in contrast with his eagerness to attain Ithaca is

---

[1] Eustathius, *Commentarius in Odysseam,* proem: ἤδη δὲ καὶ ὀξυτέρα [ἡ Ὀδύσσεια τῆς Ἰλιάδος] διὰ τὰ ἐν φαντασίᾳ ἐπιπολαίου ἀφελείας βάθη τῶν νοημάτων.

[2] Patterns of initiation are suggested as the prototype for the Cyclops and Circe episodes by Germain (1954) 78–86, 126–29, 131–32. Elderkin (1940) 52–54 also suggested that the cave on Ithaca was "simply a place of initiation into sacred mysteries." See also Carpenter (1946) chapter 6, passim. Levy (1948) finds in Odysseus' adventures a

his restraint once there, a restraint that even his patron goddess notes as remarkable (13.330–36). Again a kind of necessity prevents his immediate reunion with his family and followers: a necessity partly external— the difficulty of defeating so large and powerful a group as the suitors— and partly internal—his own need for inquiring and testing.

The poem's design controls the order and framework in which these necessities are presented.[3] Odysseus himself appears first actively only in the fifth book, on his next-to-last stopping place before Ithaca. The main portion of his overseas adventures emerges only as recounted by the hero in retrospect, not as currently lived experiences, such as the voyage from Calypso to the Phaeacians or the subsequent events on Ithaca. The greatest perils of Odysseus' return to Ithaca thus unfold among the peaceful and comfort-loving Phaeacians, amid the ease and pleasures of a banquet. This essay will begin with the significance of the Phaeacians and the placing of Odysseus' narrative among them. From here it will move out into what Eustathius called "the depths" of the poem, with particular attention to repeated narrative patterns that mark stages of meaningful loss, recovery, or passage.

The *Odyssey* deals recurrently and under many different forms with death and rebirth, change of state and the loss and resumption of identity. Some of this concern may derive from the primitive origins of epic poetry in ritual and incantation, in man's early attempts to understand the processes of life, change, and death, especially through what is the *Odyssey*'s major organizing motif, the journey.[4] In ancient poetry generally, from the *Gilgamesh Epic* onward, the connection between an individual's spiritual life and physical life is very close, and both are felt and poetically formulated as directly related to the rhythms and cycles of nature. Oral poetry probably retained some of the sacral, ritual character of proto-epic poetry. The secularized Homeric bard, after all, still takes his inspiration from the Muse or Apollo (see *Od.* 8.488).

---

series "of repeated experiences on islands which bear traces of a kindred ritual, the episode of Scheria being the most complete example" (268n. 2).

[3] For the complexity of structure of the *Odyssey* and the "boxing in" of the adventures in books 9–12, see Abrahamson (1960) 2–3; Woodhouse (1930) 11ff., esp. 15; Whitman (1958) 287ff., with 354n. 4, to whose treatment of the *Odyssey* as self-discovery and self-revelation (see 296ff.) my own interpretation owes much. My study, as is apparent, supposes the artistic unity of the *Odyssey* (including the genuineness of 23.297 to the end). The thematic and aesthetic function of the repetitions is maintained by Calhoun (1933) 1–25 and Woolsey (1941) 167–81.

[4] For the concern of epic generally with "the journeys of heroes into the world beyond, the world of the spirit" and with "the connection of man with the unseen forces of the world beyond," see Lord (1962) 205, 210.

Odysseus and the Phaeacians: Suspension and Integration

Odysseus' narrative in books 9–12 creates a world apart, a realm through which the hero has passed and from which, like Melville's Ishmael, he emerges as the sole survivor. This section of the poem has been a constant source of inspiration for poets, from Stesichorus in the seventh century B.C. to today, and it continues to draw readers in whom the spark of imagination is still alive. It has been interpreted allegorically, as readers from classical antiquity through Heraclitus and Porphyry have done, anthropologically, theologically, and psychologically.[5] This last perspective is the one I explore here, but I do so without denying the other possibilities or insisting that every aspect of the poem is accessible to late twentieth-century individualizing psychology. Instead, I focus on those aspects of the poem that involve the broad human experience of change, generational passage, loss and recovery. In this concern with a definition of human identity, my approach is anthropological as well as psychological.

The Phaeacian episode is the crucial point of transition between two very different areas of experience, the war at Troy and the kingdom of Ithaca, with its familial, economic, and political responsibilities and its intimate personal ties. If we translate the Homeric narrative into contemporary terms, the hero's entrance into the fantasy world of the sea voyage may be read psychologically as his contact with the unconscious potential of the self, a realm previously hidden or inaccessible, never easily entered, strange to and incommensurate with "reality," that is, Ithaca, the everyday, the logically predictable and rationally explicable. On Scheria, the Phaeacian island, Odysseus experiences the waning of the imaginary and the return of reality, that is, the demands of life in a human setting of city and family. In the process of making this transition, he reviews his past and thereby reintegrates the two areas of his life experience (psychologically, the conscious and subconscious dimensions of his being). More broadly, he also shapes an implicit definition of what it means to be human in this world of abrupt change and multiple identities.

[5] For the "allegorical" interpretations of Homer in antiquity, see the detailed study of Buffière (1956) 33–78 and passim. For anthropological approaches, see M. Finley (1965), Vidal-Naquet (1986), Austin (1975), and Redfield (1983). For theological approaches, see Chapter 10 below. Stanford (1954) 36–39, 42, while dismissing the "allegorical" or strictly moralistic interpretations of the ancient and later commentators, accepts the possibility of "creative symbolism, by which an artist arrives at a deeper understanding of his subject (which for Homer was human nature) by thought and intuition" (42).

In the course of returning to the familiar, human-scale realities of Ithaca and renewing and reclaiming his basic relations with parents, wife, son, friends, and retainers, Odysseus undergoes a varied series of experiences that test him as he tests those he encounters on Ithaca. His visit to the land of the dead, with its bleak vision of mortality, is the antithesis of the immortal life offered by Calypso and so the necessary preparation for the Ithacan return. Calypso's island, Ogygia, is the point from which Homer begins the tale of Odysseus' wandering and the point at which the hero himself concludes it on Scheria (see 12.450–53). The long series of trying vicissitudes is thus framed on both sides by the stillness of Calypso's island, where the hero has refused immortality but yet is far removed from mortal life.

If the return is viewed as a reclaiming of lost or uncertain identity after a major crisis, then Calypso becomes significant as a point of suspension, a point of enforced removal in which the hero's human qualities have been entirely dormant. Homer's silence about the details of Odysseus' years with Calypso may be read as reflecting the irrecoverable quality of this suspended state from which he is seeking to return. Her island is distant even for the gods (see 5.100–102). As the "navel of the sea" (1.50), it embodies the mystery, ambiguity, and remoteness of the sea itself: Calypso is the daughter of "baleful-minded Atlas who knows the depths of all the sea and himself holds up the high pillars that hold apart earth and sky" (1.52–54). Her name also suggests "concealing" (*kaluptein*). Odysseus' place of "concealment," then, is itself of the essence of the sea; and he is held by the goddess in whom are reflected the crossing and binding together of the cosmic substances—earth, sky, and sea.

This first description of Calypso shows the man who is to return to mortality against a vast, threatening scale that far overshadows his manhood. The threatening quality of this world is hinted in the epithet of Circe's father, Atlas: *oloophrōn*, "destructive-minded" (1.52). Yet Homer presents Odysseus on Ogygia at the moment when he is fully ready for his return, when all his thoughts are dominated by it. The goddess who "hides" (Kalypso-*kaluptei*) can no longer hide the hero from the human world to which his inextinguishable mortal nature draws him (see 5.215ff.). The visit to Hades marks an acceptance of mortality in general and in Teiresias' prophecy, a specific acceptance of his own death from which Odysseus can no longer turn away.

From Calypso to the Phaeacians is the longest and most perilous of Odysseus' voyages. It is twenty days in duration, twice the length of the

voyage from the Island of the Sun to Calypso on Ogygia. The two
journeys are similar. In both Odysseus is shipwrecked by a god and
travels alone, with great hardship. The first has a negative result: the
loss of all his companions and seven years of idleness, totally removed
from humanity; the second brings a positive result, an almost immediate return to the human world. The doubling of the length of the
journeys may indicate the magnitude of difficulty in finding his way
back to humanity (or the point of transition to humanity, Scheria) after
full suspension from it, in re-creating or reconstructing after loss or
removal. Psychologically, the seven-year absence on Calypso's island
can be understood as a state of shock and weakness, an inability to return to reality until he has gathered enough emotional strength and insight. But he is helpless to return until the gods, stimulated by Athena,
intervene. Among other functions, she embodies Odysseus' rationality
and patience, his clear and integrated vision of himself as the man that he
is, and therefore the reality of his bond with Ithaca and human life. She
is the vitality and resiliency of his human spirit that has not ceased to
work in his behalf, though he knows it not.[6]

To reach the Phaeacians requires a tremendous effort against over-
whelming odds. But why, to return to the question broached before,
should this passage be so crucial, and why should the Phaeacians be
chosen as the point for the review of Odysseus' adventures? The answer
requires a careful examination of the entire Phaeacian episode in the
Odyssey as a whole.

Noteworthy first of all is the juxtaposition of Calypso and the Phaeacians. The Phaeacians, with their activity, agility, and seamanship, are
antithetical to the inactivity enforced on Ogygia and to the lack of
means of transportation that Calypso alleges to Hermes (5.141–42).
Indeed, the thought of crossing "the sea's great gulf," difficult even for
ships, makes Odysseus shudder when Calypso announces that she will
send him home (5.173–79). Odysseus must create his own means of
transport from the basic materials that Calypso provides, whereas the
Phaeacians can effortlessly land him on Ithaca as soon as they agree on
his return. This is the only passage made entirely without effort on his
part, in sharp contrast with the voyage from Ogygia, where Zeus
decreed that he must return without the aid of gods or men (5.31–32),

---

[6] See *Od.* 13.221–355, especially 330–40, and the further discussion below, Chapter 3,
with note 7.

another indication that the passage from Calypso to the Phaeacians is the principal point of crisis and transition.

The loneliness and isolation of Ogygia also contrast with the Phaeacians' fondness for society and collectivity. They are first described in terms of their "community and city" (*dēmon te polin te*, 6.3), and we learn of a previous king who built walls and houses and divided fields (6.9–10).[7] Different as their way of life is from that in Ithaca, it is still recognizably human. Scheria thus forms an essential stepping-stone from the complete suspension of Ogygia to the complete involvement of Ithaca. Odysseus' activity in building a raft is not only a basic requisite for his physical passage but also the reengagement of his rational faculties and active temperament which is the psychological prerequisite for his return. It reaffirms his power to act creatively on his environment and master it for his own ends. Here he begins to reestablish the peculiarly human power of *technē* (skill, craft) which makes possible his victory over the Cyclops and which he earlier used to construct his marriage bed (23.192–201).[8] It is this same skill that established his fame in his heroic past: the building of the Trojan horse.

The departure from Calypso shows the extent to which the hero's mortal identity is inseparable from his mortal corporeality. In contrast to Platonic and Christian views of an eternal, incorporeal soul, or *psuchē*, the essence of the self lies here in the vital energies sustained by food, drink, breathing, and sleep. As Odysseus complains repeatedly in the course of his wanderings, his constant companion is the demanding belly (*gastēr*), virtually an alter ego with which he has a love-hate relation. As soon as the gods' envoy, Hermes, announces to Calypso the necessity of Odysseus' return, the hero begins to put on again these trappings of his mortal identity. He exercises his characteristic caution in asking the goddess to take an oath, eats mortal food at the table where she is served nectar and ambrosia, is addressed for the first time in the poem by his own name and patronymic (5.203), and declares his desire for his mortal wife and home in preference to immortality (5.173–224).

Once these human faculties have been reactivated, the passage over the "great abyss of the sea" (μέγα λαῖτμα θαλάσσης, 5.174), though

----

[7] The Phaeacians are frequently referred to as a *dēmos*, as are the Ithacans: see, e.g., 13.186. Scholars have frequently compared the Phaeacians to a newly founded Ionian colony.

[8] Note the similes of shipbuilding and metallurgy at Odysseus' blinding of Polyphemus in 9.384–86 and 391–93.

attended by great suffering, cannot be entirely hindered, as Poseidon knows (5.288–89). The safe arrival among the Phaeacians, therefore, cancels the paralyzing enchantment of Ogygia and marks the accomplishment of the most difficult part of Odysseus' return to humanity. Here, too, Athena, the companion of his rationally acting self, helps him directly for the first time in his overseas adventures (7.14ff., 13.316–23). There is no mention of his consciously recognizing her, however, until he is actually on Ithaca (13.322–23), where she again becomes dominant in his actions and his decisions.

The Phaeacians neutralize many of the dangers that Odysseus has met in the outlandish world between the Ciconians and Scheria. They receive him in kindly fashion, show a lively human vitality and curiosity, generously bestow gifts, and assure his return to Ithaca. Although their keen enjoyment of his tales intrudes some delay, they do not hold him by "necessity" or allure him by enchantment, as do Calypso or Circe, but agree easily to speed him on his way. For all their special skills, they are clearly human and ultimately prove subject to the same wrath from Poseidon as Odysseus. In the games of book 8, Odysseus can again assert the heroic strength of his past life, as he has not been able to do for nine years (186ff.). Yet the Phaeacians are also removed from the common sufferings and toil of ordinary mortals. It is this balance of involvement and removal (as we shall see later) that makes possible Odysseus' review of the past. He is on his way back to mortality but not yet fully involved in it and hence can reflect on and review his experiences in the nonhuman, "unreal" world before reentering the reality of Ithaca. The Phaeacians provide a restorative framework in which he can integrate the real with the unreal, the imaginary with the familiar. In the lays of Demodocus and their games (see 8.215–22), they recall his warlike prowess, which he shall have to call upon soon in defeating the suitors.

The Phaeacians face backward as well as forward: back to the adventures after Troy and to Troy itself; forward to the future struggle with the suitors. Though at peace themselves, they elicit the spirit of war and the image of heroic self-assurance that Odysseus is to renew in himself. They stand between Odysseus' great exertions on both sides of reality and provide a calm vantage point in the midst of his grim efforts. His safe haven among them is prefigured in the shelter from wind, sun, and rain provided by the olive thicket near his landfall (5.478–81); and this sheltered situation is evoked again in connection with Athena in the description of Olympus shortly after (6.42–46) and also in the favored situation of Alcinous' garden (7.117–19). Nausicaa, almost a "genius of rebirth," at once assures him, "But now, since you have come to our city and land, you will not lack clothing or anything else that befits a much-tried suppliant who has encountered us" (6.191–93).[9]

Odysseus' arrival—thrown up by the waves and awakening before Nausicaa after a safe sleep—constitutes a restoration to life after the quasi death on Ogygia. He emerges from the water entirely naked, stripped of all that has been outgrown and outlived, but ready to be reclothed for the resumption of his human life on Ithaca. The Trojan War is now far in the past, a subject of song; and even his post-Trojan adventures are seven years removed, a removal emphasized by the fact that they are presented as a tale and Odysseus, in telling them, likened to a bard (11.368). Both aspects of his past now focus on the future, and Odysseus' review of the totality of his experiences in the unreal world occurs in the very shadow of his return to reality: only one eagerly awaited dawn separates the two worlds (see 13.35).

The very act of recounting his adventures is a mark of Odysseus' readiness to return. He has lived through a full complement of experiences carrying him from the heroic to the fantastic, from the intelligible to the nonhuman, from war to inaction, from his position as a leader of men, surrounded by his companions, to total isolation in the seas off Thrinacia and Scheria. Now, no longer immediately involved, he has reached a point of integration for reentrance into his humanity. In his tale to the Phaeacians, he is making the synthesis final and strong, fixing the past in readiness for the future.

The tale to the Phaeacians is told by the man who has lived it, with its uniqueness and personal vividness in his own mind. He has not only lived it in the past but relived it inwardly and absorbed and grasped it synoptically for the future as well. What Odysseus tells, then, is re-membered experience, inwardly formed and transmuted. His tale, con-sequently, must be in the first person, and the change back to third-person narration in the thirteenth book is striking.[10]

The books of his tale (9–12) have, by contrast with the others, a

---

[9] For Nausicaa and rebirth, see Whitman (1958) 295.

[10] Stella (1955) 143–44 notes the parallel of a first-person narrative-within-a-narrative in the *Gilgamesh Epic;* but Homer's use of this device is much more subtle and far-reaching. Some of the high poetic effects of this *Ich-Erzählung* are pointed out by Reinhardt (1948) 68ff., especially in the description of landscape (77–78), in the ironic contrast between heroic and fantasy worlds (68–70, 79–83), which becomes, in the mouth of Odysseus, almost a *Selbstironie* (70).

separateness in a universe of their own which makes them appear indeed as the account of a voyage of the soul, from life to death and back to life. Whatever the meaning of the individual adventures, their presentation in the first person as a recollected totality can be taken as what the inner man has acquired, like the gifts of the outer man, in passing through a rich multiplicity of experience that cannot be communicated literally or objectively but only in the strangeness of its own terms. Here, the conditions and experiences of human life are transformed into a different plane, a key or tonality beyond and foreign to ordinary reality. Not that the actual diction or style of books 9–12 differ from the other books, but their first-person form and content and their place in the narrative as a whole mark them off as special, as does their removal from the ordinary modes of action and relation in the known world. Their interruption of the forward-moving time scheme of the poem and their function as a flashback contribute further to their "unreality." The problem for Odysseus is to bridge the gap between the two worlds, between the past accumulation of private experience (or the private aspect of all experience) and his present and future relations with the public, external, and directly communicable realities on Ithaca. If Ogygia represents a withdrawal or suspension of his relations with external reality, then his Phaeacian tale is the resifting and reerecting of his inward world to bring it into contact with the reality and objective human demands of Ithaca.

Only in the removal and transitional ground of Scheria, still partly within the magical realm of fantasy and imagination, can Odysseus give a full account of his adventures. These adventures are "true" as the subjective or personal side of his experiences; he is not merely lying, as he lies on Ithaca, for both he and the gods refer to these adventures, in whole or in part, elsewhere.[11] Yet on Ithaca he gives the full account only to Penelope, the person with whom his communication is fullest and most intimate, at the point of their reunion as husband and wife. To others he tells tales that can be recognized, in part, as the Phaeacian adventures transformed into more prosaic terms, stepped down out of the realm of imagination to the level of everyday, communicable realities.

---

[11] Stanford (1958–61) 1:63–64 raises the problem as to whether Odysseus, in his tale to the Phaeacians, emphasizes certain elements to make a more favorable impression— e.g., his love for his mother and the Catalogue of Women in book 11—that would interest and move Arete, who, as Stanford notes, is the first to speak when Odysseus finishes. Although such a suggestion is possible, there is no reason to believe Odysseus' feelings for his mother were not sincere; and the outline given in 23.310–42 confirms the general "truth" of his Phaeacian narrative.

In contrast with Odysseus' reticence on Ithaca too is his readiness to tell his story among the Phaeacians, even before his long narrative. When Arete asks about his clothes, he begins with a long and detailed account of Ogygia, Calypso, his loss of companions, and his detainment, coming to the part of the story immediately apposite to Arete's question only after some twenty lines of unsolicited narrative (7.244–66). Even the Old Man of the Sea, himself partly in the world of fantasy, tells Menelaus only that Calypso is holding Odysseus back by necessity (4.556–60), and this is the only news of Odysseus' adventures that Telemachus brings back to Ithaca (17.143–46). Earlier, before Telemachus had entered, through Menelaus, even so far into the world of Odysseus' travels, Athena had told him in the barest and most prosaic terms only that cruel and savage men were holding his father (1.198–99). Odysseus himself, in telling Telemachus "the truth" (alētheia) of his return, gives but a brief, literally credible account of his return on the Phaeacian ship: "The Phaeacians brought me, men famed for their ships, who send on their way too whatever other men should come to them," to which he appends a factual catalogue of the gifts he received from them (16.226–32). But he makes no reference to the adventures of the fantasy world.

Eumaeus, less close to Odysseus than Telemachus is, receives a tale in strictly human terms (14.193ff.), even though details such as the seven years in Egypt or the voyage to Thesprotia correspond vaguely to the seven years on Ogygia and the consultation of Teiresias, and some of the lines describing his fictitious shipwreck are identical with those in the Phaeacian episode.[12] Only to Penelope, in his meeting with her in

---

[12] Cf. 14.305–9 = 12.415–19; 14.314 = 12.447. In the whole of Odysseus' conversation with Eumaeus exists a consciously ironic interplay of falsehood and truth. Eumaeus is suspicious of beggars who deceive (14.125, 127), and then the disguised Odysseus, echoing the words of Eumaeus in 127, insists that he is not telling lies about his own return (so, too, the irony of Eumaeus' hesitation to name Odysseus who is "not present," 145). Eumaeus and Odysseus then wrangle again, after Odysseus' narrative, about the truth of the tale (14.361ff., especially 379, 387, 391–92, 400). See Eustathius' commentary on 14.199 and in general Trahman (1952) 31–43, esp. 37–39; see also below, Chapter 8. Woodhouse (1930) 132ff. regards the lies as representing the "real" return of Odysseus and hence justifying his claim to have seen "the cities of many men" (1.3). Carpenter (1946) 94–95 finds in the lies to Eumaeus a historical echo of Greek piracy in the reign of Psammetichus. Such a reminiscence, if true, would only emphasize the contrast between the experiences described to the Phaeacians and the "reality" of Ithaca. So Reinhardt (1948) 57 described the lies as "Erfindungen, die, je erlogener sie sind, umso mehr umwelthaft historische Glaubwürdigkeit, für uns 'Realität' gewinnen" ("inventions which gain all the more circumstantially historical credibility—for us, 'reality'—the more purely fictitious they are").

disguise, does he tell actual details from the Phaeacian narrative: the loss of his companions on Thrinacia and his arrival at Scheria (19.272–82); but he significantly omits any reference to Calypso until book 23 (310–42). There he gives to her the full account, beginning, as he did among the Phaeacians, with the Ciconians (9.39) and concluding with his arrival at Scheria. This narrative, following the recognition through the test of the bed and given when Odysseus is once more restored to his rightful place in it beside Penelope, marks the full integration of the fantastic adventures of the past with the present and future realities on Ithaca.

Penelope gains access to this remote world of Odysseus' travels through her special knowledge of her husband and their close relationship, which is embodied in the bed. Telemachus begins to gain access, though more limited, through the daring and effort of his voyage to the mainland and Menelaus' story of the Old Man of the Sea. But he does not get beyond this, at least within the framework of the poem, for his relationship with Odysseus is a sharing of action, the reestablishment of authority over the house by guile and force, rather than the intimate communication of Penelope. He and Laertes also share in the outward aspect of Odysseus' world the realities of heroic action and the patrimony. Penelope only, on Ithaca, shares the "truth" of his distant wanderings.

The Phaeacians' removal from the suffering that Odysseus knows so well enhances by contrast the mortality that he is to assume still more fully on Ithaca. Though the pain and toil of Odysseus are suspended as long as he is in Phaeacian hands (see 7.195–96), his involvement in suffering, by now so much a part of his being, creates a constant clash with the uninvolvement of the Phaeacians. His assertion of his human identity among the Phaeacians is the final affirmation of his resolve to return to Ithaca and, in a sense, the final test of his ability to reenter the world of human reality.

The Phaeacians, unlike Calypso, are not immortal but close to the gods (ἀγχίθεοι, 5.35). Alcinous' garden, one sign of their blessedness, is described as "the glorious gifts of the gods" (7.132), and Nausicaa is frequently likened to a god (6.16, 6.102ff., 6.150ff., 7.291). Odysseus, however, cannot be held by this quasi-divine quality. On the evening before his departure he meets the "godlike" Nausicaa for the last time (8.457) and promises to pray to her "as to a god" (467) when he returns to Ithaca. He thus distances her—and by extension his whole Phaeacian experience—from his human condition as he thinks increasingly in the terms of his mortal life on Ithaca.

The farewell to Nausicaa also reinstates the temporal stages that define a mortal life. She is the *parthenos,* the young girl at the point of transition between adolescence and the adult status of marriage; and she is compared to Artemis, as such girls often are.[13] Thanks to Athena's quasi-hypnotic suggestions, she is making active preparations for marriage, a marriage placed entirely within the human context of house and family (6.15–40, 49–70). If he married her, Odysseus would turn away from Ithaca and Penelope, but he would still have a recognizably human life (unlike the immortalizing union proffered by Calypso). Indeed, he would be renewing the earlier stage of his life, reenacting a fresh marriage to a nubile young girl. His closing address to her acknowledges the renewal that such a union might have: "You gave me life, maiden" (8.468). But in addressing her as *kourē,* "maiden," he also recognizes her youth and so calls attention to the gap between them.

Odysseus' reassertion of his mortal nature is even clearer in his first exchange with Alcinous (7.208ff.), who raises the possibility that Odysseus may be a god in disguise, mentioning incidentally the customary openness of the past visits of the gods to the Phaeacians (199–206). Odysseus replies that he is not only a mortal but also one who has suffered the most mortal woes (211–14). His statement of his mortality contains three aspects: his sufferings (211–14), the needs of his belly despite his grief (215–21), and his prayer to be sent back to his longed-for home (222–25). The first and third topics are major themes in the first half of the poem; the second becomes of great importance in the last half as a reflection of the basic and lowly human needs that Odysseus has reassumed. The entire passage recalls Odysseus' refusal of Calypso's offers of immortality in book 5 (cf. 5.210–13 with 7.208–10). He made a full and positive restatement of his mortality by refusing Calypso, and the Phaeacians fulfill this by actually restoring him to Ithaca.

The Phaeacians, therefore, are the instrument of Odysseus' return to the world of reality, but they are also the last afterglow of the fantasy realm he is leaving. They both hold its wonders and its dangers, its beckoning intimations of renewed youth as Nausicaa's bridegroom and

---

[13] Calame (1977) 1:90–92, 165–66; on the bridal imagery that pervades the scene with Nausicaa in book 6, see Hague (1983) 136–38 and Austin (1991) 235–43. The athletic contests in book 8 may also suggest marriage: see Lattimore (1969) 94ff.

its ominous hints of Calypso's moribund suspension. Their island, like Calypso's and Circe's, has hints of both an Elysium-like paradise of rest after life's trials and a Hades-like oblivion in a remote ocean.[14] This ambiguity is the source not only of their transitional function but also of the clashes that occur between them and Odysseus. They are untouched by much of the suffering that Odysseus knows. Their ships sail without effort or danger (7.556–63), and they have their sailing ability as a gift from Poseidon (7.35), the bane of Odysseus. They are called "lovers of the oar" (*philēretmos*), an epithet reserved almost exclusively from them in the *Odyssey,* at the very moment when Odysseus is being most buffeted by the waves (5.386).[15] The sea, the source of danger and death for Odysseus and hated even by the gods, is for them a means of protection (contrast 6.201–5 with 5.100ff. and 5.52). They are also removed from war. The sufferings of Odysseus and the Greeks at Troy are for them a source of aesthetic pleasure in the songs of Demodocus (see 8.83ff., 521ff.). The pain and losses of Odysseus in his post-Trojan adventures, his *kēdea* (griefs, woes), are for Alcinous a fascinating, pleasurable tale to which he would gladly listen until dawn (11.375–76), whereas Odysseus would prefer to sleep and depart at dawn (11.379ff., and see 7.222), rather than be delayed until the following sunset by another day of feasting and song (see 13.28ff.). Their fondness for games reflects the same removal from real human pain: they shun the boxing or wrestling in which Odysseus challenges them (8.206) and prefer the footrace, the dance, the lyre, and the still softer comforts of warm baths and bed (8.246–49, 253). They are surprised and shocked at the seriousness with which Odysseus takes up the challenge of Euryalus (8.158ff.), and they sit in silence after his victory boast (8.234). They are threatened by Odysseus' intensity, endurance, and anger, until Alcinous smooths all feelings by calling for a dance and the light song of Demodocus about Ares and Aphrodite (8.256ff.). They regard the highest fame (*kleos*) as resting on athletic victories (8.147–48), whereas the *kleos* Odysseus knows and has gained derives from the war at Troy, what the poets sing as the κλέα ἀνδρῶν, the "famed songs of heroes" (8.73ff.).

Through Demodocus' song Odysseus reenters the sufferings of the

---

[14] On the ambiguities of the Phaeacians, see G. Rose (1969) passim and Most (1989) 27–29. On their associations with both an afterlife paradise and Hades, see Cook (1992) passim, especially 241ff., 248ff., 266.

[15] Besides the Phaeacians, the epithet *philēretmos,* "loving the oar," is used only of the Taphians, and then just in the first book when Athena appears as Mentes, leader of the Taphians (1.181, 419).

Trojan War, whereas the Phaeacians merely take delight. The simile that describes Odysseus' weeping belongs to the world of the *Iliad:* a captive widow harshly led off as a slave, bewailing her husband's death and her fate (8.522–30).[16] The Phaeacians' aesthetic removal from Odysseus' sufferings accelerates his return to the realities of his past. His strange two-day incognito constitutes, among other things, a tacit refusal to assimilate to them. He withholds his name until their song and sport are passed; and his declaration of himself comes, as in all his identifications, in his own terms. In this case, the terms are the tears over Troy and the recollection of his previous trials (9.2ff.). He recalls his heroic past at the moment when he is to reenter, in his Phaeacian tale, the fantasy world of the nearer past from which he is just emerging. Both streams of his past will unite when on Ithaca he dons again his heroic armor to defeat the suitors and lying beside Penelope repeats to her the tale he is about to tell the Phaeacians.

Pleasure, Joy, and Grief

Odysseus' brief sojourn among the Phaeacians, I have argued, represents a clash between involvement in human suffering and removal from it, and this clash comes at the decisive point of his crossing from the limitless possibilities and discoveries in the fantasy world to reality on Ithaca. The clash has repercussions throughout the entire poem and, as we shall see in Chapters 7 and 8, reaches deeply into its poetics. It is developed partly through the significant recurrence of two key words, "joy" (*terpsis* and related compounds) and "pain" (*pēma, pēmainesthai*).

The "joy" of the Phaeacians in feasting and song (especially the latter) occurs frequently throughout book 8 (e.g., 45, 91, 368, 429, 542), but the prominence of their bard, a mark of their leisurely, pleasurable, undisturbed existence, brings only grief to Odysseus, who weeps while the Phaeacians "take joy" (90ff.), until finally Alcinous remarks publicly that the poet "is not singing to the pleasure of all" (πάντεσσι χαριζό-μενος, 538) and that Odysseus has not ceased weeping since the song began (540–41). Thus it would be better for all to "take joy" together in the song (542–43). This opposition of "grief" (*goos*, 540) and "joy" (542) introduces Odysseus' statement of his identity and his tale of the past. The adventures he relates include much that was "joyless" (*aterpes*): the

---

[16] Cf. *Il.* 19.290–94, and see below, Chapter 6.

"joyless feast" of the Laestrygonians (10.124), the Sirens who offered joy in knowledge (12.188), Teiresias' asking Odysseus if he has come to see "the dead and the joyless place" (11.94). In landing on Scheria, too, he was cast up, as he tells Arete, on a "joyless place" (7.279).

On Odysseus' last evening on Scheria, the Phaeacians are "taking joy" in the feast (13.26–27), whereas he is looking toward the mortal hardships and sufferings of Ithaca; and the contrast is emphasized by the simile of the hungry plowman to express Odysseus' eagerness to return (31–34). This simile also implies a contrast between toil and ease and between fixity on land and movement on sea (significantly, the Phaeacians are again here called "lovers of the oar," 36). In a sense Odysseus is still alone among the Phaeacians, as he has been for the seven years with Calypso. He alone knows grief, and only for him does the bard's ability to re-create suffering as well as joy have meaning. Only for him would Demodocus' loss of sight have deep significance: "Him the Muse loved exceedingly but gave him both good and bad: she took away his eyes, but gave sweet song" (8.63–64). Odysseus, himself compared to a bard (11.368), shares with Demodocus—and perhaps with Arete—alone of the Phaeacians a bond of knowledge and suffering.

The theme of grief amid joy recurs throughout the entire poem and unites the three major characters. Penelope first appears (and is first mentioned by name, 1.329) weeping and chiding the bard Phemius for singing the "Return of the Achaeans" that is "giving joy" to the suitors (1.347). Telemachus weeps covertly amid the feasting of Menelaus at the mention of his father (4.113–14), as Odysseus does at the Phaeacian feast (8.84f., 521–22). In this world of human suffering, however, Telemachus is joined by all the others (4.183–89), until Peisistratus declares that he has "no joy in lamenting after dinner" (193–94; see also 19.513 of Penelope). By contrast, the disguised Odysseus on Ithaca is at first reluctant to tell Penelope his story, lest he weep "in a strange house" (19.119). The constraint here on weeping, moreover, reflects the suitor's inhumanity, so different from the sympathetic interest of Alcinous or the shared grief of Menelaus' palace.

The suitors are usually presented as "taking joy" in feasting, song, or games (as at their first appearance, 1.107; see also 1.369, 422, etc.). Their joy in the discus (4.626) contrasts bitterly with the anxiety and grief of Telemachus on his journey. The same line in book 17 after Theoclymenus' prophecy to Penelope foreshadows the doom that is about to end all their joys (17.168). The discus also recalls the Phaeacian triumph of Odysseus (8.186ff.), and he is soon to prove the force of his arm in another contest on Ithaca. Thus the "joy" of the suitors is not the legitimate pleasure that the Phaeacians have by virtue of the favor of the gods and their remoteness from humans and human suffering but is gained by cruelty and the infliction of suffering. Such too is the "delight" (*terpōlē*) that they find in setting the two beggars to fight (18.36ff.). In contrast to the easy, god-given bounty of the Phaeacians, the suitors' feasting always shows up the toil and effort it costs: the efforts of the herdsmen who supply the animals for the feasting (14.40–42, 85–108, 415–17), the work of the servants (20.149ff., 162ff.), the added toil of the grinding woman who curses the suitors (20.105–19), and the constantly emphasized waste of Odysseus' substance. The suitors' joy also contrasts with the grim fate hanging over them, a contrast Homer exploits ceaselessly, as when they "die with laughter" enjoying the battle of the two beggars (18.100).[17]

The simple fare of Eumaeus, on the other hand, is accompanied by a true "joy" (14.443, 15.391), and swineherd and beggar may "take joy in each other's griefs, remembering them, for even amid griefs may a man take joy, even one who suffers much and wanders much" (15.399–400).[18] Eumaeus' "joy" gives suffering its place in human life and does not, as it does for the suitors, depend on the outrage and mockery of the suffering. Finally, Odysseus' recognition by Penelope is accompanied by an awareness of the balance of grief and joy in human life. She asks Odysseus not to be angry for her testing of him, because the gods have begrudged them "to take joy [*tarpēnai*] in their youth and arrive at the threshold of old age" (23.212). The joy of rediscovery is here mixed with the sadness of irreparable loss. Very different is the tone of Odysseus' farewell to Arete on Scheria, his wishing her joy "until old age and death come that fall upon men. But do you take joy in this house and your children and people and Alcinous the king" (13.59–62). To Arete, death and age are inevitable, but they are only the natural limit of a life of happiness; they leave the Phaeacians unthreatened and untroubled. When Odysseus bids Penelope to "take joy" in sleep, however, it is with the knowledge of "the measureless toil" before them (23.248–55).[19]

As Odysseus cannot share in the untroubled "joy" of the Phaeacians,

---

[17] Note also the "unquenchable laughter" sent by Athena upon the suitors, followed by the grim prophecy of Theoclymenus (20.345ff.). In 18.304–6, too, as the suitors turn to dance and song, "black evening came upon them as they took their joy," the epithet "black" having now a far more sinister connotation, as their doom approaches, than at the first occurrence of these lines in 1.421–23; note also the play on light in 18.343, 18.354–55, 19.24–25, and 19.33–35, and see in general Clarke (1962) 358–60 and Whitman (1958) 121–23.

[18] On this scene see below, Chapter 8.

[19] See below, Chapter 9.

so he cannot continue in their freedom from pain. The words "pain" and especially "painless" (apēmōn) form a recurrent pattern complementary to the "joy" discussed above. Odysseus is "the man of many woes" (1.4) who cannot be sheltered from the sufferings of his journey.[20] Calypso sends behind him a wind "painless and gentle" (5.268, 7.266), and Circe promises to aid Odysseus so that he may not "be grieved suffering any pain" (12.26–27). Even this aid cannot prevent the shipwreck of his raft or the ravages of Scylla, who brings pain to mortals (12.125) and to his companions (12.231). In the same way, Aeolus' gift cannot shorten Odysseus' wanderings. Even in offering the "painless" transport of the Phaeacians, Alcinous makes clear that Odysseus, though not suffering any pain "in between," must endure "whatever his fate and the dire spinners spun out for him on his thread at birth, when his mother bore him" (7.192–98). The last phrase in particular makes clear Odysseus' involvement in the suffering contingent on birth and mortality. His foreknowledge and acceptance of this suffering are reflected retrospectively in Penelope's speech to the suitors in book 18, in which she reports Odysseus' parting words to her: "My wife, I do not think that all the well-greaved Achaeans will return from Troy without suffering [apēmonas]" (259–60). Paradoxically, Odysseus comes back with more than if he had returned "without pain" from Troy (5.39–40, 13.137–38). His suffering enables him to bring back gifts from lands that he would not otherwise have reached.

Odysseus' involvement in mortality and pain is so strong that his suffering is reflected back on the Phaeacians, hitherto "the painless transporters of all men" (8.566, 13.174). Poseidon turns to stone the ship that brought back Odysseus, and "roots" it fixedly near the city (13.163), fettering (168) the "swift ship in the sea as it sped homeward" (168–69).[21] The Phaeacians, people of swift movement and lightness of foot, experience the fixity that Odysseus knows on Ithaca; and the people of the sea (here pointedly called "of the long oars" and "ship-famed," 166) cease giving passage to mortals. The beginning of book 13 repeats Alcinous' promise of book 8 to restore Odysseus to his country (13.128–87 and 8.565–70). In book 13 the positions are reversed: Odysseus sleeps while Alcinous, previously confident and boastful (8.556–63, 13.5–6) and easily shrugging off the prophecy (8.570–71), now in real alarm seeks to placate the gods (13.179–83).

The Phaeacians temporarily still the grief of Odysseus by taking his

[20] Note too the patronymic Polypēmonides, "Son of Much Sufferer," in 24.305, if the text is correct. For other etymologies, see Stanford (1958–61) on that line.

[21] On Poseidon and the Phaeacian ship, see below, Chapter 10, with note 27.

curse, the anger of Poseidon, upon themselves. Odysseus has thus left his mark, the inevitability of suffering, on the Phaeacians. They are affected because, unlike his other hosts, they are mortal and are still within the pale of human suffering. They cannot, like Aeolus, send him away as one accursed and "hated by the gods" (10.74–75)—but they pay the price of removing his curse. Their disaster thus breaks the last link with the untroubled fantasy realm. Their loss, with the prophecy on the one side (8.564–71) and its fulfillment on the other (13.125–87), frames Odysseus' account and recollection of his experiences there. Willingly or not, they are made to share in the suffering mortality to which Odysseus returns. The last vision of them, in the same verse as Odysseus' awakening on Ithaca (13.187), is one of trouble and uncertainty as they stand about the altar praying to Poseidon. Then Odysseus awakens and they fade, almost as if in a dream, into the past.

This past, with its fantasy world, is thus closed forever. Only the greatest effort brought Odysseus to this point of calm, wherein he could survey and relive the marvels of his journey; he leaves the Phaeacian island behind as mysteriously as he found it. It had emerged before his eyes, as welcome as life from death (5.394–98) and as elusive as the mysterious Leucothea, rising and vanishing into the waves (5.333); and it now disappears in mist and sleep. Once touched by human suffering, this remote and peaceful world ceases to be accessible to mortals. In contrast to the common fairy-tale motif, it is fairyland itself, not the returning mortal, that suffers at the crucial point of transition.

This closing of the fantasy world is accompanied by another echo of the mortal reality that Odysseus has brought with him from Troy. The verb *amphikaluptein* is used four times in close succession of the "covering over" of the Phaeacian island by a mountain (13.152, 158, 177, 183; and 8.569); but it is also employed, somewhat strangely, in Demodocus' song of the fall of Troy (sung at Odysseus' request), of how "it was fated for the city to perish when it covers over [*amphikalupsēi*] the great Wooden Horse" (8.511–12). Odysseus carries with him into the Phaeacian kingdom the pain involved even in his greatest triumph. Conversely, once Odysseus has passed out of this fantasy world into the reality of Ithaca, he cannot return. Thus Alcinous' boastful promise that Odysseus would not return to the Phaeacians (13.5–6) takes on an ironical sense after Poseidon's revenge, when the Phaeacians, to appease the god's anger (13.180–83), voluntarily desist from all further transport of mortals.

Odysseus' loss of the fantasy world, however, is a willing one; and he reaccepts the conditions of human reality and adapts to the new de-

velopments with still sharper guile and grimmer determination. Yet the
Phaeacians are important also for a restoration of another kind: they
show Odysseus that beauty, joy, and youthful gaiety still exist, and they
present a vision of the world that complements his much-enduring
spirit. Though he cannot reenter their world, he takes back the gifts and
treasures he has acquired there, articles that are fused symbolically with
the happy memories and restorative experiences that both Alcinous
(8.430–32) and Nausicaa (8.461–62) wish him to remember. These gifts
must be hidden for the nonce; they cannot be brought safely into direct
contact with the grim realities of Ithaca but must lie quiet, latent, in the
dark, misty cave (13.366ff.) so "that they may remain safe" until they
can be brought forth (13.363–64; cf. 304–5).

On the one hand, the Phaeacian episode is just another adventure,
with a hazardous landing and a safe departure, similar to the encounters
of Circe or Calypso; on the other hand, it is the point of Odysseus'
reviewing and reliving the whole of the past nine years. It embodies all
the mystery of the sea and the wanderings. It begins and ends with sleep
and the aid of Athena, who once more directly helps Odysseus. It is a
point of rest and renewal, as well as of mysterious return: renewal of his
heroic vigor in the songs of Troy, the victorious discus throw, and the
buckling on of the sword given by Euryalus (8.416). It is a renewal of
human relationships, too, in his meeting with Nausicaa—in her girlish
talk of marriage and Alcinous' actual offer of her hand in what would be
a normal union with a mortal woman in society—after the risky liaisons
with Circe and Calypso. This episode is also a return to a complex,
ordered, and highly refined society, with its comforts (see 7.336ff.) and
its protection of suppliants; and so it provides an image of the domestic
and political unity and order that Odysseus will have to restore on
Ithaca. His farewell speech to Arete as he prepares to cross the sea for the
last time to Ithaca (13.59–62) is a mortal man's turning toward old age
and death; and it balances the youth and freshness of Nausicaa that first
revived him and "gave him life" (8.468).[22]

Cyclopes and Phaeacians

The fullest antithesis to the Phaeacians is the Cyclopes. The high
civilization of the Phaeacians—their social development, shipbuilding

---

[22] There seems to be a deliberate framing effect in Odysseus' two speeches, to Nausicaa (8.461–68) and Arete (13.59–62), respectively mother and daughter, the two Phaeacian women most responsible for saving him; and both speeches begin with the farewell,
χαῖρε.

and sailing, and entertainment of guests—stands in the greatest contrast to the rudimentary social organization of the Cyclopes, their lack of ships and primitive means of sustenance, and their scorn for the gods and divinely sanctioned rights. The initial passages describing both peoples sharpen the contrasts. The Phaeacian founder, Nausithous, established the features of civilized life which are lacking among the Cyclopes: building walls and houses, founding shrines to the gods, dividing plowlands (6.9–10; contrast 9.107–15). The island across from that of the Cyclops is unpastured and unplowed because the Cyclopes lack ships to reach it (9.125–29).[23] The fertility and wildlife show the richer, more benevolent aspects of nature—calm, remote, beautiful (9.120–24, 130ff.)—whereas the Cyclopes and their island show wild nature's harsher, more savage, deadly aspect. Even the golden age richness of the Cyclopean earth contrasts with the carefully ordered, delicately fostered trees of Alcinous' garden (7.114–32)—"the glorious gifts of the gods"—in the same way that the rude cave of Polyphemus, with its great stone to close it, contrasts with the elegant palace of Alcinous with its golden doors (7.88).[24]

More important than the material differences are the moral differences. Odysseus comes upon the Phaeacians as they are reverently offering a libation to Hermes (7.136–38), and after Alcinous has seated Odysseus, they make another libation to Zeus, "who attends suppliants deserving of respect" (ὅς θ' ἱκέτῃσιν ἅμ' αἰδοίοισιν ὀπηδεῖ, 7.181). The Cyclops, however, not only scorns all the gods (9.274–76) but also specifically flaunts Zeus (277), to whom Odysseus appealed in vain as "Zeus *Xenios,* avenger of suppliants and guests, who attends guests deserving of respect" (269–71), echoing Alcinous' reverent invocation of Zeus in 7.181.

The contrast between the two peoples is made the more pointed by the curious history of the Phaeacians reported at the beginning of book 6: the Phaeacians "previously dwelt in broad Hypereia, near the Cyclopes, overweening men, who did them harm, for they were superior in force. From here godlike Nausithous led them forth in migration and settled them on Scheria, far from men who toil for livelihood" (6.4–8). Why should the peace-loving Phaeacians have such a history?[25] Nothing

[23] This passage (9.125–29) is perhaps intended by Odysseus as an encomium of seafaring as a mark of civilization which would interest and please the Phaeacians.

[24] For further discussion of the contrasts between the Cyclopes and the Phaeacians and the ambiguities of the Cyclopes as belonging to a golden age, see below, Chapter 10, pp. 202–09.

[25] Eustathius (on 6.4–8) admits that the story is "not necessary" but explains it as a transition out of Odysseus' great danger and a means of avoiding monotony; but surely

in the subsequent narrative requires it, and for an imaginary people the poet was probably free to invent or suppress details of origin. The conjunction of the Phaeacians and the Cyclopes here and the later mention of them by Alcinous alongside "the savage tribe of Giants" (7.205–6) reminds us that the fantasy world, like the Phaeacians themselves, includes both generosity and danger. Odysseus is just now escaping from its violence, cruelty, and strangeness, on which he will look back as past; and he is moving into a more comprehensible and favorable world, closer to, indeed far superior to, the real world of Ithaca.

The crucial difference, however, is just this, that Odysseus has had a personal taste of the Cyclopes' cruelty, whereas the Phaeacians have isolated themselves from it by their sea life and their high fortified walls, "a wonder to behold" (7.44–45). They seem to think of the Cyclopes now only as a remote, quasi-mythical people, like the Giants (7.205–6).[26] They have fled from an aspect of their world that Odysseus has encountered and mastered.

Among the Phaeacians Odysseus finds a high point of civilization not only in their amenities and kind treatment but also in their concern for his name, sought with sympathetic curiosity at his weeping (8.550ff.). Yet they know him most fully in the distanced, aesthetic medium of Demodocus' songs of Troy and the *kleos* of which Odysseus himself boasts (9.20). Their way of approaching the world differs profoundly from that of Odysseus. They flee from its savage elements and establish their life in the enclosed safety of their city and their walls; Odysseus encounters these elements immediately and triumphs over them through his endurance, courage, and wiliness. The Phaeacians represent for him still, therefore, a halfway point: active and social, unlike Calypso or Circe, not murderous and callous, like the Cyclopes, but still removed from the savage realities that Odysseus has known and will again confront.

Odysseus' defeat of the Cyclops is a victory of human intelligence over primitive force and the brute power, the sheer *bia,* of untamed nature (see 6.6). His putting out of the Cyclops' eye is described in images

---

the following account of Nausicaa (6.15ff.) serves these functions, and besides, such an explanation does not account for the content of the history. Legends and conjectures about Hypereia and the "prehistory" of the Phaeacians are reviewed by Eitrem (1938) 1527–28.

[26] For another aspect of the relation between the Phaeacians and Giants here, see below, Chapter 10, pp. 203–04.

of the arts of civilization, metalworking and shipbuilding (9.384–86, 391–93), whereas the Cyclopes' lack of shipbuilders was especially remarked (9.126). Even in appearance Polyphemus is "not like a man, eater of bread, but like a wooded crag of high mountains which appears alone apart from the others" (9.190–92), another image of wild nature (see also 9.292); but Odysseus departs shouting his human name and birthplace.

Through his exercise of intelligence, Odysseus defeats Polyphemus and regains the heroic identity of which the brutality of the Cyclops had deprived him and of which the adventure in the cave marks the lowest ebb. Polyphemus allows him no rights, treats him almost as one of the animals he keeps, and inquires of his name merely to assure him that he, too, will be eaten as were the others, only later. He must become temporarily "No-Man," without identity, until, after winning his freedom and his life, he again defiantly announces himself as "Odysseus sacker of cities, son of Laertes, having his home on Ithaca" (9.504–5). Reassuming his identity, however, exposes him not only to the dangers of the Cyclops' missiles but also to all the subsequent sufferings that Polyphemus' prayer to Poseidon will bring down. Polyphemus can curse Odysseus only when he knows his name, but simultaneously, his name carries with it the associations of pain (*odunai;* cf. 17.567, 19.117) and hatred (*odussesthai;* cf. 19.275–76, 407) with which his Ithacan existence is connected.[27] His nearly fatal declaration of his name to Polyphemus appears further oriented toward the human world: "If any one of *mortal* men ask you" (9.502)—a boast that almost destroys his return to "mortal men."

The Loss of Troy

Odysseus' return to the real world is measured also in terms of his relationship with his companions. He is gradually divested of them—as

[27] For the odium that Odysseus' name carries on Ithaca, see Eupeithes' enumeration of the disasters Odysseus has caused, 24.427–29. Stanford (1952) 209–13 discusses 19.407–9 and concludes that the passive sense of *odussesthai* predominates and Odysseus is therefore "the man of divine displeasure" (see 1.62), "the man doomed to odium." The scholiast on 19.407 explains *odussamenos* as *misētheis*, "hated." The connection with *odunē*, "pain," is stressed by Dimock (1956) 52–70: Odysseus must accept what is implied in his name. For another suggested etymology, see Carpenter (1946) 131. On Odysseus' name and on naming in general in a poststructuralist perspective, see Peradotto (1990) 101–19, 123–31, 153–55.

of his ships, clothes, and all his Trojan accoutrements—through increasing emotional estrangement. The unreality of the fantasy world is reflected in the instability of these relationships, which are based only on temporary circumstances and a common desire for self-preservation. The bond begins to dissolve as the companions' desire for self-preservation weakens. The fantasy world tests both the companions' hold on life and their relation with Odysseus. Both give way, and even Odysseus' wish to save them, along with his former position of authority, becomes increasingly meaningless.

The *Odyssey* begins with the hero's strong sense of responsibility for his men: "Many pains in his heart did he suffer on the sea, winning his own life and his companions' return; but not even so did he save the companions, desirous though he was" (1.4–6). He is concerned that none of them be left behind among the Lotos-eaters (9.102), and he takes futile measures to pass Scylla without loss of men (12.111–14). Indeed, his concern for them seems to increase as the dangers become greater; but simultaneously, as he enters deeper into the fantasy world and approaches his seven-year "suspension" on Ogygia, his links with his Trojan past weaken and with it his relation with his men. This concern for them is partly an aspect of his heroic identity and partly a remnant of his leadership at Troy. But from the very beginning, the Ciconian debacle, he can no longer fulfill the functions of protective king and general, and he becomes increasingly less able to save his men from the ravages of this dangerous world. Their increasingly mutinous behavior reveals the inadequacy of the relationship, until their total disobedience on Thrinacia severs them from Odysseus completely. This breakdown of the former martial discipline accompanies the loss of the other survivals from the war, until when Odysseus arrives alone among the Phaeacians the war is but a subject for song.

The clash and strain of wills appear from the very first. The companions refuse to obey (*ouk epithonto*, 9.44) Odysseus' suggestion of immediate departure from the Ciconians. Later, Odysseus' disregard of their plea, when "they did not persuade [his] great-hearted spirit" (οὐ πεῖθον ἐμὸν μεγαλήτορα θυμόν, 9.500), brings near disaster from the Cyclops' missiles (9.494ff.). The parallel is further emphasized by the repetition of the line "lest one go away disappointed of an equal portion" in both episodes (9.42, 9.549). The Aeolus episode is the most painful failure of trust between Odysseus and the companions and precipitates Odysseus' moment of greatest despair (10.49–52). On Circe's island Odysseus has twice to argue with the factious Eurylochus (10.266ff.,

424ff.). In the latter instance, in a rare loss of temper and control, he even draws his sword in murderous anger (10.438–42), for a moment looking more like Achilles in *Iliad* 1 than his usual self. The same Eurylochus forces Odysseus to land on Thrinacia (12.278ff.) and instigates the disastrous slaughter of the Sun's cattle (12:339–65).[28]

This episode brings a total rupture of relations. Odysseus, the true leader, is ignored and "forced" (*biazete,* 12.297, the word used of his experiences at the hands of the suitors in 13.310) to act against his better judgment, indeed his certainty of the evil consequences of such action. But the men, lacking Odysseus' "iron" determination (12.280), are destroyed by the attrition of their will to survive, by their sheer weariness and acquiescence in death (12.341ff.). The extraordinary nature of their situation requires a degree of cooperation that diminishes increasingly. Odysseus can still count on his men to bind him when they pass the Sirens, assuring them that they will face the coming dangers with full knowledge (12.156–57), thus ostensibly avoiding the error of the Aeolus episode. Yet he shrewdly withholds information about Scylla, lest their fright cause them all to perish (12.224–25). But it is his men who recall him from Circe to the necessity of returning to Ithaca (10.466–75).

Mutual interdependence alternates with disastrous mistrust, but the fluctuation only betrays the instability of the relationship. In recalling him from Circe, the crewmen speak with a still living attachment to home and mortality, but their loss is the gradual disappearance of the remnants of the war and the temporary, limited human relations it creates. In this respect the *Odyssey* inverts the *Iliad*'s perspective on the bonds created by war. In the *Iliad* the Greeks' ties to home and family take second place to the bonding among the male warriors, and family ties are part of the tragedy of Troy. The *Odyssey* views the ties to wife, son, and parents as the truly lasting relationships and those among the comrades of the war, though important, as less essential to the definition of its protagonist's identity. These latter dissolve through their own internal tension and instability until there is nothing left. Odysseus is isolated not only by the violent end of the companions but by the increasing privacy of his adventures as well. The encounters with Circe and the Sirens and the meetings in Hades all in some way exclude the companions.

In the voyage from Troy to Scheria and then to Ithaca, Odysseus

---

[28] For other aspects of the Thrinacian episode, see below, Chapter 10.

loses the booty gained in war alongside his companions and instead brings back the gifts he obtained alone among the peace-loving Phaeacians. The vessels that carried him to Troy are not sufficient to carry him back, but he returns on a mysterious ship, not his own, by an unknown route to a land that he does not at first recognize. He has lost not only the ships, garb, and companions of the war years and the wandering but also the means of wandering further, and the very ship that returned him is "fettered" as a rock. His journey is a continual separation from the casual and fortuitous, through which the wanderer finds his way back to the essential and lasting. Yet he accomplishes the transition from unsettledness to peace only by a final act of violence, and he reassumes his proper role in Ithaca only by a final movement of nakedness, the throwing off of his rags (*gumnōthē*, 22.1) as he commences to slay the suitors.

CHAPTER 3

The Phaeacians and Odysseus' Return: Part 2, Death and Renewal

Mortality and Hades

Odysseus' return is a return to humanity in its broadest sense. For the early Greek, however, humanity subsumes and is essentially linked with mortality; and life is defined by the awareness of death. "Look always to the last day," the generations of men like that of leaves, men as a "shadow's dream."[1] So, too, the *Odyssey* is permeated by an undercurrent of death: the honorless, unheroic death of Agamemnon; the horror of death expressed by Achilles; the lurid horror of Hades itself; the culmination of the poem in the death of the suitors, felt and presented in its grimness and necessary brutality, and their spiritless shades in the underworld.[2] The death of Odysseus himself, "mild," "coming from the sea" (or, by another interpretation, "far from the sea"), announced to him by Teiresias in Hades,[3] mars even the joyfulness of his return (23.248–55) and hangs over his days to come, a deep and sad expres-

---

[1] See, for example, *Il.* 6.145–49, Pindar *Pythian* 8.95f., Sophocles *Trachiniae* 1–3 and *Oedipus at Colonus* 1224–28; see, in general, Wankel (1983) passim.

[2] For the brutality of the slaughter, see especially Stella (1955) 291–93, who considers it as "l'ultimo atto, in certo senso l'epilogo, della 'luttuosa guerra' " ("the final act—in a certain sense the epilogue—of the 'grievous war,' " 291) and finds throughout the *Odyssey*, unlike in both the Germanic and the Near Eastern epics, a humane pity for the horror of death (293ff.; also 228–29). Whitman (1958) 305–6 also sees the slaughter of the suitors as a primitive survival from the intractable raw material of the tale.

[3] Later mythographers even fulfilled Teiresias' prophecy through an Etruscan enchantress, a runaway maidservant of Circe called Hals, "Sea": see Westermann (1843) 191.

sion, characteristically Homeric, of the mixed and limited nature of all human happiness, of the inevitable involvement of man, even after his most strenuously attained and hoped for successes, in time, change, and death.

Odysseus' acceptance of his mortality before his departure from Ogygia (5.203–24) colors the rest of his adventures. He voyages forth as a man who knows he will suffer and die and accepts it (see 221–24). Homer makes his mortal position even more pointed in the interview with Calypso: Odysseus follows "in the tracks of the goddess" (193); they come to the cave "a goddess and a man" (194, θεὸς ἠδὲ καὶ ἀνήρ), and he sits where the divine Hermes sat before, not eating the nectar and ambrosia that Calypso offered Hermes (5.93) but "such food as mortal men eat" (οἷα βροτοὶ ἄνδρες ἔδουσιν, 197) while she is served nectar and ambrosia (199). The difference between "man and god" (194) is made as clear as possible, and Odysseus' refusal of immortality is to reinforce this separation. Even the formulaic epithet "divine Odysseus" (*theios*) in line 198 may convey a touch of irony that strengthens this separation.[4] When Odysseus, still tossing on the waves, sees the Phaeacians' land rising before him, the simile prefigures the mortal life to which he is moving closer: "As when the life of their father appears dearly welcome to children, their father who lies in the powerful grip of sickness, suffering pains, for long wasting away, and some hateful power [*daimōn*] has assailed him, but the gods, to their welcome joy, have loosed him from ill, so joyfully welcome to Odysseus were earth and woodland" (394–98). The basic, touching human situation marks his passage back toward the world of men: a rebirth, a new entrance into life, crossing the waters—sweet and bitter waters, waters of life and death—but also a rebirth into mortal life, with its pain and struggles.[5]

The crossing of waters to Ithaca is calm and gentle, unlike the rough, angered seas through which Odysseus had to fight his way to Scheria. In many myths it is exactly this crossing, the hero's reentrance to the

---

[4] Note also that at the beginning of the Calypso episode, Zeus tells Hermes that the Phaeacians will honor Odysseus "as a god" (5.36), a phrase used of Arete (7.71, and see 7.69) and later of Odysseus himself (disguised) in speaking to Penelope (19.280). Then in 23.339, after the slaughter, Odysseus, now in his own person, uses it again of himself, recalling 5.36 (as well as 19.280) and thus marking the completion of his return to Ithaca and the restoration of his rightful position as the good king and of the political harmony of which the Phaeacians presented a model.

[5] The water imagery, like the motif later of swimming through the river channel to arrive at the Phaeacian shore, may suggest the physical process of birth: see Newton (1984) 12–14.

mortal world after a long sojourn in the world beyond, that is the most dangerous. In some myths the hero even falls dead when his foot touches mortal soil again.[6] But Odysseus has already made the transition, physically and inwardly, among the Phaeacians, and they absorb the danger of his crossing.

It is Athena who greets him and gradually restores to him the true image of Ithaca, dispelling the mist with which she herself has concealed it (13.189–96, 352). She serves as an objective correlative of his inner wholeness, his ability to act with rational comprehension of and full orientation in the human world. Thus she is the goddess who sees through his disguises. As his personal protectress, she is visible to him alone (16.160–63); and she restores to him his old heroic image, the strength and beauty of his recovered being, when he reveals himself to son and wife (16.172ff., 23.156ff.). But she also elicits his characteristic traits of cunning, deception, and restraint by testing him in a battle of wits in which her disguise as a shepherd lad (13.222) forces him into the first of his Ithacan lies. She does not remove the mist over Ithaca until she has penetrated his disguise and revealed herself, in the form of a beautiful woman (288–89), as his helping goddess (299–302).[7] He recognizes her before he does his homeland. Thus a kind of inner self-recognition precedes the outer recognition of Ithaca (he does not actually kiss the earth as the sign of true acceptance until line 354). Unlike Calypso, Athena "hides" only to reveal more fully. With the reappearance of Athena come the resumption of his orientation in the human world, the certainty of his aims, the reawakening of his rational powers and his strength to endure, and the confident grasping of himself as he is (see 303–10). Athena's own guile, which matches that of her protégé, sets the stage for the display of Odyssean *mētis* (wiliness) that she both admires and calls back to life. His recognition of her inaugurates the long series of recognitions to follow.

The man who would have the fullest experience of life must acquire the bitter knowledge of death. And conversely, before knowing death, Odysseus expands his knowledge of life. He enters Hades only after he

---

[6] For the danger of the return from the beyond, see Germain (1954) 299, who cites the story of Nechtān in the voyage of Bran as a myth of this kind. Germain takes up the suggestion, made at least as early as Friedrich Welcker, that the Phaeacians may be some kind of ferrypeople of the dead, here performing the reverse function in returning Odysseus to life (298–99).

[7] On the meeting between Athena and Odysseus (especially 13.236–351), with its complex humor and ironies, see Hart (1943) 273–77 and Clay (1983) 188–208.

has completed many perilous adventures and has voyaged far into the beyond. His journey to Hades is immediately preceded by the renewal of erotic experiences and the year of sensuous enjoyment with Circe. From her island of physical fulfillment (see 10.460–68), he enters the gloomy realm of lifeless, disembodied shades; and after, amid the pleasures offered by Calypso, he can only weep (5.151–58). The sharp contrast between the bodily satisfactions of Circe and the bodiless ghosts of Hades points up the impermanence of a liaison with an enchantress for the hero returning to the human world. Her year-long delights can only postpone, not prevent, his journey to Hades, of which she has presumably known all along. Later in his voyage, on Calypso's island of Ogygia, after he has experienced the passage from Circe to Hades, his departure and separation from a beautiful enchantress have long been willed and desired by the hero himself. In the case of Circe it took the intervention of his human companions to make him want to leave (10.471–74). Yet the departure itself from Calypso requires help from the highest authority on Olympus (1.48–87).

Like the Phaeacian episode as a whole, the visit to Hades faces both forward and back. It is the only adventure imposed on Odysseus as a task or preliminary requirement (ἀλλ' ἄλλην χρὴ πρῶτον ὁδὸν τελέσαι, "But first you *must* accomplish another journey," 10.490). This journey is accepted voluntarily, though with lamentation (10.496ff.), but it is not demanded by geographical necessity or caused by chance. It requires, in fact, a detour outside the course leading directly onward to Ithaca. Yet, paradoxically, this detour across the dark sea to Hades brings him into closer touch with Ithaca and his human life than do any of his adventures hitherto. When he and his men return to Circe, they are together called, alone of mortals, "twice dying" (12.22); yet Odysseus alone among these returns to the land of the living, bringing his heavy burden of death back to the world of life.

His experience of Hades begins with the unnamed souls of the dead, from every range of life: "young matrons and bachelors and much-enduring old men and tender maidens with their newly grieved hearts, and many men wounded with bronze-fitted spears, men slain in battle, wearing bloodied armor" (11.38–41). This generality of death is followed by the meeting with Elpenor, a specific experience of death close at hand, in a companion recently seen alive. Here Odysseus is personally touched by death, and Elpenor entreats him in the name of his living kin, his wife and the father who reared him and "Telemachus whom you left alone in your halls" (66–68). Odysseus' first reaction to the mass of anonymous dead had been "pale green fear" (43), but the sight of Elpenor fills him with a deep pity: "When I saw him I wept and pitied him in my heart" (55). Odysseus repeats the line twice more, on meeting his mother (87) and Agamemnon (395). The formulaic repetition not only creates a forward-moving rhythm of accumulating grief but also marks the continual deepening of his compassion and sorrow as he sees the ravages of death on those closer to him. By awakening Odysseus' direct personal sympathies, Elpenor begins to excite the pity and grief that continue throughout the *Nekyia,* the underworld journey.

Elpenor is also a kind of Everyman. His story is the ever present, accidental possibility of death that occurs when least expected, when there is no risk, at a moment of leisure and forgetfulness. His death was remarkably unheroic, almost foolish, in contrast to those of the heroes and heroines Odysseus will meet or the slain in war, with "bloodied armor." Elpenor, indeed, has little of the heroic about him: he is the youngest of the companions "and not in any way very valiant in war or of very firm intelligence" (10.552–53). His weakness makes him a kind of ritual scapegoat for Odysseus' journey to the dead but simultaneously brings out the sincerity of Odysseus' grief and his individual concern for even this feeblest and most worthless of the companions.

Odysseus' bond with Elpenor is not deep; but it is nevertheless significant, and Odysseus responds. It is externalized in part by the oar that Elpenor requests to have set up on his grave, "the oar with which I used to row when I was among my companions" (11.77–78). The oar embodies the participation in common toil and risks, the sharing of the years of wandering. The proper burial of Elpenor at the dawn immediately after their return to Circe (12.8–15) fulfills this bond and carries the experience of Hades over into the further adventures in the upper world. Immediately afterward, Circe welcomes them with the "bread and abundant meats and bright red wine" that their mortal condition requires (19); but, in calling them *disthanees,* "twice-dying" (22), she reminds them that as mortals they will all make a second trip to Hades—a trip that will be fatal.

The close connection of Odysseus' personal feelings and his recognition of the universality of death continues as he travels further back into his past, from the still recent death of his mother to the remote heroines and then to his companions at Troy. Yet the whole remainder of his exploration of the land of the dead is colored also by his own death, presented in the prophecy of Teiresias (11.100–137). In the figure of Teiresias, the prophet of disaster and tragic fate, he meets his own mortal destiny.[8] When he asks Teiresias how he may address his mother's shade, he calmly faces his own death: "Teiresias, these things have the gods themselves spun out," he begins (138). His mother's presence in Hades closely overhangs his discovery of his own fate. She appears briefly immediately before Teiresias and immediately after (84–89, 152ff.). The presence among the dead of the woman who gave him birth places his life in the biological cycle of the coming and passing away of generations. But through her he also renews his direct contact with Ithaca and with his closest human ties. After answering her questions, he asks quickly about her death (170–73) and about his father, son, and wife (174–79). Odysseus thus reexperiences the human world in its most poignant terms: he looks out at it through death and suffering, his own fate in the foreground. Through this meeting, surrounding as it does Teiresias' prophecy, he reaccepts his human ties on Ithaca in the light of his acceptance of his own death.

Here, too, the general blends with the personal, for at the end of the interview, after he has twice tried unsuccessfully to embrace his mother's shade, she addresses him in the anguish of their personal situation: "Ah me, my child, ill-starred above all mortals" (11.216). She then goes on to explain the general "way of mortals [dikē brotōn] whenever anyone dies" (218), how only the shade (psuchē) is left, "like a dream" (222). Odysseus is thus instructed fully in all that pertains to death; but he also undergoes the emotional experience of trying to clasp his mother's ghost. In this empty grasping he experiences what he missed on Ithaca, the full sense of loss, the complete unattainability of the dead, however tangible and real they seem to the survivors who love them. Anticleia's loss is also due specifically to his wandering: she has

---

[8] On Teiresias' prophecy see Reinhardt (1948) 126–27: "Als Gestalt einer Oedipodie oder Thebais tritt Teiresias in das Leben des Odysseus: als der Seher tragischen Verhängnisses, als Warner vor dem Zorne der Götter. . . . Er weiss von Schuld und Sühne, Fluch und Segen" ("Teiresias enters the life of Odysseus like a figure out of an *Oedipodeia* or *Thebais*: as the prophet of tragic fate, as a warner against the anger of the gods. . . . He knows of guilt and expiation, curse and blessing"). He notes also the paradox "dass der grösste Unglücksseher, den die Sage kennt, am Ende aller Mühsal, die er prophezeit, ein so versöhntes Sterben kündet!" ("that the greatest prophet of misfortune known to tradition announces such a reconciled death at the end of all the travail that he prophesies") (132). Woodhouse (1930), though regarding Odysseus' dismissal of the prophecy as almost "flippant," sees it as an insight of Homeric psychology that Odysseus is concerned "with the more trivial facts" of the situation on Ithaca rather than with his own still remote death (148). These concerns, however, are perhaps not so trivial for him, nor is his acceptance of his own death any the less firm for his concern about his mother, wife, son, and father. For other aspects of the prophecy, see below, Chapter 9.

died out of longing for him, and his absence caused her death (202–3). The world that the hero has left is subject to aging and death; though he finally returns, he cannot expect to find all those whom he left alive. The empty embrace is the emptiness of absence during the years of wandering, the loss of the years that might have been spent together. The catalogue of heroines that follows suggests an alternative to death in the continued fame of beautiful women who had union with the gods, but it also shows the extension of death even to the remote, glorious past.

Homer interrupts Odysseus' account at this point to recall the narrative framework, the hero among the Phaeacians (11.333ff.). They are deeply impressed, offer more gifts, and try to persuade him to stay another day. Odysseus replies politely, accepts, saying he could gladly stay a year,[9] but he makes it clear that even his acceptance of gifts has a homeward purpose, to reenter Ithaca "with a fuller hand" and be "dearer and more respected" by his people (11.359–61). When the hero has been so deeply immersed in mortality, he is not threatened by staying another day. He is sure of his purpose and beyond further temptation. He is still willing to store up as much "wealth" as he can from the fantasy world he is leaving, but he is certain of being able to limit the attraction of this world on him. Hence, this delay is quite different from that with Circe or Calypso; Odysseus allows it solely in view of the return itself.

Odysseus' vision of death expands still further as he encounters the Greek heroes of Troy: death again among the close connections of the past. Grim meetings all, especially the garrulous Agamemnon's tale of his treacherous murder and Ajax's angry silence. Achilles' preference of the most toilsome poverty to death continues the mixture of general and personal. Yet Odysseus' years of removal and subsequent experience of life and death have left their mark. He treats his former companions with tenderness and has gentle words of commiseration and reconciliation for each.[10] Heracles, the last of the shades, reminds him of the toils that lie ahead. The wild animals and scenes of "combats and battles and slaughter and the killing of men" that adorn his baldric (11.610–12) recall Odysseus to the fact that he must come to grips again with violence and death in the upper world. As the greatest of heroes who

---

[9] That Odysseus' statement that he would gladly stay a year (11.356) is only a polite compliment appears also from Telemachus' similar reply to Menelaus' offer (4.595) when he, too, is bent on departing.

[10] See 11.391–96, 478, 482–86, 506–37, 553–62.

attained immortality but still left a mortal part of himself in Hades, Heracles seems to sum up finally the inevitability of death.

Sea and Land

Odysseus' acceptance of his own death and of mortality generally is also an acceptance of fixity and a relinquishing of the sea; and both are closely connected in Teiresias' prophecy (11.119–37). He is to seek out the men "who know not the sea nor eat food mixed with salt" (123), where his oar is taken as a winnowing fan (128), an instrument of settled life on land. Here he will fix the oar, fastening that which carried him over strange seas, as a binding of himself to the earth (γαίη πήξας εὐῆρες ἐρετμόν, "fixing in the earth the well-fitted oar," 129) and as the acceptance of the death of a part of himself, just as he fixed the oar of the dead Elpenor on his grave. The oar has sometimes been taken as the necessary instrument for crossing "the river or ocean of death";[11] hence it would also mark the final passage, the last journey of human life.

When Odysseus finally regains his house, the instruments of voyaging reestablish his fixity on Ithaca: Philoetius fastens the doors of the hall with "the rope of a double-curving ship" (21.390–91); and after the slaughter the treacherous maidservants are hanged with "the landing cable of a dark-prowed ship" (22.465). When Penelope at last acknowledges the victorious stranger as her husband, her emotion is likened to the joy of shipwrecked men at the sight of land (23.233–38). Their meeting thus appears as an image of safety from the sea. The simile recalls Odysseus' landing on Scheria in book 5, the accomplishment of the most difficult part of his return to reality. Now, as the return is complete, he leaves the sea not for a remote land halfway between the fantastic and the mortal worlds but for the circle of his essential relationships and the toils to come (23.248–50).

A grimmer and more prosaic simile of the sea expresses the harsher side of the return. As Odysseus surveys the scene of carnage after his battle with the suitors, the bodies are compared to fish caught in nets drawn up on shore, "and all of them, longing for the sea's waves are poured forth, and the blazing sun took away their life" (22.384–88). And later, when the Ithacan relatives come to claim the bodies, Odysseus sends the non-Ithacan corpses "to fishermen to bring [home],

---

[11] For the oar as necessary for the crossing to the land of the dead, see Knight (1936) 41, who also compares the punting poles of Gilgamesh and the tiller of Palinurus (25).

loading them on their swift ships" (24.418–19)—a sea-crossing very different from Odysseus' Phaeacian voyage.

Yet Odysseus' voyage is also the triumph of life over death and especially over easy surrender to death. Once, it is true, at a low point of despair, Odysseus contemplates suicide when the companions disastrously open Aeolus' gift (10.49ff.); "But I endured and remained" (53), he says, as his *tlēmosunē* (enduring spirit) overcomes his despondency. Elsewhere, too, when shipwrecked off Scheria, he wishes that he had been killed at Troy and had at least received heroic honors (5.306–12), and in his tale to Eumaeus he wishes that he had perished in Egypt (14.274–75). While he is toiling homeward, those on Ithaca despair of his return and would prefer him to have been killed at Troy rather than perish ingloriously at sea (e.g., 1.236ff., 14.365–71). Only Penelope endures, though she too has moments of despair and wishes for a gentle death like a deep sleep (18.201–5).

Odysseus' firm hold on life is explicitly contrasted with the fate of the other Trojan leaders. Agamemnon envies Achilles his glorious death (24.36–97), and Achilles himself would now gladly exchange his fame in Hades for the paltriest bit of life above (11.488–91). Unlike Agamemnon, Odysseus adapts to and masters the situation at home, bringing the restoration of order, not its dissolution. Unlike Achilles, he returns to reestablish peace. Achilles almost steps beyond the bounds of mortal life in receiving honor from the sea and his immortal sea mother (24.47–49, 58ff.); but for Odysseus the sea is the source of wandering, which he flees to return to human finitude. Menelaus, too, has endured a long voyage and hardships before his return, but he did not enter the fantasy world or encounter Hades, and he will eventually escape the ultimate necessity of the mortal condition in his translation to "the Elysian plain and the limits of the earth" (4.561–69). Odysseus' return is the hardest and longest because it involves the fullest overcoming of death and the fullest emergence into life. His tenacious attachment to the human ties on Ithaca, conciliatory spirit, and adaptability all separate him from the harsher ideals of the doomed heroes of the *Iliad* and begin to shape a heroism of another kind.

Images of Death

In his non-Iliadic heroism, Odysseus undergoes an experience of death different from that in Hades. Hades is physical death, empty and horrible, although through the counsels of Circe he can cope with it. Just as dangerous is the spiritual death that he undergoes on Calypso's island. Here, his rational faculties are paralyzed; he is totally helpless until the gods interfere, at Athena's instigation. Calypso is a "dread goddess" (*deinē theos*, 7.246, etc.)—like Athena (7.41) or Circe (10.136)—who "holds him by necessity" (*anankē*, 4.557, 5.14, etc.). "His sweet life was ebbing away" (6.162), and all he can do is weep (5.81–84). Though he resists Calypso's offers, his human energy is sapped and his resourcefulness, gone.

Odysseus' landing on Calypso's island is preceded by the loss of the last remnants of his Iliadic identity, his companions and ships, and by a loss of orientation in his passage through the whirlpool Charybdis (12.430–44). He is suspended "like a bat" (433) over a void, clinging to the only sign of life and protection in sight, the saving fig tree. To this he holds, high in the air, "nor did I have any place to fix my feet firmly or to climb upon it, for its roots were far off, and its branches were hanging high away from me" (433–35). His hanging is an image of disorientation: nothing is firm any longer, almost all contact with the natural and human world is gone, save for the "great tree blooming with leaves" (12.103).[12] Hanging like a bat is also an image of death, for the gibbering of the suitors as they are led to Hades in book 24 is compared to the squeaking of bats as one drops off from the hanging chain (24.6–9).[13] Yet the death image for Odysseus is only partial; the

---

[12] Odysseus' position over the abyss, within sight of the sheer rock of Scylla (see 12.73–79), is perhaps similar to the psychological position described in a classical Egyptian text "The Letter of the Scribe," cited (in another connection) by Stella (1955): "*You are alone, you have not a companion with you,* nor a friend within you. Resolve to go on even if you know not the road. Terror seizes you, your hair stands on end, your soul stands in your hands. *On one side you have the abyss, the mountain on the other.* The sky has opened and you believe to have your enemies within you. Begin to tremble, and know the taste of suffering" (135: emphasis added). Compare also the void and suspension in Blake's *Marriage of Heaven and Hell* (1914): "Thro' the mill we went, and came to a cave. Down the winding cavern we grouped our tedious way, till a void boundless as a nether sky appear'd beneath us, and we held by the roots of trees, and hung over this immensity. But I said: 'If you please, we will commit ourselves to this void, and see whether Providence is here also. If you will not, I will.' . . . So I remain'd with him, sitting in the twisted root of an oak. He was suspended in a fungus, which hung with the head downward into the deep" (256).

[13] For the association of bats with death, see Stanford (1958–61): "There was a common belief in antiquity that bats were the souls of the wicked dead, as in the legends of Vampires" (2:411). Carpenter (1946) 109 also suggests that Charybdis might be one of the entrances to the underworld, a further connection with death, and cites a parallel from *Beowulf;* see 147. The whirlpool might be connected with the maze or labyrinthine pattern of mysterious and dangerous entrance, especially from life into death: see Knight (1936) passim.

vitality of the fig tree, like the olive tree that protects him on Scheria and on Ithaca, saves him.[14] He is suspended from human life for seven years but never breaks the bond with his humanity. All he can do consciously is negative, to refuse Calypso's immortality; but Athena above is contriving his return.

After the perilous voyage from Ogygia to Scheria, the subsequent reliving of his adventures in the fantasy world among the Phaeacians provides a synoptic view of his past and reactivates his conscious efforts at reaching reality, Ithaca. The actual transition, however, occurs in sleep, "painless sleep, wakeless, sweetest, most like to death" (13.79–80, also 119). The passage between fantasy and reality is mysterious; it requires all the preceding effort, but the exact point of crossing is hidden in unconsciousness. The transition is also ambiguous: it is a recovery of what has been long sought, but also a loss of the fantasy world, a "death" of the part of Odysseus that has been wandering in return for the rebirth of his fully human self, the renewal of his mortal life on Ithaca. The sleep is restorative—in it are summed up and then purged all his previous sufferings: "Thus [the Phaeacian ship] swiftly moving cut the waves of the sea, bearing the man who had counsels equal to the gods, who previously suffered very many woes in his heart, breaking through wars of men and grievous waves; but then he slept in quiet, forgetting all that he had suffered" (13.88–92). At the same time, it also has a transformative function, so that he does not recognize Ithaca when he awakens (13.194–96).[15] The pain of the past is soothed, but something new and at first strange appears in its place.

This transitional function of sleep has an interesting parallel in a famous passage of Dante's *Purgatorio*. There, too, sleep comes after the conscious passage through the trials of Purgatory, when Dante can proceed on further by conscious or rational effort (as represented by Virgil). After passing through the purifying fire and before entering the Earthly Paradise, he sleeps and dreams of Rachel and Leah. The sleep itself, however, anticipates the good that is to come after the toil of the ascent.

---

[14] See 5.477 and 13.122, 346, 372. For the saving aspect of the olive tree for Odysseus, note also the axe handle of olive wood given by Calypso (5.236), the olive-wood stake in the Cyclops' cave (9.382), and the bed of olive wood (23.190ff.). Note too the comparison of the saving Nausicaa to the Delian palm tree (6.162ff.). See also below, note 31.

[15] For Odysseus' reawakening as a return to consciousness expressed through the root meanings and associations of *nostos* (return), *noos* (mind), and *neomai* (come back), see Frame (1978) chapter 3, especially 137–65.

> Sì ruminando, e sì mirando in quelle,
> mi prese il sonno: il sonno che sovente,
> anzi che 'l fatto sia, sa le novelle.
>
> (27.91–93)

So meditating and marveling upon those [stars], I was seized by sleep, the sleep that often, before the deed exists, knows the news of it.

Later, in canto 31, under the severe reproach of Beatrice, he faints and awakens in the River of Lethe, held by Matilda, who then leads him to the divine visions on the other side (88–93; also 32.64–72). As in the *Odyssey* there is a mysterious crossing of water, unconscious, to reach a much sought goal. For Dante, this is the innocence, purity, and hope of salvation that he had lost in later life; for Odysseus, it is the past and the full human life that he had left behind for Troy and his travels. For both, the journey is difficult, and the actual crossing is administered by forces beyond their control: a crossing into the unfamiliar, which is then made known and familiar again and is taken once more into the reintegrated self.[16]

Recognitions

The whole of the second half of the *Odyssey* consists in Odysseus' rediscovery of the familiar through alienation, of himself through being other than himself. This rediscovery is nothing less than his re-creation of his entire mortal life, the whole range of his human ties. Having passed through the realm of the removed, nonhuman, and incommunicable, he needs the human bonds, personal and social, to be whole, to be again Odysseus, prince of Ithaca. He needs to bring the inner world into the external world of human converse; and this he does in part, through his unique relation with Penelope and the possibility of sharing with her his strange adventures. He gradually rebuilds around himself the close circle of relations he left behind, testing them now as he was tested in his wanderings. They must meet and know him as he has found and won them. It is through their aid, finally, that he completes his task of taking full possession of his house, his wife, his patrimony. He gradually reconstructs his entire human past, reviewing and reliving the whole course of his life on Ithaca, as among the Phaeacians he reviewed his experiences beyond Ithaca.

[16] On the transitional function of sleep, see below, Chapter 4.

The recognition by Eurycleia and the narrative of the scar (19.392–475) bring back not only his early youth but his birth and infancy, memories shared with the nurse who placed him on his grandfather's knees to be named (399–412). The perspective from which the scar's history is told, in fact, here seems to shift from Odysseus to the nurse.[17] In the previous book Penelope's recollection of his speech to her as he left for Troy (18.259ff.) takes him back to his early married life up to the interruption of their relationship by the war. It also anticipates the point of recommencing after separation. At the same time, the figure of Penelope calls up the irreparable loss of the happiness of their youthful maturity, canceled by Troy and the sea. Her suffering and longing span and parallel his own, from her first appearance, lonely and weeping when Athena sends sweet sleep (1.328–36, 363f.), to her fainting recognition of Odysseus, as she complains that "the gods have given us grief, who begrudged us, remaining by one another, to have joy of our youth and arrive at the threshold of old age" (23.210–12). She is part of the beautiful past from which the male warrior-voyager is estranged but which, after suffering, he wins again.

Finally, in visiting his father, Odysseus completes his involvement in the cycle of life.[18] Finding Laertes in squalor, "worn by old age, holding great grief in his breast" (24.233), in his weeping (280) and pouring dust over his head when "the black cloud of grief covered him" (315–17), Odysseus experiences the misery of extreme old age. Yet it is a misery that he claims for himself in his own weeping and hesitation under the pear tree (234–40) and finally in his embrace when he can endure no longer (318–26). Here, more than in the previous meetings, Odysseus has deliberately fixed by previous plan and decision the mode of recognition; he is the initiator and the tester, as he was not with Penelope (cf. 216–18, 235–42). But this is one of the few times in the poem when he overestimates his power of self-control. The man of resolve and intellect relaxes and gives way to uncontrollable feeling when the final link of his humanity has been fastened (315–26).

[17] See Peradotto (1990) 125–26.

[18] Eumaeus' description of the unhappiness and grief of Laertes to Telemachus in the presence of the disguised Odysseus (16.139–45) perhaps prepares Odysseus for this meeting, sketching out for him the field of past relationships—and their present condition—which he must re-create. Eumaeus' concern that Laertes be told may, in fact, be unnecessary if Laertes, according to 4.754, was never actually informed of Telemachus' departure. The significance of the meeting with Laertes at the end of Odysseus' trials and self-revelations is well pointed out by Whitman (1958): "And it is by no means tactless of the poet to have saved Laertes till last, incidentally, for recognition by one's father is, in a way, the final legitimation which establishes a man in his world" (296).

As Odysseus relived the beginnings of his life in the scene with Eurycleia, so here he extends his experiences of human suffering into extreme old age. In the meetings with his parents, one in Hades, the other in misery on Ithaca, he fixes the biological roots of his life amid death and suffering. He also reestablishes the natural cycle of his own life, from birth to death, backward to the generation of his grandfather and forward to his son. The meeting with Laertes takes place too amid the cycles of the natural world: the rows of vines each "bearing in succession" (24.342) and the grapes, unlike the ever-blooming fruit of the remote Phaeacian garden, appearing "when the seasons of Zeus fill them full from above" (344). The cycles of mortal life are bound to those of the fields and the earth, for these are the orchards which Laertes gave to Odysseus and which Odysseus will give to Telemachus.

The hero is now defined not by the sea but by the earth, with its cycles of growth and death, as he fills out the frame of his human life. Each relationship is won back amid the acceptance of change, aging, and death. As Penelope reminds him of the loss of their youth together (23.210–12), so he recalls to her that they have still "measureless toil" ahead (23.248–50).[19] This possession of a deeply felt and involving past is the mark of a full humanity. The suitors, lacking knowledge of the past and of Odysseus' rule and character (4.687–95), also lack this dimension of human understanding. These young stay-at-homes have no experience of the loss and recovery through which Odysseus has passed. The ingratitude of Antinous is especially remarked (16.421–32), and ingratitude was one of the concomitants of the total inhumanity of the Cyclops (9.355–70).[20]

Another series of simple recognitions in part precedes and in part accompanies the major, more complex ones. The first of these is the kissing of the earth and the prayer to the Nymphs or Naiads (13.354–60). The latter are especially close to the life-filled aspects of Ithaca and of Odysseus' past there, with its closeness to the earth (here "grain-giving," *zeidōron,* 354). He promises to give the Nymphs gifts, "as before" (358), thus renewing his ties with the fruitful past. At the end of his prayer to them, he hopes that Athena "will allow me to live and will increase for me my dear son" (360). In this simple prayer Odysseus

---

[19] See below, Chapter 9.

[20] The reference here to Antinous' lack of reverence for suppliants protected by Zeus (16.422–23) perhaps reinforces the connection with the inhumanity of the Cyclops, who likewise pays no regard to suppliants' rights (9.266–78).

reestablishes his old sympathies with the propitious spirits of fertile nature and their life-giving forces in his own life and its extension in his son's. The recognition itself takes place by "the misty cave," a fit setting for the re-creation of a distant, now dim set of associations.

As Odysseus' reference to his son in 13.360 looks ahead to his re-establishment of his rightful place on Ithaca, so the whole setting of this first recognition—the cave and the Nymphs—looks back to the past adventures (13.96–112). The description of the harbor of Phorcys and the cave of the Nymphs calls up, vague and transformed, the world of fantasy through which Odysseus has voyaged. Phorcys himself is the grandfather of the Cyclops Polyphemus (1.72). The two precipitous headlands (13.97–98) suggest Scylla and Charybdis (see 12.73ff.). The shelter from winds (13.99–101) evokes the island across from that of the Cyclops (9.136) or, indeed, any of the easy landing places, such as Laestrygonia (10.87–94). The "slender-leaved olive" (13.102) has associations with significant appearances of the olive previously (5.236, 5.477, 9.382) and also with the saving fig tree "blooming with leaves" (12.103) over Charybdis. The cave itself, "lovely and misty" (13.103), is but one of many caves that Odysseus has known: those of Calypso and the Cyclops; the cave of Scylla, also "misty" as here (see 12.80); the "hollow cave" in which he falls asleep on Thrinacia, where there are "seats and dancing-places of Nymphs" as well (12.317–18). These earlier caves, though likewise places of crucial and perilous passage, brought disaster, whereas the Ithacan cave is a place of safety for him and his gifts and, with its two doors, divine and human, a place of reentrance to his human life.[21] The stone looms and the weavings recall the weaving of Calypso, Arete, and Circe.[22] Within these similarities, however, there is an interesting alignment of female weaving, for the looms of the seductive and dangerous goddesses of the fantasy world resemble one another (5.61–62 = 10.221–22, of Calypso and Circe, respectively), whereas the half-line describing Arete's weaving is recalled for the looms in the cave of the life-giving Nymphs on Ithaca (6.306b = 13.108b). The Nymphs, then, are closer to the helpful, if mysterious, Phaeacians in their saving role than to the clinging temptresses of fairyland.

---

[21] See also the suggestion of Elderkin (1940) 52–54, that the cave was a place of initiation to sacred mysteries and hence a place of rebirth. For the association of caves generally with initiation, rebirth, and "a change of state," see Knight (1936) 30, 38, 46ff., 169, and passim.

[22] For looms and weaving, see 5.62 of Calypso, 6.306 of Arete, and 10.222 of Circe.

Odysseus' Phaeacian voyage is still a mysterious transition, blanketed in a deep, deathlike sleep (see 13.80, 187–96); but the clear human reality begins to crystallize out of the mist of the Phaeacians and the fantasy world in the tangible clarity of "conspicuous Ithaca" (*Ithakēn eudeielon,* 13.212; contrast the "mistiness" of 13.103, 150, and 176 with the "mist" that Athena initially pours over the still-unrecognized landscape in 13.189–91). Harking back to the dangerous caves of the sea world—those of Calypso, Polyphemus, and Scylla—the Nymphs' cave is a condensation of the mysterious passages of the fantasy world and also a link with the geographical realities of Ithaca. It enables Odysseus to enter the real world without losing his experiences of the fantasy world. These latter, however, have been transformed in his mysterious sleep, as if by the unconscious workings of his mind at a crucial transition. They rest stored there, as the gifts remain in the misty cave, until the return is complete, until with the reintegrated wholeness of his life he can again bring forth his fantasy experiences in his narrative to Penelope.

The simpler aspect of Odysseus' reestablishment of his relations with his homeland continues in his meeting with Eumaeus, the first of his genuinely human contacts on Ithaca. Here he encounters the total trust and devotion of the servant, who in his first words speaks of his "godlike lord" (14.40ff.). Eumaeus, who has one of the most direct relationships with Odysseus, is connected, too, with the property and material position that Odysseus is to reclaim. So he catalogues his master's wealth (14.99ff.) and spends the night with the pigs, at which "Odysseus rejoiced, because he looked after his property though he was far away" (14.526–27). Eumaeus' offering to the Nymphs (and to Hermes, 14.435) also places Odysseus amid the earthy, fruitful associations that Odysseus first renews on recognizing Ithaca. He does not identify himself to Eumaeus until he is about to slay the suitors, but he establishes their relationship by asking his life story (15.381ff.). This is not merely to pass the time; he communicates with a simple man, through the deeper fellowship of suffering that both know.[23]

As Odysseus, in the company of Eumaeus, approaches his palace, he encounters the Nymphs again: "And they came to a spring, artificially made, well-flowing, from which the citizens draw water, which was made by Ithacus and Neritus and Polyctor, and round about was a grove of water-nourished poplars, circling all about, and cool water flowed

---

[23] See Chapter 8, below.

from a rock above, and above it was built an altar to the Nymphs at which all passersby did sacrifice" (17.205–11). The fertility of Ithaca appears here in a more civilized and communal aspect than at the cave by the shore: this is the water that the "citizens" (*politai*, 206) draw;[24] and the naming of the eponymous founders, Ithacus and Neritus, evoke the long-established sanctions of much lived-in places, the traditions of the land.

Odysseus' contact with the Nymphs in the "misty cave" of book 13 was a re-creation of private associations, for he was still in the mysterious, transitional ground between reality and fantasy. Now he encounters their more public aspect, their communal significance, the dynastic connections with the founding heroes who gave their names to the land and its mountains.[25] As the king who maintains communal order and enforces the sanctions, who has recently recognized and acknowledged the son who is to inherit his position, it is fitting that he encounters these divinities in this public aspect. The good king, in his personal relation with these deities of the fruitful land, mediates for his whole society; and he unites public and private in his own person (see 19.109–14). Their favoring presence as he approaches the palace that he must win back bodes well for his success. After Melanthius' insult, Eumaeus invokes the Nymphs and mentions the previous sacrifices of Odysseus (17.240ff.; see 13.358). He thus places the fruitfulness of the Nymphs, the simple vitality and piety of the country—the land and its traditions—on the side of Odysseus. And revivifying water, the fresh water of local springs, a sign of safety and welcome (see 5.441ff., 6.85ff., 7.129–31), marks another transition and a closer approach to the full return.

The Bow and Victory

Odysseus comes still closer to reestablishing the communal aspect of his connection with Ithaca in the trial of the bow. The bow belongs to the maturity and authority of the prince in a settled community, with

---

[24] The spring here perhaps recalls the civilized order of Scheria and Alcinous' garden (the last half of 17.206 is the same as that of 7.131).

[25] Ithacus and Neritus, at least, are eponymous heroes. See Stanford (1958–61) on 17.207ff. Also interesting in this connection is that when Odysseus identifies himself to the Phaeacians, he mentions both Ithaca and Mount Neritus in close conjunction with his own and his father's name (9.19–22).

the strength and ability to enforce his commands. It takes Odysseus into his youthful past, before Troy and the disorder on Ithaca. He acquired it on a public errand, serving the *dēmos* (21.17).[26] It was the gift of a man killed in violation of guest rights and the sacredness of sharing a table (21.27ff.), and it will be used now by Odysseus to avenge the suitors' violation of these rights (see 21.98–100), which the *dēmos* permitted in his absence.

The bow is also connected with Odysseus' settled life, for he "never took it upon the black ships when going to war, but it lay in his halls as a reminder of his dear friend, and he carried it in his own land" (21.38–41). It belongs to the peace and order of a strong king. When the disguised Odysseus requests it, it is to try "his hands and his strength" and to see "whether I still have such might as was previously in my bent limbs or whether my wandering and lack of care has now destroyed it" (21.282–84). Antinous mocks this request, as he mocked earlier when Eumaeus and Philoetius wept on seeing the bow (21.82f.). They weep because the bow embodies the strength and authority of the master they love, and its possession by others means the loss of Odysseus. The bow involves them in a deep emotional and personal bond that the suitors, with their callous lack of respect for the past, cannot comprehend. Antinous indeed admits a faint memory of Odysseus (21.91–95) but with no deep associations; nor has he absorbed the full reality of Odysseus' strength, for he "was still a helpless child" (95).

Of all those who attempt the bow, only Odysseus stands in a personal relation to it. When it is finally placed in his hands, he touches it lovingly, "turning it in every way, trying it here and there, lest worms might have eaten the horn while the lord [*anax*] was away" (21.393–95). Whereas the others have been heating and greasing it, Odysseus treats it with care, love, and a masterful familiarity (see 21.396–400). The bow to him is not simply an instrument, a necessary means for winning a coveted prize, but a part of his human past and of a life he is about to reclaim. It is not merely an appurtenance of his outward strength and authority; his close bond to the bow is the innate and acquired rightness

---

[26] There is no reason to regard the past history of the bow as an interpolation. Gabriel Germain (1954) 12, note 3, follows August Fick, Jan Van Leeuwen, Victor Bérard, and others in deleting 21.13–41 (or 13–52) on the grounds that the geography is not "Homeric." If Messenia is not mentioned elsewhere by Homer, it may simply be that he never had occasion to refer to it except in this little local Ithacan legend. The lines are not questioned by the Alexandrian editors. Eurytus also (21.14, 32, 37) is mentioned previously as a great bowman, fittingly by Odysseus, in 8.224, which Germain would then have to remove as well, which he is prepared to do (38n. 3).

of his claim to the kinship and Penelope. It is part of his nature and his heritage as good king and "gentle father."

The comparison of Odysseus stringing the bow to a bard who "understands the lyre and song" (21.406–9) reinforces this personal relation. The peaceful associations of the bard, which evoke harmony and a quiet, well-ordered house (one is reminded of Demodocus singing at Alcinous' command), mitigate—one might almost say justify— the harshness and brutality of Odysseus' ensuing use of the bow. This simile, however, has other ramifications. We recall the song of Phemius in the first book which brought tears to Penelope (1.325–44); Demodocus' songs about the heroes at Troy which had a similar effect, for different reasons, on Odysseus; Alcinous' comparison of Odysseus himself to a bard as he recounted his journey to Hades—his encounter with his dead heroic past—in the removed, peaceful Phaeacian palace.

The poet's lyre is the means of bringing together past and present, and in this role it recalled Odysseus to his heroic past at the point when he revealed his identity to the Phaeacians (8.521–56). Now Odysseus reaffirms that past not through the medium of song but through the actual function of the bow as a deadly weapon of war. Homer carefully reminds us of its accompanying "grievous arrows" (21.12) and its violent, murderous past (21.26–33). In the first book, Mentes-Athena told Telemachus of Odysseus' search for poisoned arrows (1.260–66), thereby reactivating the bow's deadly past with the first movements of the return. The lyre simile of book 21, however, fuses the contradictions of peace and violence in Ithaca, of apparent helplessness (both the bards Phemius and Demodocus are physically ineffective) and actual strength in Odysseus. The lyre helped the Phaeacian bard sing the famed deeds of war as something remote; the bow, compared to the lyre, helps the old Iliadic warrior to the harsh deeds that will reestablish peace in the immediate present. In disguise he takes up the bow as a weapon of destruction, but he will use it as a bard uses a lyre, to create the "harmony" of order on Ithaca and to reveal and assert the truth and vitality of the past.[27]

The bow also foreshadows the due succession of Telemachus and hence the continuing vitality of Odysseus' line. Telemachus almost succeeds at bending the bow but desists at a nod from Odysseus (21.113–29), at which he ironically declares his weakness to defend himself (21.131–33). These are the same two lines that he spoke when he first

---

[27] On the lyre and the bow see below, Chapter 5, pp. 98–100, with note 32.

entered Eumaeus' hut and felt overwhelmed and helpless at receiving the disguised beggar (16.71–72). His position is now the reverse, and his actions are soon to belie this alleged helplessness. The bow thus serves as the means for Telemachus also to prove his heroic identity as Odysseus' son that he sought at the beginning of his voyage (see 1.214–20, 2.270–80). Later, in declaring it his privilege to give the bow to whomever he wishes, he frees himself from his mother's authority: "The bow will concern all the men, but especially me, to whom belongs the power [kratos] in the house" (21.350–53 = 1.361–64). He repeats here the verses that he used in book 1 for male authority over song; now he faces the more serious male authority over war (21.352–53). He also vindicates his future right of succession after Odysseus' reestablishment of order in the house and in the kingdom.

The bow fuses the public and private aspects of Odysseus' re-creation of his life on Ithaca. The idea of the trial of the bow originates with Penelope (19.572ff.). It is her second "test" of Odysseus, the first being her questioning him, in his guise as a beggar, about his clothing (19.215ff.). With the bow she tests his more essential qualities—his strength, manhood, and cleverness—on the superiority of which rests his position as king of Ithaca. To win her back he must prove again those manly and heroic qualities; then he may essay the final and decisive test of the bed. To complete their recognition, he moves again from the public back to the private world; after the slaughter he is bathed again by his old nurse (23.153–63) and from warrior becomes, finally, husband.

By his absence Odysseus has suffered irreparable loss in his closest personal ties, a loss represented in part by the emptiness of his embrace of his mother in Hades. He experiences comparable loss in his simpler relations, most poignantly in seeing the misery of his old dog Argus, who recognizes but lacks the strength to approach his master and expires in the very act of unacknowledged recognition (17.291–327): "And then the portion of black death seized Argus as soon as he had seen Odysseus in the twentieth year" (326f.). He is first described as "Argus, the dog of Odysseus patient of mind, whom he himself once reared but had no joy of him, for first he went off to holy Ilium" (292–94). Argus belongs to the simple joys of a country prince who keeps fast dogs at his table "for brilliant display" (aglaiēs heneken, 309–10) and takes joy in the hunt and the woods (295, 316–17). But man and dog have a deeper bond of suffering: both are in misery, cast out of their rightful place by usurpers. Argus' age and death and the pathos of his futile efforts to greet Odysseus (302–4) mark the using up in war and wandering of the twenty years of youthful vigor and past quickness, the twenty years of possible joy and vitality on Ithaca, that cannot be reclaimed.

Although Odysseus has lost the goodness of the intervening years, he returns with more than he would have had "if he came without harm from Troy" (5.38ff., 13.137–38). In one sense, these losses form the subject of the poem: first the losses, before arriving on Scheria, of men, ships, and clothes—important but less essential parts of himself; then the loss of his mother, of twenty potentially happy years, and of his youth on Ithaca. Athena's aging of him at the end of book 13 (429–38) is compensated for, it is true, by the beauty and firmness she pours over him after he slays the suitors (23.156–63). But in the interval between the two transformations, he has come to know hunger, beggary, and insult. Through his adaptability and adhesion to life, nevertheless, he can regain much that is lost. As Athena repairs the ravages of the disguise, so Odysseus, having slain the suitors, begins to repair their inroads on his property. The wasted goods comprise those losses that can be healed; and Odysseus' readiness to recommence his Ithacan life appears in his orders for the maintenance of his remaining property and his plans to make good what the suitors wasted (23.354–58). The deed of death done, he turns again fully into life.

Gains and Gifts: Perspectives on the Past

Is there, then, an actual development in Odysseus' character throughout the poem? A difficult question, and one not to be answered fully here. His initial qualities—adaptability, stability, and resourcefulness—seem fixed parts of his nature from the beginning;[28] yet through these qualities he is able to reach his extraordinary fullness of experience, voyage beyond reality and come back, and in the process broaden his knowledge of the range of human suffering, from himself outward. He

---

[28] Woodhouse (1930) notes the developments in Telemachus' character and remarks: "It is interesting to find the conception of character-development in this the earliest extant literary creation of Greece" (212ff.); but he regards Telemachus as "the only personality of dynamical quality" in the poem (213). His development is, of course, the most striking because it is the most obvious. Odysseus has less to learn and is far more formed and stable initially and hence perhaps seems "static" when his "growth" is compared with that of Telemachus.

does not attain a new state of being but reestablishes the old on deeper foundations. His journey does not have the upward movement of Dante's, completely transcending his previous life, nor does it, like that of Aeneas, bring a permanent settlement in a new land in accordance with a historical mission. Odysseus, unlike Aeneas, who loses his wife along with Troy, comes back to the humanity he left behind. His fate is not only a voyage but also a return; it has the nature of a circling spiral that returns upon itself at a deeper level, after circumscribing a broad new area.

He does, in the course of his voyage, learn from the past. Returning as the last of the heroes, he can profit from the experiences of those who preceded him, notably Agamemnon. Although he later acts on Agamemnon's suggestion that he return in secret (11.455), he pays little heed to his injunction "never to be gentle to your wife" (11.441). He does not have Agamemnon's leaning to cruelty. Caution and intelligence do not banish his capacities for affection and trust. His long wanderings also seem to have changed some of his perspectives on the past. He weeps when Demodocus sings of his quarrel with Achilles (8.74ff.), and when they meet in Hades, he tries to console him. He takes a conciliatory attitude toward Ajax, whom he addresses "with pleasing words" (11.552). To the Phaeacians, in introducing the episode, he utters the wish that he had never won the arms (11.548). The competitive spirit at Troy has been replaced by a greater appreciation of the bond between men, even though Ajax's shade is unreconciled and "strides off after the other shades into Erebos" (11.563f.).

Odysseus has also won from his toils a knowledge of his ability to endure, and he can call on his past suffering to aid him in new crises. In leaving Calypso, he states his readiness to add the "endurance" (tlēsomai) of shipwreck to his previous sufferings of war and the waves (5.221–24). When he is mocked by the suitors, he calls on his heart to endure, as it endured the Cyclops: "For once you endured something more shameless still, on that day when the Cyclops, resistless in might, devoured my strong companions" (20.18–20). Far from wearing him down, his past sufferings are a source of fortitude for the future; they reinforce the qualities that enable him to return. It is, in fact, his capacity for suffering that links him with the human world and enables him to return to it.

Odysseus' one tangible gain from his wanderings are his Phaeacian gifts. Yet paradoxically they are the most intangible of all. No sooner is he back in control than he must concern himself with replenishing his wasted possessions, with no thought of the gifts to which he previously gave so much care.[29] His return is very different from that of Menelaus, who realized an immense fortune on the gifts he brought back and who then settles down to a most comfortable middle age in plush surroundings, with his beautiful—and repentant—wife.

But what of Odysseus' gifts, the treasure from the Phaeacians that he so solicitously hid in the Nymphs' cave? Commentators have been troubled by their disappearance after book 13.[30] *An hoc loco bonus dormitat Homerus?* If, however, the Phaeacians and the fantasy world generally point to an inward, personal dimension of experience, then it is perhaps possible to understand the disappearance of the gifts. They are the accumulated but ultimately intangible "wealth" of understanding and experience brought back from this remote world and hence are not easily assimilated to the terms of the "real" world. Menelaus did not actually enter the fantasy world; his gifts, therefore, are fully convertible into tangible substance—they can be brought back and made known in Sparta.

The closest Odysseus comes to bringing forth these gifts is in the telling of his fantasy adventures to Penelope, for here he unites at last the two worlds of experience. Here he does mention the gifts, so that Homer has not merely forgotten them. They form, in fact, "the last word" of his tale before he falls asleep (23.341–42). Yet the actual gifts continue to lie in "the misty cave," where Athena placed them (13.366–71). They are still in an ambiguous position between fantasy and reality. They are on Ithaca but remain shut away from the "real" world by the rock closing the cave entrance (370), a civilized version of the way Polyphemus would have enclosed his cannibal's treasure of captive sailors. Unlike the guest-gifts that Menelaus and Helen offer to Telemachus or the other gifts given in heroic exchange, these are not stored up as solid, conspicuous *keimēlia* (guest-gifts) in the palace. Embodying perhaps the deepest levels of incommunicable experience that Odysseus brings back from his wanderings, they remain just out of touch with

[29] Odysseus' concern for gifts appears notably in his adventure with Polyphemus (9.229) and in his suave reply when offered more gifts by Arete and Alcinous (11.354ff.). The importance of gifts in the former episode is well brought out by Podlecki (1961) 125–33, who emphasizes the close intertwining of the gifts and the theme of *outis* (No-Man) throughout the book.

[30] See, for example, Scott (1939): "These gifts are the only unused major poetic mechanism in Homer. . . . They are the only important unfinished detail of Homeric poetry. Did Homer forget, or did he leave all this to the imagination of his hearers?" (103).

reality, just below the threshold of consciousness, their location known to Odysseus alone.

By being placed in the cave of the Nymphs and, first, "by the base of the olive tree" (13.122), where Odysseus and Athena later sit to plot the fulfillment of his return (372), the gifts are brought into contact with the life-giving, fertile aspects of his existence on Ithaca, his private, joyful relation with the vitality of the land and his early life there.[31] In this favoring context they can remain safe and protected, sheltered from harsher or more prosaic aspects of Ithacan reality. In fact, no one from Ithaca itself touches them. The Phaeacians lift them out of their ship to the olive tree "outside of the road, lest any man, passing by, come up and harm them before Odysseus awakens" (123–24). Later Athena conceals them in the cave. The attention the gifts receive both from Odysseus, who counts them solicitously (217–19), and from Athena marks them as valuable and also as vulnerable.

They are protected, however, not only by Athena but also by their own nature, their privacy and uniqueness, set apart by the knot of Circe that both protects them and keeps them in touch with the fantasy world from which they came. Arete, in giving the gifts, has asked Odysseus to tie them, "that no one may harm them on the journey when you sleep a sweet sleep traveling on the black ship" (8.444–45); and he ties them with a "clever knot that once lady Circe taught him in his mind" (447–48). The fantasy world from which Odysseus brought them itself provides the means of safeguarding them and preserving them as uniquely his own. Odysseus is able to use his very experiences in this fantasy world to bring back to Ithaca some of the "wealth" that he acquired there. He employs this knot at the conclusion of his adventures, when assured of a safe return, and Arete stipulates that he and no one else tie it. It will not be untied like the silver cord of Aeolus (10.23–24), for there are no longer discordant forces about Odysseus to delay his return: he has lost them all in his journey. To him alone were the gifts given; alone he returns, and alone he binds up the acquisitions that will remain isolated on Ithaca.

These gifts made their first appearance in the poem in book 5, when

---

[31] Wilamowitz (1884) regards this tree as "einen heiligen Ölbaum" ("a holy olive tree," 106, with note 17). It may be that Athena and the olive tree are interchangeable, complementary symbols of safety and security for Odysseus. For the favoring significance of the olive throughout the poem, see above, note 14, and in general Germain (1954) 211–15, 308ff. For the religious significance of the olive tree, see Pease (1937) 2020–22 and also 2015ff. for its connection with Athena. For trees generally as symbols of the favoring goddess, see Levy (1948) 120.

Zeus set Odysseus' return into motion. He there described the gifts as so much gold, bronze, and clothing; but he adds that they make up more than Odysseus would ever have got from Troy, "even if he had come home painlessly with his share of the booty" (38–40). The gifts, then, appear as a kind of compensation for what was lost at sea, for the fruitless interval between the division of the spoils at Troy and the landing on Ithaca. But they are also totally incommensurate with their material counterparts in the real world. Only the gods and the Phaeacians seem to know of them; and Zeus, in introducing them, mentions them almost in the same breath as the "honor like that of a god," the aura of divinity with which they were surrounded among the Phaeacians (36).

Athena's part in caring for the gifts is also interesting. Homer makes a special point of repeating that the Phaeacians gave Odysseus the gifts "because of great-hearted Athena" (13.121). Connected with Odysseus' unified rational consciousness and full human identity, she safeguards this precious acquisition of his voyaging. Her part in protecting them complements that of Circe: Circe's enchantment keeps them safe in Scheria and on the mysterious passage; Athena's power protects them on Ithaca. As the force that directed Odysseus' return to reality, Athena assures the safety and preservation in the "real" world of what was gained in the world beyond reality. But in the cave they remain, known only to Odysseus and, vaguely, to Penelope, never brought out of the mist into the full light of Ithaca. Thus, though on Ithaca, they never lose their magical contact with the mist-covered ships that brought them (8.562)[32] or the "misty sea" over which they mysteriously traveled. They remain suspended, as it were, between fantasy and reality, Scheria and Ithaca. Perhaps this suspension is the only form in which Odysseus, once returned to Ithaca, can keep them.

Conclusion: Poetry and Reality

Throughout the *Odyssey* Homer has kept apart the worlds of fantasy and reality only to interweave them again, as they are interwoven in

[32] The epithet "covered with mist and cloud" occurs only once more, of the equally mysterious Cimmerians, whom Odysseus passes on the way to Hades (11.15). Autrain (1938), in 2:194, connects the name of the Phaeacians etymologically with mist (*phaios* means "dark," "dusky"), with "la brume légendaire recouvrant, depuis ce temps, leur pays et ses habitants" ("the legendary mist that, from this time on, covers this land and its inhabitants"); see also Whitman (1958) 299. But see, *contra*, Germain (1954) 316–17.

Odysseus' mind and in the human mind generally and, hence, in all poetry. From the dreamworld in which the logic of ordinary human expectations is suspended, Odysseus returns to the stringent demands of the situation on Ithaca, a situation that enforces a conscious and determined suppression of identity. What occurred because of the strangeness and remoteness of his surroundings on the voyage must be effected by will and effort on his return. And as the concealment of identity on Ithaca is an act of will and inner strength, so its revelation requires courage and imagination, warlike force and humane insight.

There is perhaps a further level of unreality in the fantasy world implicit in the nature of exile from home, always regarded as a terrible fate by the ancient Greeks. For the man out of touch with family and country, cut off from his roots in the known and familiar ties that tell him what he is, nothing is quite "real"; there is no firm, clear point of reference either for victory or for defeat. In this sense, too, Odysseus' return, as for any voyager, is a reclaiming of self.

Yet there is more. The voyage carries Odysseus into areas not ordinarily open to men, the creation of which is the product of the fantasy powers of the poetic, myth-making mind. In this sense, as I have suggested, the voyage can be interpreted as man's penetration of his inner world at levels that he cannot reach by the normal processes of reason or waking life or the everyday activities of his land existence (Ithaca). Each of these realms has a separate set of characters, but Odysseus' return links the two; in fact, he is the only person who passes from the one to the other (and there can be only a one-way passage). His voyage and his person bind the two worlds.

In returning to his human reality on Ithaca, Odysseus passes through the crucial intermediary realm of the Phaeacians; and it is significantly there that he relives his fantasy past. This review before his crossing to the "real" world is quite unlike Dante's review of his past journey in *Paradiso* 22.124–54 when he is "near to the ultimate salvation": Dante, the Christian poet, sees his voyage as an upward progress and a gradual relinquishing of his earthly life—"the threshing floor that makes us so fierce"—from which he is now free (see *Paradiso* 22.154: "Then I turned my eyes to the beautiful eyes"). Odysseus surveys his past not at the end but at the midpoint of his journey, when the strenuous task of return to humanity and the full reintegration of the two worlds still lie ahead.

I should not claim that all the meanings and interpretations suggested in this essay could be consciously "intended" by Homer. Homer has no concept of, indeed no word for, the unconscious, let alone the "self."[33] But the fact that he could not name them does not mean that, at some level, they did not exist for him. He conveys their existence and meaning through poetical language and his mythical narratives; and it is through these, with their beauty and suggestiveness, their fusion of the concrete and precise with the intangible and indefinite, that the reader (and interpreter) enters the world of the *Odyssey*. As Goethe wrote,

> Wer den Dichter will verstehen
> Muss in Dichters Lande gehen.

Whoever wants to understand the poet must go to the poet's land.

It is of the essence of poetry and poetic myth to know and reveal more than the physical life, to penetrate below the external surface of the materially apprehended and practically, logically lived-in world. Freud regarded man's myth-making faculties as "the step by which the individual emerges from group psychology" and achieves psychic independence. Freud himself created a myth in order to understand and explain the growth and nature of the individual self.[34]

Myth, too, is removed from the logical criterion that a thing is either such or not such; it conforms rather to the psychological but "illogical" truth that a thing—or a person—may be many opposites at once, like Homer's Old Man of the Sea, whose form contains the possibility of becoming "all the creatures that are born onto the earth," including the elemental opposites "water and divinely blazing fire" (4.417–18). In the same way, Odysseus' secrecy about his name in the fantasy world and his disguises on Ithaca dramatize his being both "himself" and "not himself" simultaneously. Myth and its formal expression in poetry work through its Protean knowledge of the multiplicity and contradictoriness of human identity and motivation, the paradoxes of our being

[33] For the lack of the idea of a central "self" in Homer, see Snell (1953) 8ff. and also 213, where he notes, "The problem is comparable to that of the soul which did, in a certain sense, exist even for Homer, but of which he was not cognizant, whence it did not really exist." Snell does, however, admit that myth may contain psychological truths and thus serve "to make human nature better understood": "Mythical causality controlled a territory which was later, after the discovery of the soul, surrendered to psychological motivation" (223; see also 224).

[34] See Freud (1922) chapter 12. For Freud's own "myth," see his *Totem and Taboo*, part 4.

and consciousness. It draws on the deep reservoirs of human experience over millennia and reveals truths about the human self that the language of prosaic reason—of psychoanalysis as well as of literary analysis—cannot fully express. If it could, poetry would cease to be written or to be read.

CHAPTER 4

Transition and Ritual
in Odysseus' Return

Passage, transition, change: this phenomenon is the most familiar of human life and also the most difficult to comprehend. It is no wonder that this theme, in one form or another, is one of the central concerns of Greek philosophy, from Heraclitus and Parmenides to Plato and Aristotle. In placing at the center of the *Odyssey* the hero's passage from the marvels of Phaeacia to Ithacan reality and probability, Homer sets out in high relief, for the first time in European literature, the sense of the inexhaustible mystery of the changes of state or being, outward and inward, that constitute human life.[1]

The universal fact of change in human life is symbolized in the *Odyssey,* as throughout European literature, by the journey itself.[2] Yet Homer's hero, unlike Dante's or Tennyson's Ulysses, does not simply travel in search of new experiences. His journey is a return. Thus in the first four books we are anchored in the world of his human past, Ithaca and the Greek mainland, before we are allowed to follow Odysseus over distant seas. We are first shown the past that is to be regained and the threatened order that is to be restored.

In most societies, changes of state are marked by rituals that define change, visibly confront its reality, and orient the individual in the new world he or she has entered. Such rituals, or rites de passage, follow a more or less constant pattern and show three major phases. These

---

[1] For the significance of the Phaeacian episode and the hero's reclaiming of his human identity, see above, Chapters 2 and 3.

[2] For the symbolic implications of the journey in the "epic of quest," see Levy (1953) chapter 5 and passim.

consist, according to Arnold van Gennep, of *rites of separation, rites of transition,* and *rites of incorporation.*[3] This division is useful for analyzing Odysseus' return. The journey between Troy and Ogygia constitutes a gradual *separation* from his Trojan warrior past (compare the widespread concern for the desanctification of the returning warrior most familiar, perhaps, from the Roman practices of lustration). The sojourn with the Phaeacians is a primarily *transitional* situation, succeeding the total suspension from "reality" on Ogygia and preceding the reentrance into Ithaca. The Ithacan adventures are mostly concerned with his re*incorporation* into the society he left behind and fittingly culminate in a reenactment of marriage. The analogies should not be pressed, and there is a certain overlapping, inevitably, between these ritual functions and the different stages of Odysseus' journey. Yet both the schema of the ritual and the structure of the poem share a common perception of a fundamental experience in human life.

The poem's transitional situations are reinforced by a number of recurrent themes or motifs that are well known in almost every mythic journey: the crossing of water, the changing of clothes, the sharing of food. Such themes in their various repetitions throughout the work gain a deepening significance, an effect that is totally consistent with the nature of oral epic, which proceeds in terms of repeated themes or groups of themes—contracted, expanded, or elaborated, as the poet requires.[4] The verbal repetition of the particular formula or formulas involved in such motifs often underlines the thematic repetition.[5] Indeed,

[3] Van Gennep (1960) 21 and passim. See also the introduction by Solon T. Kimball, vii ff.

[4] For the recurrent theme in oral epic, see Lord (1960): "Each theme small or large—one might say, each formula—has around it an aura of meaning which has been put there by all the contexts in which it has occurred in the past. It is the meaning that has been given it by the tradition in its creativeness. To any given poet at any given time, this meaning involves all the occasions on which he used the theme, especially those contexts in which he uses it most frequently; it involves also all the occasions on which he has heard it used by others, particularly by those singers whom he first heard in his youth, or by great singers later by whom he was impressed. To the audience the meaning of the theme involves its own experience of it as well. The communication of this supra-meaning is possible because of the community of experience of poet and audience" (148). See in general chapter 4, "The Theme," and especially 89–91 and 109 for ritual elements in recurrent epic themes; on the level of the formula rather than the theme, see Whitman (1958) chapters 1 and 6.

[5] The simplest definition of the formula in Homer is a recurrent expression of fixed metrical value, such as "rosy-fingered dawn" or "so speaking he went off." I use the term "formulaic," however, somewhat more broadly here, to apply also to the repeated passages of one or more lines that describe certain standard actions, for example, bathing, eating, and the embarkation of ships. On the formula in general, see Lord (1960) chapter 3.

the Homeric oral formulaic style itself almost ritualizes such actions by presenting them as fixed and stylized into a set pattern. These formulas provide a familiar and constant background for the newness that Odysseus is ever encountering in the exotic world of his adventures.

There is a latent tension between the formulaic language of the *Odyssey* on the one hand and the richness of the hero's experiences and the fabulousness of the poem's far-flung geography on the other. The very forces that were causing the loosening of the severer structure and style of the *Iliad* may also have contributed to the poem's interest in the primitive reaches of mythic lore behind elements such as Ogygia, Circe, the Cyclops, and the Phaeacians. The *Odyssey*'s greater openness of style, by comparison with the *Iliad*—for which Cedric Whitman, among others, has suggested analogies with the Proto-Attic style in pottery—leaves it receptive to the strange, shadowy figures of the preheroic past and to those primitive strata of myth and ritual that have so intrigued scholars such as J. A. K. Thomson, Gertrude Levy, and Gabriel Germain. These ritual elements should be considered in close connection with folktale and with the common Mediterranean (and Bronze Age) storehouse of fable and legend. The blending of these common Aegean elements with the formal, demanding qualities of the Greek epic hexameter makes the *Odyssey* a poem that, like its hero, straddles two worlds, whereas the *Iliad* plants itself gigantically and immovably in one.

Underlying the themes of transition is a mythical pattern fundamental to the epic of quest, namely, the cyclic alternation of life and death; the rediscovery of life after a period of sterility, darkness, and imprisonment; and the ultimate victory of life over death, of order over disorder. This kind of epic, of which *Gilgamesh* is the prototype, embodies the experience, to quote Levy, "of loss and segregation, the temptations of love and fear, the vision of death and the return of the hero to the starting point, changed by the knowledge and acceptance of defeat."[6] The *Odyssey*, though undoubtedly based on such a mythic pattern, transcends it by turning its significance away from the originally ritually enacted death and rebirth of cosmic divinities to the realities and possibilities of human action and human nature. Yet beneath the human-centered action the underlying mythic structure still makes itself felt and gives the poem what Northrop Frye calls the "encyclopedic range" of high epic, an inclusiveness that embraces the totality of human experience.[7]

[6] Levy (1953) 21–22.
[7] Frye (1957) 218ff.

I define "ritual" in this context as a regularly performed action carried out in a stylized manner to indicate a significant contact with supernatural powers that are felt to embody essential and mysterious features of our existence. Some of these transitional situations in the poem may dimly echo actual transitional rituals of a remote past. I am not concerned with survivals of actual rituals but rather with the literary function of situations of transition in the poem as a work of art. Even in this limited sense, the ritual elements open into the realm of the sacred and the numinous and thus add an important dimension to the poem's meaning. For a society such as Homer's, the sacred and the profane are still closely united, and the division between a person's physical and spiritual life is much less clear than in modern Europe or America.

We can follow the unfolding of the return through an examination of recurrent motifs that involve or accompany transition. Those that I shall consider are sleep, the bath, purification, and the threshold. All, as will appear, are associated with the mystery of passage between worlds, and all belong to the realm of experience where known and unknown cross. Only two, purification and the bath, can properly be said to be of a ritual nature. The other two, sleep and the threshold, can be described simply as themes of significant transition. All four, however, reflect important stages of the return, the hero's gradual reclaiming of all that is his own.

Sleep

Sleep is perhaps the most obvious means of transition between the real and unreal worlds. Odysseus' return from the Phaeacians is an awakening out of a sleep "likest to death" (13.80). Like any passage or change of state, sleep is ambiguous. It can be like death or it can restore to new life. On his wanderings in the fantasy world, Odysseus is wary of sleep. As he sails from Calypso's island, Ogygia (5.271), he is the man of alert wakefulness who has learned not to trust sleep. When he has yielded to it, it has brought disaster, as on the voyage from Aeolus' island (10.31–55) or on Thrinacia (12.38). It is only when he arrives on Scheria, the Phaeacians' homeland, that sleep becomes positive and restorative. At first he resists it, as he did earlier in the wanderings, fearing wild animals (5.470–73); but the olive thicket saves him, and Athena "poured sleep upon his eyes, that she might ease him soon of his toilsome weariness" (5.491–93). The next night he sleeps in Alcinous' palace in perfect security, "on the well-bored bed, under the resounding portico" (7.345). As he emerges from the fantasy world, or at least from its more dangerous aspects, he can yield to sleep in safety. On his last voyage, when his struggles with the sea are over, he sleeps on the Phaeacians' ship, though they pay dearly for the effortlessness and safety of his passage (see 13.134–87). His reawakening (13.187), however, is a return to consciousness and to life.[8]

Sleep frames Odysseus' entire return. On Scheria, the bridge between the fantasy world and reality, he sleeps on arrival and departs in sleep. Later, in the repetition of his Phaeacian adventures to Penelope, the theme of sleep frames his tale. His account to her is introduced thus: "And she took pleasure in hearing, nor did any sleep fall upon her lids until he had related everything" (23.308–9). His tale ends: "This was the last tale he spoke of when sweet sleep that looses the limbs came upon him, loosing the cares of his heart" (23.342–43).

Hermes, bringing the message that sets in motion Odysseus' return from Ogygia, carries "the wand with which he charms the eyes of whomever he wishes and awakens them, in turn, when sleeping" (5.47–48). He then reappears as escort of the dead with the same wand (and almost the same two lines) immediately after the reunion of Odysseus and Penelope at the beginning of book 24. Hermes and the dead suitors mark the threatening complement to the life Odysseus has regained. As the god of both sleep and awakening, Hermes unites in himself the poles of failure and success, dream and reality. We may compare his function of guiding Priam through the limbo between the two camps in *Iliad* 24. On the one hand, Hermes is connected with sleep, dormancy, death— Odysseus' state during his "concealment" on Calypso's island. On the other hand, the god makes possible the hero's conquest over a powerful enchantress: he shows Odysseus how to overcome Circe. It is fittingly Hermes and his wand that appear at the beginning and end of the journey. Through him the magical potency of sleep marks the initial stages and the final fulfillment of the hero's return.

These passages and the recurrence of Hermes and his wand at the two ends of the journey home make the entire return appear under a great metaphor of sleeping and awakening. Part of Odysseus sleeps and rests until Athena begins to promote the awakening into the real world. On the divine level, she is the real motive force behind the return; she initiates it, unlike Hermes, who is only an agent, a mechanism fulfilling

[8] See above, Chapter 3, note 15.

that which has already been set into motion by the will of the gods. Athena, too, is often the dispenser of sleep in the *Odyssey,* and there is perhaps a deeper connection between her other functions in the poem and her ministrations of sleep. It is perhaps *because* she is the divine force most clearly behind the return that she controls the mechanism of sleeping and waking, knowing when withdrawal and stillness are necessary and when, the process of recovery and integration complete, the mind may again awaken to the light of reality. Sleep marks a kind of moral awakening as well, for in the closing episode of the poem, the herald Medon wakes up just in time to explain to the enraged parents and relatives of the slain suitors that Odysseus acted with the assistance of the gods (24.439–49, especially 439f.: "Medon and the divine singer approached from the hall of Odysseus since sleep left them").

Sleep has a special importance for Penelope. She, indeed, is more frequently associated with sleep than is anyone else in the *Odyssey.* Her sleep often follows grief and weeping. It is a constant reminder of the emptiness of her bed and, hence, perhaps a retiring back into herself until Odysseus comes. Athena, as the ministrant of sleep for her, may be associated with her trust in the return of her husband and her full identity as the wife of Odysseus. Her sleep, therefore, as a communion with that trust through the goddess who is contriving her husband's return, is often restorative and soothing (see 4.839–40, 18.187).

Conversely, sleep is also a sign of her reduced life and the static condition of her world without Odysseus. In her sleep she is acted on by Athena, as in the two passages just cited. Sleep, however, is not a means of change and passage for her in the same way that it is for Odysseus (as in books 6 and 13). Crucial events occur while she sleeps, such as Telemachus' departure for the mainland at the end of book 4 and especially the slaying of the suitors. In the latter case, in fact, she says she has never slept so soundly since Odysseus left for Troy (23.18–19). Her sleep during the struggle with the suitors has some analogies with Odysseus' landing on Ithaca: she awakens (or rather is, to her displeasure, awakened, 23.15–17) to find reality changed, to be told of the fulfillment of the hoped for return; and like Odysseus in book 13, she cannot recognize the truth until later. For her, however, sleep is more correctly a sign of the suspended condition of her life as she waits in quiet endurance and hope rather than the direct renewal of strength for positive action of her own. Her task is to hold out in hope, and sleep keeps her fresh for the time when the return is accomplished.

Her sleep, as a communion with her past, also keeps fresh the beauty that Odysseus knew before the war. In the deep sleep that precedes her tempting of the suitors in book 18, Athena carefully enhances her beauty (187–96). With the return of her beauty of past years comes also the resurgence of her longing for her husband. Here her recollection of Odysseus' departure is keenest, and she relates at length his parting words of twenty years before (257–70). Penelope not only reports at great length—which she never does elsewhere—an intimate moment with her long-absent husband but also does so at the very time when she is coaxing gifts from her wooers. It is more interesting still that Odysseus, present in disguise, should be pleased (281–83). It is as if her sleep and Athena's ministrations have reawakened in her a more vivid sense of the past, through which Odysseus recognizes in truth the wife he left behind. He knows, as the suitors do not, that "her mind is eager for other things" (283).

This unexpected flashback of Penelope's into the past also brings an ironical foreshadowing of the near future wherein the past will in fact be restored. The desire that Penelope arouses in the suitors is described with the metaphor of "loosing their knees" (τῶν δ' αὐτοῦ λύτο γούνατ', ἔρῳ δ' ἄρα θυμῷ ἔθελχθεν, "There were their limbs loosed, and they were made spellbound with desire in their hearts," 18.212). The phrase refers not only to erotic desire but also to death or to the sinking despair at the fear of death. Telemachus echoes the phrase in this sinister sense shortly afterward, praying that the vanquished Irus' fate might be extended to the suitors (λελῦτο δὲ γυῖα ἑκάστου, "and the limbs of each would have been loosed," 18.238). The same metaphor describes the suitors' reaction when Odysseus prepares to turn the deadly bow on them (τῶν δ' αὐτοῦ λύτο γούνατα καὶ φίλον ἦτορ, "Thereupon were their knees and hearts loosed," 22.68).[9] There are other ironic foreshadowings here in book 18, as when the suitors "die with laughter" (100). It has sometimes been suggested that from this point on there is

[9] Note also the similar "and their knees were loosed" in a sinister sense elsewhere in book 18, e.g., 238, 242, and 341. This mixture of the sinister and the erotic in the "loosing of the knees" is taken up later in the book in Odysseus' banter with the maids who have become paramours of the suitors. He assures them that he will be able to supply light for all, even if they wish to stay up until dawn: οὔ τί με νικήσουσι, "They will not conquer me," or as Fitzgerald (1963) translates, "They cannot tire me out" (18.319), at which the maids laugh and glance at one another (18.320). This possible double entendre in "loosing the knees" is reflected in the twofold use of the closely related adjective lusimelēs, "loosing the limbs," an epithet of sleep and death, on the one hand, and of love, on the other: cf. Od. 20.57, Hesiod Theog. 121 and 911, Sappho fragment 130 Lobel-Page (1955), and Carmina Popularia 873.3 Page (1962); also Alcman 3.61 Page (1962).

operating within Penelope an intuitive or subconscious recognition of her disguised husband that prepares her for the "real" recognition in book 23.[10] If so, it is again sleep that creates the setting for this prerecognition, serving as the essential mediator between past and future, illuminating past happiness with the stark light of present longing.

Penelope's sleep in book 18, like Odysseus' in book 13, is compared with death: "I wish that chaste Artemis would send so soft a death" (18.201–2). Sleep, death, and change form a related cluster of motifs in the return but differ in their significance for Odysseus and Penelope. Her sleep after Telemachus' assertion of his authority over the bow (21.354–58) and during the slaughter does, in fact, mark a crucial passage, but one of which she remains oblivious until later. As a woman in a patriarchal society, Penelope lacks Odysseus' freedom and initiative; and so the transitions for her are veiled in sleep. Unlike Odysseus, she does not even know that a transition is being made. Yet for her, as for Odysseus in book 13, sleep marks a communion, through a kind of death, with her suspended status as wife and queen and precedes its vital awakening into life.

The Bath

The bath is a long-established sign of welcome (see Gen. 18:4) and mark of accepting a stranger into a new environment. It indicates to the newcomer a point of crucial entrance, and washing by water probably retains a certain ritual significance as the ceremony for this tradition. It is also obviously connected with birth and hence rebirth. Like other transitional situations, the bath has an essential ambiguity. It is physically pleasant (cf. the Phaeacians' pleasure in warm baths, 8.249) yet involves a potentially dangerous exposure. This latter aspect of the bath is familiar from the post-Homeric version of the return of Odysseus' less fortunate companion, Agamemnon. Through the bath changes can also occur, both in appearance (as frequently in the *Odyssey*) and in mood.

Here too the formulas underline the ritual element involved, for, as one would expect, similar formulas are used in nearly all the bathing scenes. There is, of course, a great deal of variety, but practically the

---

[10] For discussion of Penelope's recognition of Odysseus in book 18, see Amory (1963) 100ff.; also Harsh (1950), esp. 10ff. For a different interpretation, see Else (1965) 47–50 and Russo (1982) passim, especially 11ff.

same pair of lines occurs near the beginning of each instance of bathing ("X washed Y and anointed him with oil and put a beautiful cloak around him").[11]

Like sleep, the bath, through its outward function as a sign of welcome, can emphasize the danger of the passage to a new situation. Such is the bath Helen gave Odysseus at Troy when he entered the city in disguise (4.242–56). A bath may also be only partially accepted. Thus Circe has Odysseus bathed as a sign of her acceptance of him and his successful passage through the danger of her enchantments (10.348–53). Her bath has all the sensuous accompaniments that a bath by Circe should have (see especially 359–60, 362–63), including the four maidservants born "from springs and groves and from sacred rivers" (350–51). But still all this "pleased not" Odysseus' heart (173), and his grief for his companions disturbs the usual smooth flow of formulaic motifs. Here the purely physical restorative powers of the bath do not operate on the man who seeks a restoration of another kind. When the companions are changed back, however, all are bathed (449–51) and happily spend an entire year with her.

There is even a figurative bathing in a situation of dangerous passage in 12.237, where the seething of Charybdis is compared to water boiling in a caldron (*lebēs*). In the next book, however, though seven years later, the Phaeacians in 13.13 make the friendly gift of a tripod and caldron, the implements regularly associated with bathing. The Phaeacians, too, are addicted to the comfort of warm baths (8.249).[12]

Two instances of bathing are of especial interest, that on Scheria in book 6 and Odysseus' bath by his nurse in book 19. In the first passage Odysseus, for the only time in the poem, is bathed in "the flowing streams of a river" (6.216), the "beautifully flowing river" that saved him from the sea and the rocks (5.441–44). The sweet waters succeed the "salt water";[13] and Odysseus' washing off of the "salt seawater" (6.219, 225–26) marks his return to safety, the end of his duel with the sea and Poseidon. Yet he refuses to let Nausicaa's maids bathe him, out of reluctance to be seen nude by "fair-tressed maidens" (220–22), especially after the ravages of the sea ("he appeared frightful to them, all

<hr>

[11] See 3.466–67, 4.49–50, 4.252, 6.227–28, 8.454–55, 10.364–65, 17.88–89, 23.154–55, 24.366–67.

[12] For the soothing and gentle connotations of bathing, see also Pindar *Nemean* 4.4–5.

[13] Note the use of the phrase "salt water" three times in close succession of Charybdis: 12.236, 240, 431. Compare also the single occurrence of the phrase "sweet water" of the safe harbor on Thrinacia (12.306). Thrinacia is, in fact, a place of shelter as long as the Sun's cattle are not harmed.

befouled by the sea," 137). His refusal is perfectly in keeping with the situation: he shows a tactful delicacy of feeling in not offending the young girls on whom his salvation depends. Yet such an attitude toward nudity is unusual in the epic.[14] Odysseus' refusal, then, may be more than embarrassment. It may indicate also his hesitation to be drawn into his new environment more than is necessary, bathing being the sign of welcome and acceptance. When he was luxuriously bathed by Circe, after all, he spent a whole year. Now, ready for his return to Ithaca, he wishes to keep his distance from new involvements. Hence he bathes alone and thus keeps outside of the gaiety, youthful beauty, and carefree energy of the Phaeacian girls. He is bathed later by Arete's servants only when he is assured of his return (8.449–57).

The bathing by Eurycleia in book 19 (343–507) is, like the first Phaeacian washing, a ritual that is not fully or perfectly performed. Again Odysseus holds back, permitting himself to be washed solely by an old servant, "who has endured in her heart such things as even I have endured" (347). His refusal to let himself be washed by the younger servants, as in the Nausicaa episode, marks his insistence on reentering his world only under the sign of the suffering and aging that have become integral parts of him. Thus he seeks out the servant with whom he has the greatest bond of suffering (see 360, 374, and 378). The bath here has a double function: both ritual entrance and the means of revealing identity.

When Eurycleia drops the basin with a loud clang as her hand touches the scar (19.467–70), she spontaneously interrupts the proper ritual and thus inadvertently reveals the ambiguity of Odysseus' position—what should be a welcoming and safe gesture, the bathing of the master in his own house, is, in fact, fraught with danger. The reentrance is a perilous one and accordingly so indicated. Correspondingly, the revelation of his identity would be dangerous, as Odysseus firmly points out to his nurse (479–90). When Odysseus has overcome the danger, the familiar formula recurs ("she washed him and anointed him richly with oil," 505), but with the added details that Odysseus draws his stool closer to the fire to warm himself and "covered up the scar with his rags" (506f.).

This scene of bathing, by far the longest in the poem, recalls a corresponding situation of danger from which Odysseus escaped tri-

[14] For the usual absence of such self-consciousness about nudity and bathing, see Stanford (1958–61), on 3.464. Germain (1954) 310ff. would explain the irregularity of this modesty by the influence of the Near East and the oriental sacral significance of nudity.

umphantly: his bathing by Helen in Troy (4.252–56). The similarity is bitterly paradoxical, for on Ithaca he is now as much in the house of his enemies as he was at Troy. The clang of the basin may also serve as an evil omen for the suitors (like the clanging of the pitcher in 18.397), for the ritual of the bath marks Odysseus' official "entrance" into the life of the palace.

Odysseus' final bath in book 23 seals the fulfillment of his return and immediately precedes his recognition by Penelope (152–65). Here at last he is bathed openly in his own house without mishap and no longer, as in book 19, as a stranger. Athena, directress of his return to himself, enhances his beauty in lines repeated from the similar scene at his arrival in Scheria (23.157–62 = 6.230–35). Thus the beginnings of his return are brought full circle with its completion. Both crucial entrances are marked by a welcoming ceremony and divine aid. Washed up from the sea on Scheria, however, and among strangers, Odysseus bathed himself alone, in a river; here, on Ithaca, he is washed by his housekeeper, Eurynome, not merely under the shelter of a regular human dwelling but in his own house as well. After isolation, wandering, and exposure to the elemental forces of a mysterious world, he is now ensconced in the stability and safety of a reestablished social order. Athena presides over both scenes as the constant element. She reveals in the grizzled warrior the young husband who left twenty years before. The decisive recognition through the trial of the bed can thus follow immediately thereafter (23.171–208). The supernaturally enhanced beauty of the bathed Odysseus both in book 6 and in book 23 carries associations of nuptial imagery, the radiance of the newly married couple.[15] In book 23, however, the "wedding" is fully appropriate and figuratively takes place soon after, when the old nurse, Eurynome, leads the couple into their chamber, carrying the torch, just as in the nuptial ceremony (289–96).[16]

Finally, in book 24, the bathing of Laertes marks the extension of the process of rebirth and rejuvenation brought about by Odysseus (365–71). This passage also shows how the formulaic style reinforces the ritual repetition. The formulas used of Laertes here repeat those used in the bathing and miraculous enhancing of Odysseus' stature in the preceding book: $\mu\epsilon\acute{\iota}\zeta o\nu\alpha$ δ' $\mathring{\eta}\grave{\epsilon}$ $\pi\acute{\alpha}\rho o\varsigma$ $\kappa\alpha\grave{\iota}$ $\pi\acute{\alpha}\sigma\sigma o\nu\alpha$ $\theta\mathring{\eta}\kappa\epsilon\nu$ $\mathring{\iota}\delta\acute{\epsilon}\sigma\theta\alpha\iota$, "She made him larger and stouter to look upon than before," 24.369;

***

[15] Note especially the allusion to the hair like hyacinth in lines 6.231 = 23.158 and Sappho's epithalamion, fragment 105c Lobel-Page (1955).

[16] On this scene see below, Chapter 5.

and μείζονά τ' ἐσιδέειν καὶ πάσσονα, "larger and stouter to look upon," 23.157. The same formula, naturally, also introduces both bathing episodes:

> τόφρα δὲ Λαέρτην μεγαλήτορα ᾧ ἐνὶ οἴκῳ
> ἀμφίπολος Σικελὴ λοῦσεν καὶ χρῖσεν ἐλαίῳ
>
> (24.365–66)

Then a Sikel maidservant washed and anointed with oil great-hearted Laertes in his own house.

> αὐτὰρ 'Οδυσσῆα μεγαλήτορα ᾧ ἐνὶ οἴκῳ
> Εὐρυνόμη ταμίη λοῦσεν καὶ χρῖσεν ἐλαίῳ
>
> (23.153–54)

Then Eurynome the housekeeper washed and anointed with oil great-hearted Odysseus in his own house.

For both men, this bath marks a return to their rightful position of authority in "their own house." Both recover a lost vitality as father and king. The archetypal pattern of the restoration of the dead or maimed king is operative, in a sense, for Laertes as well as for Odysseus. Odysseus, to be sure, is now king (see, e.g., 24.501: ἄρχε δ' 'Οδυσσεύς, "Odysseus led them"); yet Laertes performs a kingly action, as of old, in being the first to strike down his enemy (24.520ff.).[17] Odysseus' reentrance into the fullness of his past life, with its human ties, also recreates those lives that wait on his; and they, too, are washed of their previous sufferings and prepared to resume a fullness of existence that had been lost.

Purification

The bathing episodes can be seen as a ritual cleansing as well. But it is fire that replaces water as the purifying element in the crucial transition after the killing of the suitors and their accomplices (22.481–94). Odysseus refuses Eurycleia's offer to exchange his rags for more decent garb and insists on first purging the house with fire and sulphur: "Let there

---

[17] Note that earlier (24.353–55), too, Laertes is the first to assess the danger of reprisal from the suitors' families.

first of all [*prōtiston*] be fire in my halls" (24.491). It is perhaps felt that only the violence of fire, by a kind of homoeopathy, is sufficient to cleanse away the destructive aspects of the return that culminate in the suitors' death. Indeed, the thoroughness of this purgation—the only one of its kind in the *Odyssey*—is possibly the poet's indication that he recognizes and wishes to mitigate the brutality involved in the suitors' slaughter, the maids' execution, and the mutilation of Melanthius.

For Odysseus, too, fire is the final exorcism of the violence of the past years. Now leaving behind the war and the destructive monsters of the journey home, he must nevertheless reenter his house as he left it, a warrior, under the sign of violence—the blood-spattered lion and the purifying fire. Odysseus as a blood-splattered lion at the end of the slaughter is the image that Eurycleia reports to Penelope at the beginning of the following book: "You would have been warmed in spirit," she tells her just-awakened queen, "to have seen him splattered with blood and gore, like a lion" (23.47f.). The lion image evokes again the Iliadic world that the hero has been so long in leaving. At the same time, it is natural for the elderly servant to see in Odysseus the terrible warrior who has made good his return. She sees the outward, grim, one might say official aspect of Odysseus. The warrior, too, though speaking kindly words, was Penelope's last picture of her husband, as it recurred to her mind in book 18. But in the final recognition between them, she will look deeper into the past for another image: "For we have signs," she says, "hidden, which we alone know, apart from others" (23.109f.).

The fire at the end of book 22, ordered by the returned master from the faithful servant, helps make the palace his own again and rids it of the intrusive influences of the past. Only gradually, however, will Odysseus undergo the stepping-down process to become once more the familiar husband and "gentle father." He is curt and imperious in rejecting the clothes Eurycleia offers (485–91) and perhaps implicitly rejects also the bath that would naturally accompany such a change of raiment. The other participants in the slaughter wash immediately after the deed and the execution of the delinquent maids: "Then washing off their hands and feet they went to Odysseus in the house, and the deed was accomplished" (478–79). It is at this point that Odysseus calls for sulphur and fire. There is no bath for him until line 154 of book 23, immediately before the recognition near the bed. For him, the destructive, purifying force of fire precedes restorative waters at this point of crucial transition. It is only *after* this purgation that he is ready to reassume the positive elements in his life, to shed his rags (23.155), claim the living bed (23.181–206), and appear again as Penelope's husband.

This purification of the past parallels and completes another loss by fire and sulphur in the past, the blasting of his ship by Zeus' lightning off Thrinacia at the end of book 12: "The ship was filled with sulphur, and the companions fell from the ship" (417; cf. also Odysseus' tale to Eumaeus, 14.305–15). Ship and companions, the unstable remnants of his Trojan past, are purged before the hero undergoes the total isolation of Ogygia. This purgation is necessary and implicit in the preceding adventures, wherein Odysseus moves further and further from the heroic world into experiences of an increasingly private nature (Circe, the Sirens, the visions in Hades, Calypso). This sulphurous fire leaves Odysseus totally alone, cut off from his remaining human ties, "suspended" (12.432–36) over the abyss, surrounded by death. It also marks the transition to his greatest point of isolation, the seven years with the goddess Calypso, who would complete his separation from the mortal world and make him, like herself, immortal.

The sulphur and fire in his halls, however, mark the end of his isolation and the return to his full human position. He himself commands that the sulphur be brought: he is again in a world that he can understand and control, and in it he has reestablished his rightful authority. With the return of the legitimate king, order is restored and disorder purged. In book 12 the purgation is followed by loss and death; in book 22, by recovery and life. Both have been necessary, and the second naturally succeeds the first; but both also constitute a purgation of the forces that prevent the full return.

Odysseus' successful purgation through blood and fire contrasts with a bloody death of a different outcome, the murder of Agamemnon, as the victim describes it in Hades. The blood of the murdered king "seethed upon the ground" (δάπεδον δ' ἅπαν αἵματι θῦεν, 11.420).[18] The contrast between Agamemnon's return and that of Odysseus is not only between death and life, failure and success, but also between pollution and purification. The parallel is pointed up by the repetition of this half-line about the bloody ground in the slaughter of the suitors (11.420 = 22.309); and the half-line occurs but once more in Homer,

---

[18] The verb thūein (probably the same root as "Thyiad") means literally "rushed forth," "flowed," but there may also be some association with "smoke" or "steam" (cf. Latin *fumus*), which might suggest a connection with fire and purification: see Stanford (1958–61) on 11.420, Heubeck and Hoekstra (1989) on 11.420, and Caswell (1990) 52–63.

when the suitors describe their death to Agamemnon in Hades (24.185 = 22.309). There is a significant inversion of the theme in this repetition, for it was first Agamemnon who described to Odysseus the "seething" of his own (and his companions') blood (11.420); it is now Odysseus' vengeful shedding of blood that is described to him (24.185).

The parallels are part of a carefully developed antithesis between the two returns. Both Agamemnon and the suitors are slaughtered at a banquet, amid tables and feasting. The death of Agamemnon, however, is a sinister, perverted ritual. He is, as it were, "sacrificed" like an ox ("as one would kill an ox at the trough," 11.411 = 4.535, and cf. Aegisthus' sacrifices, 3.273–75). Agamemnon fails at his point of crucial transition as Odysseus succeeds at his. Both returns at their completion contain ritual elements involving fire and sacrifice. In Agamemnon's return this significant entrance and the ritual motifs accompanying it have their full measure of potential destructiveness. For him these purgative and ritual associations bring only defilement and pollution. For Odysseus, the "seething" blood and sulphurous fire are succeeded by water and the restorative, cleansing bath.

The Threshold

Because it marks the passage between known and unknown, the crossing of the threshold is, like bathing or the receiving of guests, a significant, danger-fraught act. Even in today's industrialized and rationalized societies, the threshold retains its symbolic value as a critical transitional point, safeguarded by magical representations or good-luck charms. It is but one example of the many dangerous entrances or guarded gates to be encountered in every epic journey into the unknown, from *Gilgamesh* on. The threshold in the *Odyssey* serves as the human, comprehensible counterpart to such mysterious entrances as the double-portalled "misty cave" on Ithaca in book 13, the crucial juncture between worlds.

At the beginning of the human action in the poem, when Athena sets in motion Odysseus' return and Telemachus' journey, she appears to the latter "on the threshold of the court" (1.104) as he is thinking of his father's return and the expulsion of the suitors. Inviting her within the house is the initial sign of his new spirit of manly independence that will now take him to the courts of the heroes on the mainland.

In Odysseus' journey the threshold is more involved with dangerous and supernatural elements. The Cyclops' great stone bars his threshold (9.242) and makes the passage out one of the greatest tests of Odysseus' wit and courage. In his entrance into and passage out of the Phaeacian kingdom, the crossing of thresholds receives special attention. Alcinous' threshold, like Aeolus' palace, is of bronze, and Odysseus approaches it with anxious thoughts (7.82–83), to be succeeded by wonder (see 7.134), until he crosses it to find the Phaeacians engaged in pious libations (7.135–38).

For the Phaeacians as well as for Odysseus, this entrance produces a tense situation, for the treatment of a stranger is always a delicate and dangerous matter. Coming from the unknown and potentially hostile outside, he must somehow be incorporated into the familiar, made *philos,* a part of what is "friendly" and so part of "one's own" normal reality (the double meaning of Homeric *philos*). For Odysseus, there is also his accumulated experience of other ways, not all friendly, in which a stranger may be treated. Thus at this point of crucial transition, the Phaeacians' remarkable silence emphasizes the tension and the in-between state of Odysseus (7.154). The tension is resolved and the full entrance effected by a succession of ritual acts. Echenaos breaks the silence with the suggestion of a libation to Zeus "who attends suppliants worthy of respect" (7.165). Then King Alcinous takes Odysseus by the hand (a significant establishment of physical contact: cf. 3.36–39) and seats him on a "bright chair" in the place of his own son, Laodamas (7.167–70). Odysseus is then washed (172–74); a table is set, and a common meal, shared (175–77). The due libation to Zeus "who attends suppliants worthy of respect" (181 = 165) is then carried out (179–81). Here, not only the ritual acts themselves but also the familiar formulas by which they are described strike a reassuring note and mark the successful completion of an important stage in the return.

When Odysseus is about to leave Phaeacia and make the final crossing of waters back to the mortal world, the threshold once more underlines the significant passage. His last conversation among the Phaeacians is with Arete, their queen: " 'Fare you well, O Queen, all the time until old age and death come which come upon men. But I depart. Do you in this house take joy in children and people and Alcinous the king!' So saying, over *the threshold he crossed,* noble Odysseus" (13.59–63). He then boards the swift ship and embarks for Ithaca, his mind fully turned, in this conversation, toward the human world he is about to reenter.

Later, on Ithaca, Odysseus approaches his palace disguised as a beggar and actually sits *on* "the ash-wood threshold within the doors" (17.337–40). He now occupies in squalor the very point of entrance to what he has so long sought. Later, in 20.258, Telemachus seats Odysseus further inside, "by the stone threshold," but still just barely within his house. Then, in the contest of the bow, Telemachus tries it at the threshold (21.124), whereas Odysseus, in slaying the suitors, shoots from his seat to the door (21.420–23). He thus not only demonstrates his masterful ease with the bow but also establishes his rightful position *inside* the palace. Finally, at the beginning of the slaughter, Odysseus "lept upon the great threshold" (22.2), and later "the four stand upon the threshold, but within the house are many men and noble" (22.203–4). Here, the proper place of inner and outer is again reversed, and the rightful possessor must for the last time make good his claim and establish his identity through a dangerous passage. Here, also, the transition to a new condition is underlined by a throwing aside of clothing: Odysseus throws off his rags (22.1) to reveal himself to the suitors and leaps on the threshold.

Afterward, when Penelope is informed, she wonders "whether she should address her dear husband from a distance or stand beside him and kiss his head and take his hands." She then "crosses over the stone threshold" and sits "opposite Odysseus" (23.86–89). These lines also recall Odysseus' significant entrance among the Phaeacians in the seventh book, where he hesitates before crossing the threshold (7.82–83 = 23.85–86). The description of Penelope sitting "in the light of the fire" (23.89) also recalls Arete sitting by the fire in that scene of book 7 (cf. 7.153–54; also 6.305).[19] There, Odysseus supplicated the Phaeacian queen directly after crossing the threshold into Alcinous' hall and then sat himself "on the hearth by the fire" (7.153–54).[20] A striking combination of transitional themes thus connects the two episodes: in both, the hero confronts a queen, and in both, hesitation at the threshold is combined with sitting by the fire. Here, too, the beginnings of the return in the emergence from fairyland are joined to its completion on Ithaca. Now, however, Penelope rather than Odysseus initiates the

---

[19] The theme of sitting by the fire is developed in the first meeting of Odysseus and Penelope as well. First, in 17.572 Odysseus sends word to Penelope through Eumaeus that it would be better to meet him in the evening, "seating me nearer the fire." Then, in 19.55, when Penelope comes down from her chamber, she is given a seat "by the fire." Finally, Odysseus, just before she addresses him and immediately after his bath by Eurycleia, draws his stool "closer to the fire" (19.506). The theme of meeting by the fire thus prepares for and is duly completed by the final meeting "by the fire" in book 23.

[20] For this scene as a situation of ritual rebirth, see Newton (1984) 8–9.

crucial passage back to reclaim what has been lost. After the man has won his way back by his strength and endurance and by the constant exercise of his will and reason, the final movement of acceptance, the spontaneous rekindling of the intimate tie between them, is left to the woman. She will test the man who has been the tester on so many other occasions.

The return of Odysseus has been described above in terms of a reawakening. It appears also as a rebirth. The theme of bathing, as suggested earlier, has obvious connections with birth and rebirth. Occurring at points of significant entrance, it naturally accompanies the exchange of age and debility for youth and freshness. One of the most crucial entrances makes the connection explicit. The nurse who bathes Odysseus in book 19 is an obvious maternal figure, and she vividly remembers the actual birth of Odysseus and his naming by his grandfather (19.399–409, and cf. especially 400, "newborn child," and 482–83, "Why do you wish to destroy me, my nurse? For you yourself nursed me at your breast").[21]

Birth and death, then, the most mysterious passages of human life, underlie the overall rhythm of the return and oscillate ambiguously in it in a kind of contrapuntal movement. To obtain passage back to mortal life, Odysseus must visit the land of the dead. The knowledge of his own death gained from this visit is present to him even at the moment of the joyful reclaiming of his human life and his spouse: "O wife, we have not yet come to the limit of our trials, but afterward there will be still measureless toil, much and difficult," he begins (23.248), and goes on to tell her, reluctantly, of Teiresias' prophecy of his death (263–84). Earlier, Odysseus regarded his Phaeacian landing as a rebirth and thanked Nausicaa for "giving him life" (8.468). It is fitting that the fresh princess should be the restorer of life to the exhausted warrior; yet his sleep on the ship that brings him back to the mortal world and fulfills the Phaeacians' promise is "most like to death" (13.80). In the same contrapuntal fashion, the dead suitors are paraded off by Hermes, "leader of souls" (*psuchagōgos* or *psuchopompos*) as the grim counterpart to Odysseus' successful return to full "life."

Odysseus' rebirth is also a source of life for those who waited: son, wife, and father. It is a rebirth for Odysseus' line as well, marked in the

---

[21] The connection between Eurycleia's bathing of Odysseus and the theme of birth is stressed by Baudouin (1957) 45ff., who would go so far as to regard the scar as a "signe de naissance."

joyful utterance of Laertes, himself rejuvenated after his bath (24.365–82), when he sees "son and grandson striving concerning excellence" (24.515). The renewal of Odysseus' life is here fulfilled in terms beyond himself; and he stands in the middle as the link between generations, between past and future. This rebirth is transferred also into moral and social terms at the very end of the *Odyssey*: the interference of the gods ends the cycle of strife and assures "wealth and peace in abundance," as Zeus had promised Athena (24.486). The poem thus ends with the order of Zeus with which it began; and the promised restoration of the land comes with the return of the rightful king and "gentle father," as foreshadowed in Odysseus' first words with Penelope on his return, when he addresses her, disguised as a beggar, in the darkened halls:

> My lady, never a man in the wide world
> should have a fault to find with you. Your name
> has gone out under heaven like the sweet
> honor of some god-fearing king, who rules
> in equity over the strong: his black lands bear
> both wheat and barley, fruit trees laden bright,
> new lambs at lambing time—and the deep sea
> gives great hauls of fish by his good strategy,
> so that his folk fare well.
>
> (19.107–14; Fitzgerald's translation)

Though Penelope and Odysseus have not yet explicitly recognized each other, they meet here both as the individual characters they are and as the archetypal king and queen, the partners in a sacred marriage. In terms of Frye's "encyclopedic range" of epic, their union symbolizes the ever-renewed fertility of the earth and the fruitful harmony between society and cosmos.

These ritual elements not only imply this larger dimension of meaning but also point to an artistic function behind a basic component of the poem's style: the ritualizing quality of the repeated formulas. Through the repetition of the verbal formulas, the recurrent acts of sleep, bathing, entrance, and departure stand out in a suggestive ritual character, with the overtones of meaning carried by that ritual character for a society such as Homer's. One may regard this cooperation of matter and style as a happy by-product of Homeric language. Yet there may be an inner congruence between the material and the style, a congruence that grows out of the culture itself and its means of apprehending and ordering the world. The outwardly inflexible demands of the oral style, in other words, seem to suit the ritual modes of thought that doubtless helped to create the style in the first place. These are modes of thought in which recurrent cycles of loss and regeneration, alienation and re-discovery, and death and rebirth are celebrated as the fundamental facts of existence and form an organic link between human life and the natural world. Such cyclical patterns are both metaphor and reality; and the ritual patterns discussed here help unite the two, for ritual itself partakes of both play and seriousness, both imaginary projection and realistic confrontation.

The very fabric of Homer's language, then, presents the expected, reenacted situations that make up the return through the equally pre-dictable, crystallized, ritualized expressions that make up the formulas. These recurrent formulaic expressions themselves intimate the steady sameness, the shared narrowness, and the richness in limitation that form the substance of that for which the hero has journeyed back to Ithaca. The contrast between the circumscribed, formulaic language of the *Odyssey* and the richly varied, brightly colored adventures it de-scribes also reflects the poem's movement between exploration and return, between the exotic and the familiar, and between the open possibilities of the free traveler who consorts with goddesses and the accepted constraints and rewards of the land dweller who is bound to a mortal woman.

CHAPTER 5

Kleos and Its Ironies

Heroic glory, κλέος, occupies a central place not only in Greek epic but in the entire Indo-European epic tradition as well.[1] In the *Iliad* a warrior's *kleos* is more important than life itself, as Achilles' ultimate choice makes clear. In a shame-culture, like that depicted in Homer, where esteem depends on how one is viewed and talked of by one's peers, *kleos* is fundamental as a measure of one's value to others and to oneself.[2] Both the Homeric poems, however, although based on this value system, also comment on it and even explore its limits. Achilles does this explicitly in *Iliad* 9;[3] so does the *Odyssey,* although less directly. The complexities and ironies in the *Odyssey's* view of *kleos* form the subject of this chapter.

The *Odyssey* is remarkable for its self-consciousness about the social function of heroic poetry, the contexts in which such poetry is performed, and the rapport between the bard and his hearers.[4] On three occasions, situations of bardic recitation are described in detail: the song of Phemius in book 1, the songs of Demodocus in book 8, and the *apologoi* recited by Odysseus himself, especially in book 11. When he

---

[1] See Schmitt (1967) 61–102, Schmitt (1968) 337–39, Durante (1960) 244–49 = Schmitt (1968) 283–90, Pagliaro (1961) 11–13, Benveniste (1969) 2:58ff., Ritoók (1975) 137, Nagy (1974) 229–61, and Nagy (1979) chapters 1 and 6. A motif equivalent to that of *kleos* also plays a role in the *Gilgamesh Epic:* see tablet 4, 6, 29–41 (Gilgamesh's speech to Enkidu before the attack on Humbaba) in Pritchard (1955) 82.

[2] See Dodds (1951) 17ff., Russo and Simon (1968) 483–98, and M. Finley (1965) 125ff.

[3] See *Il.* 9.318ff. and Whitman (1958) 188ff.

[4] Fränkel (1962) 8ff., Marg (1971) 11ff., Schadewaldt (1965) 54–87, and Germain (1954) 583ff.

introduces the disguised Odysseus to Penelope in the palace, Eumaeus also compares his storytelling skill to that of a bard (17.518–21). These passages relate the values of heroic *kleos* directly to the bardic tradition that keeps it alive: they show that tradition operating before our eyes (and in our ears) in the songs about great deeds of the past which poets sing and which humans "hear" from generation to generation.

In the first two of these situations, the songs of Phemius and Demodocus, a curious reversal takes place: instead of the *terpsis,* the joy or delight that song should bring, these songs bring grief, pain, and tears.[5] Odysseus, compared explicitly to a bard by King Alcinous (11.368), held everyone in silence, like Phemius in book 1 (11.333 = 1.339). His song, like that of Phemius, casts a spell or enchantment (*kēlēthmos,* 11.334; cf. *thelktēria,* 1.337).[6] Alcinous compliments him not only on his skill in general (ἐπισταμένως, 11.368) but also specifically on the beauty of his verbal expression as well as on the wisdom or good sense of its contents (σοὶ δ' ἔπι μὲν μορφὴ ἐπέων, ἔνι δὲ φρένες ἐσθλαί, 11.367).[7] Now, a hero or bard may sing of the "glorious deeds of men," the κλέα ἀνδρῶν, as Achilles does in *Iliad* 9 or Demodocus in *Odyssey* 8.73.[8] But what elicits Alcinous' praise here (as more naturally Arete's in 11.336–41) is a tale about women. This interruption of Odysseus' narrative, the only one that occurs, immediately follows the Catalogue of Heroines.

This inversion in the hero's "bardic" role as a singer of the *klea andrōn* takes on a broader significance in the light of the passage in which Odysseus announces his heroic identity at the beginning of his tale:

> εἴμ' Ὀδυσεὺς Λαερτιάδης, ὃς πᾶσι δόλοισιν
> ἀνθρώποισι μέλω, καί μευ κλέος οὐρανὸν ἵκει.
>
> (9.19–20)

"I am Odysseus, son of Laertes, who to all men am a concern by my wiles [or, am a concern to men by all my wiles], and my fame reaches the heavens."

[5] See 1.336–52, 8.62ff., and 11.333–69.

[6] On the importance of poetry's "spell" in Homer, see Lanata (1963) 16–17, with the references there cited. Circe's combination of song, magical spells, and love also brings together the "magic" of poetry and the seductive magic of love's power, with a suggestion of the danger inherent in both: see Segal (1974) 142–44.

[7] For the theme of Odysseus as a bard, see Rüter (1969) 237ff. See also Seidensticker (1978) 14ff. for Odysseus' role as a paradigm for the poetics of Archilochus.

[8] For the *klea andrōn,* "der vornehmste und vorzüglichste Gegenstand der epischen Dichtung" ("the most prominent and choicest object of epic poetry"), see Schmitt (1967) 93–95 and Schmitt (1968) 341–43. Cf. also Hesiod *Theog.* 100 and the remarks of Bradley (1975) 285–88.

These lines have several noteworthy features. First, with one partial exception, to be discussed later, this is the only place in the *Odyssey* where a character speaks of his own *kleos*. It is also the only place in Homer where μέλω, "be a concern to," common in the third person in this sense, occurs in the first person.[9] The closest parallel in this association of μέλει with enduring fame or *kleos* is Circe's brief allusion to the Argo as πᾶσι μέλουσα, "the Argo that stirred the concern of all" (12.70), a usage appropriate to a ship famed in legend and probably already celebrated in epic song. In using the verb in the first person here in book 9, Odysseus calls attention to the fact that he is, in a sense, singing a *kleos* that normally would be recited in the third person *about* him.

The Homeric hero is generally unreticent about his own achievements.[10] His *kleos*, however, the fame that is "heard" among men (cf. *Il.* 2.486), lives in the mouth of the bard, not of the hero himself. Wide-reaching and lasting fame, as Walter Marg puts it, is the "great desire of the Homeric hero"; and it is the singer above all, the repository and transmitter of knowledge and lore about the past, who can fulfill this desire.[11] This *kleos* is for others to sing, for "strangers to carry around the wide world," as Penelope says (19.333), or to spread "wide over Greece and the midlands of Argos" (1.344 = 4.726 = 4.816) or for gods to embody in "graceful song among men who live on the earth" (24.196; cf. *Il.* 6.357f.). As the parallels in the Indic epic tradition suggest, κλέος ἄφθιτον, "fame imperishable," is not merely a human creation but something akin to the eternal elements of the world, possessed of an objective existence in the lives of societies and their traditions.[12]

In the *Iliad* it is rare for a hero to speak of "my glory," *emon kleos*, in the first person. A hero may talk of "winning *glory* for myself," for example, as Hector boasts of his martial prowess when Andromache urges him to hold back from the war.

"To me too are all these things a concern, my wife; and yet terribly do I feel shame [αἰδέομαι] before the Trojans and the long-robed Trojan

[9] The closest parallel is Theognis, 245. Song can be the subject of *melei* (is a concern to), but always, of course, in the third person: see *Od.* 1.159, 358f., Hesiod *Theog.* 61, and Homeric *Hymn to Hermes* 451. Cf. also the proper name Astymeloisa, in Alcman fragment 3.73 Page (1962).
[10] See Stanford (1958–61) on 8.19–20.
[11] Marg (1971): "Ruhm, weiter und dauernder, über den Tod hinaus, ist das grosse Verlangen der homerischen Helden. Ihn gibt vor allem der Sänger, der die Kunde befestigt und weiterträgt" (20).
[12] See Nagy (1974) 241ff.

women if like a base coward I shun battle; nor did my spirit so bid me, since I learned to be noble always and to fight among the first of the Trojans, winning the great glory of my father and of myself [ἀρνύμενος πατρός τε μέγα κλέος ἠδ' ἐμὸν αὐτοῦ]."

(Il. 6.441–46)

Even here *kleos* is something to be won and is closely associated with the father as well as the individual hero.

Parallels to Odysseus' phrasing occur at two moments of special heroic intensity in the *Iliad*. Achilles in 9.412–16 contrasts the *kleos aphthiton* (glory imperishable) that he will win if he fights at Troy with long life and loss of *kleos* (ὤλετό μοι κλέος ἐσθλόν, "my fame is destroyed," 9.415). Even here, where the pronominal adjective "my" is not actually used, the hero's *kleos* is not something achieved and final. Quite the contrary, it seems remote and beyond his direct control. Hector's challenge to the Greek army in *Iliad* 7 offers a closer parallel: his opponent will die, Hector boasts, "but my *glory* will not perish" (τὸ δ' ἐμὸν κλέος οὔ ποτ' ὀλεῖται, 91). Here, too, as in *Iliad* 6.446 cited above, the hero is in the process of creating that *kleos*. Similarly, Achilles in *Iliad* 9.415 stands at a moment of crucial decision that will determine whether or not that *kleos* will exist in the future.

The situation of *Odyssey* 9.19–20 is very different. Odysseus is not involved in action or decision. He is, in fact, far from the heroic world, safe among the soft, luxury-loving Phaeacians. He is not creating that *kleos* by fighting but rather re-creating it by the *Ich-Erzählung* (first-person telling) of the long, bardlike narrative that is to occupy the next four books.[13] As both hero and bard, he is in the unique position of being the singer of his own *kleos*. His *kleos,* in other words, gains both a subjective and an objective aspect. The interlude in book 11 makes this double function explicit.

The anomalous position of Odysseus as the reciter of his own *kleos* brings together two aspects of *kleos* that are usually kept separate. First, as Gregory Nagy has suggested, *kleos* is "the formal word which the Singer himself (*aoidos*) used to designate the songs that he sang in praise of gods and men, or, by extension, the songs that people learned to sing from him."[14] Second, *kleos* is also the objectification of the hero's personal survival in epic song, the "imperishable fame" that lives among the people and keeps alive the hero's name. Thus, as Nagy points out,

[13] See Reinhardt (1948) 58ff.
[14] Nagy (1974) 248 and in general 245–52.

the usual translation of *kleos* as "fame" is inadequate, for "fame" indicates only "the consequences rather than the full semantic range,"
whereas, in fact, the relation between the actual fame of the hero and the
medium that preserves that fame is more complex: "The actions of gods
and heroes gain fame through the medium of the Singer, and the Singer
calls his medium *kleos*."[15]

By removing Odysseus far from the locus of his great heroic achievements at Troy and even from the adventures of the more recent past, the
poet views *kleos* retrospectively. It is already fixed as part of a heroic
tradition. That tradition can itself be held up for reflection, examination, and criticism. Odysseus' encounters with the Cyclops and with
Scylla, for example, reveal the inappropriateness of the traditional heroic response of straightforward battle in this strange world of fabulous
monsters (9.299–306, 12.226–33).[16]

Aware of the increasing discrepancies between the heroic world of
the epic cycle and the contemporary world of his audience, the poet of
the *Odyssey* calls attention to the fact that the glory of heroic deeds exists
only through song: it is truly *kleos* in the sense of the tales that men
know by hearsay (κλέος οἶον ἀκούομεν, "we hear only the fame," *Il.*
2.486). The great deeds of the past, in other words, are now especially
designated as a part of heroic song qua song. Their "objective" existence as unquestioned events that the audience accepts when it is under
the "spell" of the poet's magic (*thelxis, kēlēthmos*) yields momentarily to
an awareness of the form that makes possible that spell. The magic of
the singer is necessary to call these deeds into being and give them their
life. The "message" appears, for a moment, as the creation of its "medium." Hesiod, looking at the epic tradition from a certain distance, can
even go so far as to suggest that the poet's Muses can speak falsehood
that resembles "truth":

> ἴδμεν ψεύδεα πολλὰ λέγειν ἐτύμοισιν ὁμοῖα,
> ἴδμεν δ᾽, εὖτ᾽ ἐθέλωμεν, ἀληθέα γηρύσασθαι.
>
> (*Theog.* 27f.)[17]

We know how to say many lies like to true things and we know how to
speak the truth when we wish.

---

[15] Ibid., 250.

[16] See Reinhardt (1948) 59 and Whitman (1958) 300, both on the inappropriateness or
ineffectuality of the heroic stance against Scylla.

[17] On these lines and their problems, see Pucci (1977) chapter 1, with the bibliography
there cited; Lanata (1963) 24–25.

Odysseus, in book 11 able to tell tales with the skill of a bard, can also tell stories that make falsehood seem like truth after the manner of Hesiod's Muses (ἴσκε ψεύδεα πολλὰ λέγων ἐτύμοισιν ὁμοῖα, "In speaking he knew how to make many lies like to true things," *Od.* 19.203).

The *Iliad* offers a few glimpses of *kleos* as a self-conscious creation of bardic tradition. Helen reflects on the fame in song (ἀοίδιμοι) that she and Paris will have in the songs of later times (*Il.* 6.356–58). Achilles, at a crucial point for his own *kleos,* sings the *klea andrōn,* the famed songs of heroes (*Il.* 9.189). On the other hand, later poets such as Ibycus, are quite overt about the distinction and the interdependence between the objective *kleos* of heroes that the poet transmits and the personal "fame" that the medium confers.[18]

Odysseus' formulation of his *kleos* in 9.19–20 has yet another anomaly. His *kleos* derives not from heroic deeds achieved in the forefront of the battle, as did Hector's in *Il.* 6.446, but from their opposite, *doloi,* "wiles" or "tricks." A syntactical ambiguity accompanies the ambiguity of the *kleos:*

εἴμ' 'Οδυσεὺς Λαερτιάδης, ὃς πᾶσι δόλοισιν
ἀνθρώποισι μέλω, καί μευ κλέος οὐρανὸν ἵκει.

I am Odysseus son of Laertes, who am a concern to all men by my wiles, and my fame reaches the heavens.

The word "all," *pasi,* is so placed that it can modify either "men," *anthrōpoisi,* or "wiles," *doloisi.*[19] Odysseus' *kleos* can be a universal fame ("all men") or a fame won for the thoroughness of his trickery, the totality of his immersion in unheroic guile ("all ruses").

Odysseus' description of himself here is to be connected with the sinister side of himself contained in his name: identity as "the man of pains" (ὀδύναι) or the man "doomed to odium" (ὀδύσ[σ]ομαι).[20] Odysseus'

---

[18] Ibycus fragment 282, line 47, Page (1962). See the paraphrase of this poem in Nagy (1974) 250.

[19] See Stanford (1958–61), on 9.19f.; Rüter (1969) 254, sees in *pasi doloisi* a reference a reference to the Trojan horse sung by Demodocus, as well as to the *doloi* that the hero will exhibit again on Ithaca, the whole constituting a self-conscious praise of the *Odyssey* and the *Odyssey*-poet. See also Peradotto (1990) 141–42.

[20] Cf. *Od.* 1.62; 5.340, 423; and 19.275, 406–9. See Stanford (1958–61) on 1.52, Stanford (1952) 209–13, Dimock (1956) 52–70, Austin (1972) 1–19, and above, Chapter 2, note 27.

very name, as George Dimock and Norman Austin have pointed out, so deliberately concealed or revealed, associates him with the ambiguous practices of trickery and his descent from the trickster Autolycus. That ambiguity is perhaps also present in μέλω, whose unique Homeric occurrence in the first person I have already noted. Μέλω can mean "I am a subject in song to men" but also "I am a care to men," that is, a "worry," "concern," or "problem" to men in a more negative sense (cf. *Od.* 5.6).

Odysseus' representation of himself as an ambiguous hero of *dolos* is all the more striking in the light of Penelope's very different view of him and his *kleos* at the end of book 4. She fears the loss of her noble and courageous husband, whom she describes as

> endowed with all the virtues among the Greeks, noble, whose fame is widespread in Greece and the middle of Argos.

> παντοίῃς ἀρετῇσι κεκασμένον ἐν Δαναοῖσιν
> ἐσθλόν, τοῦ κλέος εὐρὺ καθ᾿ Ἑλλάδα καὶ
> μέσον Ἄργος.
>
> $(4.725f. = 4.815f.)^{21}$

Viewing Odysseus nostalgically from the needy perspective of Ithaca, Penelope endows him with the traditional heroic *aretai* (virtues) and the traditional wide-spreading *kleos*. Odysseus himself, fighting his way out of the strange fairyland world of his sea travels, sojourning among the unwarlike Phaeacians, has come to experience and value a very different aspect of himself. Encounters with monsters such as Polyphemus, whom he will soon describe, have taught him the futility of the Danaan *aretai* that Penelope praises and the emptiness of the *kleos* that spreads far and wide over Hellas and the midst of Argos. His still wider world requires a larger, more universal, more convertible form of *kleos*. He must now exercise skills that have an ambiguous value among the warriors at Troy.

Odysseus' formula here, κλέος οὐρανὸν ἵκει, "my fame reaches the heavens," reflects another peculiarity of his *kleos*. Because fame is so central to both epics, one would expect this formula to be of frequent occurrence.[22] In fact it is found only once in the *Iliad,* significantly of a

---

[21] Austin (1972) comments on some of the peculiarities of *Od.* 4.725f. = 4.815f., but he does not connect them with the anomalies of 9.19f.

[22] See the useful brief survey by Marg (1956) 27n. 3. Though the formula describes physical movement into the sky frequently in the *Iliad*, it is used of *kleos* only in *Il.* 8.92.

solid, durable, but not otherwise particularly famous object, Nestor's shield (*Il.* 8.192). It occurs only two other times in the *Odyssey* (8.74 and 19.108), in neither case of the martial glory of a traditional epic hero. The first passage does not refer to a warrior at all but to song: the Muse inspires Demodocus to sing a "lay whose *kleos* mounts to the broad heavens" (8.73–74).

The other occurrence is more striking still. It describes Penelope, whom Odysseus, disguised as a beggar, addresses for the first time in the darkened halls of his palace:

> ἦ γάρ σευ κλέος οὐρανὸν εὐρὺν ἱκάνει,
> ὥς τέ τευ ἢ βασιλῆος ἀμύμονος.
>
> (19.108–9)

Truly your fame reaches the broad heavens, like that of some blameless king.

This simile applied to Penelope is one of several that reverse gender roles.[23] It, too, places heroic *kleos* in a new and unfamiliar light: a noble queen keeping her fidelity to her lord absent from the palace has *kleos* as does a warrior facing his enemies on the open field of battle. Though nothing overt is said, a situation is created in which each recognizes and begins to revivify the obscured *kleos* of the other. Here, the threatened queen, beset by dangers, approaching desperation, lacking a firm protector in her house, receives this formula of heroic honor from the king who is in the guise of a starving, homeless beggar. Not only is he without *kleos* at this point but he is even without name. He explicitly asks Penelope not to inquire about his lineage or his homeland:

> μηδέ μοι ἐξερέεινε γένος καὶ πατρίδα γαῖαν,
> μή μοι μᾶλλον θυμὸν ἐνιπλήσῃς ὀδυνάων
> μνασαμένῳ· μάλα δ᾽ εἰμὶ πολύστονος.
>
> (19.116–18)

Ask not my race and my fatherland, lest you fill my spirit all the more with pains as I remember, for I am indeed a man of many woes.

Marg suggests that its usage in the *Odyssey* reflects the poet's self-conscious attempt to claim a place of honor for his work beside the *Iliad* (27–28), an idea developed by Rüter (1969) 254. At the other end of the vertical scale, the "deep fame" (= *bathu kleos*) of Indic epic, used by Pindar *Olympian* 7.53, seems not to have appealed to the Homeric poet: it occurs only in the proper name Bathuklēs, at *Il.* 16.594: see Schmitt (1967) 75–76.

[23] On reverse similes see Foley (1978) 7–26, especially 11ff.

In characteristic Odyssean fashion, the concealment of the name cryptically reveals one of its meanings, Odysseus/*odunai*, "pain." The situation, however, utterly reverses heroic practice. The traditional warrior who guards his *kleos* as his most precious possession proudly boasts his name, his race, his origins, and his native land, as for instance Glaucus does in his encounter with Diomedes in *Iliad* 6. 150–211. Here, Penelope makes the appropriate reply: for the only time in the poem besides 9. 19–20, a character speaks of *kleos* in the first person. Repeating lines that she had used to the suitor Eurymachus in the previous book (18.254f.), she says of Odysseus and her *kleos*:

εἰ κεῖνός γ᾽ ἐλθὼν τὸν ἐμὸν βίον ἀμφιπολεύοι,
μεῖζόν κε κλέος εἴη ἐμὸν καὶ κάλλιον οὕτω.

(19.127f.)

If he should come back and look after my life, my fame would be greater and nobler thus.

Now, she continues, instead of the *kleos* that should give joy, she has only ἄχος, "grief" (19.129 = 18.256, νῦν δ᾽ ἄχομαι, "now I have grief"). In the speech in book 18, she spoke mournfully of the difficulty of Odysseus' return and complained of the suitors' behavior, but here she tells the story of her web (19. 137–56). Her tale reveals that her *kleos*, like that of Odysseus in 9. 19f., has its basis in *doloi*: in fact, she precedes her account of "weaving" the shroud with her "weaving of guile" (ἐγὼ δὲ δόλους τολυπεύω, 19.137).

This combination of *dolos* and the highest heroic *kleos* again points up the paradoxes and contradictions in Odysseus' "heroism." A woman can be expected to use *doloi* for her *kleos*, but a hero should win his *kleos* in fair fight on the battlefield. Yet for the woman, too, *dolos* is ambiguous: it can lead to the exact opposite of *kleos*, namely, shame and disgrace, αἰσχύνη and αἶσχος. The notorious example of this latter is Clytaemnestra, whose "guileful" planning (δολόμητις, 11.422) and fashioning of guile (δόλον ἤρτυε, 11.439), as her murdered husband in Hades complains, "poured down shame [*aischos*] on herself and on all women after her" (11.433f.). Both Penelope and Odysseus tread the fine line where *dolos* can lead to "glory" instead of "shame." In this respect, as in so many others, Odysseus and Penelope complement and parallel each other.

This complementarity of *dolos* and *kleos* for them both is especially clear in the second *Nekyia*, the poem's second account of the underworld (24.1–204). The slain suitor Amphimedon gives Agamemnon the full account of Penelope's "guile" (note *dolos* in 128 and 141; cf. *polukerdeiai,* "wiliness," 167). He at once contrasts her with Clytaemnestra (196–202), praising Penelope's "great *arete*" (virtue) and "good sense" and declaring that "the glory of her *arete* will never perish" (τῷ οἱ κλέος οὔ ποτ' ὀλεῖται ἧς ἀρετῆς, 196f.). The gods will make her a subject of "lovely song" (ἀοιδὴν χαρίεσσαν, 197f.), whereas Clytaemnestra will be a subject of "hateful song" and bring "harsh repute" to women (στυγερὴ ἀοιδή, 200, and χαλεπὴν φῆμιν, 201).[24] Penelope can use *dolos* but still win the *kleos* and *arete* that are diametrically opposite to Clytaemnestra's "hateful song" and "harsh repute." Odysseus, on the other hand, master of disguise and trickery, nevertheless fights a real battle (24.178–90), whereas lordly Agamemnon dies "a most pitiable death" (11.412), unable even to get his hands on his weapon (11.423–25). This latter scene contrasts with the heroic exertion of Odysseus' son at the crucial moment of battle:

αὐτὰρ ἐγὼ ποτὶ γαίῃ χεῖρας ἀείρων
βάλλον ἀποθνῄσκων περὶ φασγάνῳ.

(11.423f.)

And I on the earth, lifting my hands, threw them around my sword as I was dying.

ἀμφὶ δὲ χεῖρα φίλην βάλεν ἔγχει.

(21.433)

And he threw his own hand around the sword.

Agamemnon's heroism cannot cope with a woman's *doloi;* Odysseus, meeting Penelope on her own ground, can enlist their separate *doloi* jointly in the restoration rather than the destruction of their house and their *kleos.* At the crucial transition between fairyland and Ithaca in his landing on Scheria, Odysseus had praised the "good fame" that husband and wife enjoy when they live together in "harmony of spirit," *homophrosunē* (6.180–85): μάλιστα δέ τ' ἔκλυον αὐτοί ("they themselves

---

[24] Note *aoidē,* not *kleos* here: see Nagy (1974) 260–61, Nagy (1979) 36–39, and Rüter (1969) 233n. 9. Note the repetition, 24.202 = 11.434: the same contrasts are implicit in both passages, but the full contrast between Penelope and Clytaemnestra and between Odysseus and Agamemnon is spelled out only here. For a stimulating reexamination of this contrast and of Penelope's *kleos* generally, see Katz (1991), especially 3ff. and 20ff.

have the greatest fame," 185). That remote prayer for Nausicaa and her prospective husband now becomes relevant for Penelope and himself, fulfilled in the reaffirmed *kleos* of his Ithacan wife.[25]

The poem defines heroism through a series of symmetries and inversions: Odyssean *doloi* contrast with Agamemnon's *kleos,* the success of the one with the failure of the other. The house-destroying *dolos* of Clytaemnestra also contrasts with the house-preserving *dolos* of Penelope, as *aischos* contrasts with *kleos.* Simultaneously, the *kleos* of Odysseus, paradoxically achieved through *dolos,* parallels the *kleos* of Penelope: she is a woman who weaves guile (19.137) but, woman though she is, still gains the *kleos* usually reserved for male heroes. He, a hero of the Trojan War, possessing the masculine *kleos* of the warrior, wins that *kleos* through *dolos* and, in this poem, through a deed executed in the interior space of the house, the realm usually associated with women. The Iliadic warrior at once announces his name to his antagonist; Odysseus wins his major triumphs by circumspectly (and often unheroically) hiding his name.

Odysseus' "fame" that "reaches to the heavens" in 9.20 recurs later in that same book in an exploit that contains one of his most brilliant *doloi* and forms one of the most important parts of his *kleos,* namely, in his first face-to-face encounter with the monstrous Cyclops. He addresses Polyphemus, for the first time, as follows:

> ἡμεῖς τοι Τροίηθεν ἀποπλαγχθέντες Ἀχαιοὶ
> παντοίοις ἀνέμοισιν ὑπὲρ μέγα λαῖτμα θαλάσσης,
> οἴκαδε ἱέμενοι, ἄλλην ὁδὸν ἄλλα κέλευθα
> ἤλθομεν· οὕτω που Ζεὺς ἤθελε μητίσασθαι.
> λαοὶ δ' Ἀτρεΐδεω Ἀγαμέμνονος εὐχόμεθ' εἶναι,
> τοῦ δὴ νῦν γε μέγιστον ὑπουράνιον κλέος ἐστίν·
> τόσσην γὰρ διέπερσε πόλιν καὶ ἀπώλεσε λαοὺς
> πολλούς.

(9.259–66)

We are Achaeans, *tossed off our course* from Troy by winds of every kind over the great abyss of the sea, as we sought our way homeward, and we came on another road and other ways, for so did Zeus somehow wish to devise it. And we boast to be the men of Agamemnon son of Atreus,

---

[25] On the importance of *homophrosunē* in the *Odyssey,* see Austin (1975) 181, 188–89, 203–4; also Murnaghan (1987) 43.

whose fame is greatest under the heavens, for so great a city *did he sack* and destroy its many people.

Odysseus here presents himself in terms both of his helpless wanderings on the vast sea and of the heroic glory of his Trojan exploits, the capture and destruction of a great city which constitute the "greatest *fame* under the heavens" of his leader. That same configuration—wanderings and the capture of Troy—introduces the hero in the poem's very first lines:

> Ἄνδρα μοι ἔννεπε, μοῦσα, πολύτροπον, ὃς μάλα πολλὰ
> πλάγχθη, ἐπεὶ Τροίης ἱερὸν πτολίεθρον ἔπερσε.
>
> (1.1–2)

Sing me, Muse, the man of many turns, who was *tossed* much after he *sacked* Troy's holy city.

Far from Troy and Trojan heroism, however, this "greatest fame beneath the heavens" (*megiston hupouranion kleos*) has little meaning. It certainly makes little impression on the Cyclops, who "with pitiless spirit" dismisses his appeal for suppliant rights (9.272–80). Odysseus replies with "guileful words" (δολίοις ἐπέεσιν, 9.282): he begins to understand that one may hark back proudly to martial deeds at Troy, but in this post-Trojan world, the hero will have to achieve *kleos* by new means.[26]

The narrative context of the breadth of *kleos* in 9.264 contains another irony. "The greatest distance possible," Austin remarks apropos of the spatial field of Homer's world, "Homer expresses in the proportion: Agamemnon's glory is as widely dispersed beneath the sky as the city was great that he destroyed."[27] Odysseus borrows from his leader at Troy a *kleos* that embraces the sky and the earth. But Odysseus speaks of the great abyss of the sea (μέγα λαῖτμα θαλάσσης, 260) and of this vast *kleos* under the heavens at the point when he is trapped in a cave that, though "wide" (237), is nevertheless a dark and rather crowded enclosure (cf. μυχὸν ἄντρου, 236; also 219–23). He is dwarfed by the giant who towers above him (cf. 257) and uses his massive strength to seal that enclosure with a rock that not even twenty-two wagons could

---

[26] At his first meeting with Polyphemus, Odysseus addresses him only with "words," *epessin*, without a modifier (9.258): there would seem to be a progression to the "guileful words" and then the "insults" of 9.282 and 474, respectively.

[27] Austin (1975) 89. It is interesting that the definition of *kleos* by its breadth (*euru*) occurs only in the *Odyssey*, though it is well established in the Indo-European epic tradition: see Schmitt (1967) 72–73.

budge (240–43). The rock both makes the enclosure definitive and renders futile traditional heroic battle with the sword (299–305).

There is one further irony. Odysseus invokes with pride and confidence the *kleos* of a leader whose death, as he will relate in the *Nekyia* of book 11, was anything but glorious (11.406–34). Agamemnon's own fate illustrates the failure and inadequacy of the traditional *kleos* in this post-Iliadic world. Citing him, Odysseus will also find an alternative.

To defeat the Cyclops, Odysseus has to resort to the extreme form of guile, *dolos:* he temporarily negates his personal identity and becomes *Outis/Mētis,* "No-Man" (9.366), which is also the *mētis* of his guile or *dolos.*[28] The pun on *mē tis* ("no one," the negative of Outis) and *mētis* (guile) associates the abandonment of heroic identity with the guile on which he has increasingly to rely in this strange world. He later resumes the traditional heroic stance and boasts like an Iliadic warrior over a defeated enemy. But it is a mistake to address the Cyclops "with insults" (*kertomioisi,* 9.474) rather than with "guile" (9.282). The result is disastrous: in possession of his enemy's name, the Cyclops can call down the curse of Poseidon against him (9.530f.; cf. 504f.).[29]

In this passage Odysseus assumes the heroic, warrior epithet "sacker of cities," *ptoliporthios.* He thereby identifies himself with the Iliadic *kleos* of his leader in whose name he introduced himself to the Cyclops in 9.265: "He sacked so great a city" (τόσσην διέπερσε πόλιν). May one speculate that by the time Odysseus has reached Alcinous' court he is more aware of the incongruity of that martial epithet in this marine realm? As discussed above, he has now learned to regard himself less as a "sacker of cities" than as a man of guile and tricks (*doloisi,* 9.19–20).[30] In achieving the final restoration of his heroic status, Odysseus will need *doloi* more than the martial prowess of a "sacker of cities."

The converse of Odysseus' inappropriately heroic address to the Cyclops occurs in the next book. Landing on another unknown island, Odysseus confesses his disorientation (10.189–97): he does not know the celestial coordinates of east and west, sunrise and sunset, and finds himself at a loss for his usual *mētis.*

> ἀλλὰ φραζώμεθα θᾶσσον,
> εἴ τις ἔτ᾽ ἔσται μῆτις. ἐγὼ δ᾽ οὐκ οἴομαι εἶναι.
>
> (10.192–93)

---

[28] See Podlecki (1961) 125–33 and Austin (1972) 13–14; also Chapter 2, above.
[29] See Brown (1966) 193–202, especially 196; see also Austin (1972) 3–4.
[30] On Odysseus' narrative as a retrospective interpretation and understanding of his previous actions, see Chapter 2, above; also Bradley (1976) 137–48, especially 144.

But let us quickly take thought if there will still be any devising. But I
think that there is not.

At this declaration, his men's spirit is broken as they remember the
violence (*biē*) of the Cyclops and Laestrygonians (10.198–200), and they
weep miserably (201f.). Not only is there an antithesis of *mētis* and *biē* as
acted out in the Polyphemus episode but also, with the absence of
Odysseus' *mētis*, closely akin to his *dolos*, a resulting loss of speech: his
men can only "wail shrilly" and lament (κλαῖον δὲ λιγέως θαλερὸν
κατὰ δάκρυ χέοντες, "they wailed shrilly, pouring down abundant
tears," 10.201f.). "Guileful words," *dolia epea*, are the saving device of
Odysseus' *mētis* against brute force (9.282). Shortly before, his "honeyed words" of encouragement (*meilichia epea*, 10.173) kept his men
from grieving about death (10.172–78). Now, in the absence of his
mētis, words give way to inarticulate and helpless grief (ἀλλ᾽ οὐ γάρ τις
πρῆξις ἐγίγνετο μυρομένοισιν, "and nothing practical came from
their lamenting," 10.202). Soon afterward, these dispirited companions, lacking the guidance of Odyssean *mētis*, lose their human voice
(*phōnē*, 10.239) and in their bestial transformation by Circe are penned
up "wailing" (*klaiontes*, 10.241).

Odysseus' formal declaration of his heroic identity at the beginning
of book 9, as we have seen, has associations with the bardic view of *kleos*
as something past and definitively formed: he sings as his own a *kleos*
that ought to come from another's mouth. In book 11 Odysseus actually performs as a bard who skillfully sings a warrior's deeds. In the
Phaeacian perspective of aesthetic distance, martial exploits and painful
suffering appear only as art.[31] But when Odysseus faces his great task of
restoring order on Ithaca and regaining name and kingdom, he sets up
just the reverse relation of art and action. No longer the soldier doing
the work of a bard but a beggar in disguise, he elicits from his regal
weapon the sound that is music to the warrior's ears. Holding the great
bow, finally, in his hands, he handles it as a poet handles a lyre:

ὡς ὅτ᾽ ἀνὴρ φόρμιγγος ἐπιστάμενος καὶ ἀοιδῆς
ῥηϊδίως ἐτάνυσσε νέῳ περὶ κόλλοπι χορδήν,

[31] See Marg (1971) 16–17 and 20 and Lanata (1963) 17. Rüter (1969) 243 and 237 makes
the point that Odysseus, unlike Demodocus, moves deeper into his grief as he sings; he
gains a certain distance from his grief that he had not had before. All the while the
Phaeacian audience enjoys his tale as if it were merely the song of a bard. Burkert (1960)
also stresses the contrast between the light Olympian world depicted by the Phaeacian
bard and the serious side of Olympus shown in the *Iliad* (141–43).

ἅψας ἀμφοτέρωθεν ἐϋστρεφὲς ἔντερον οἰός,
ὣς ἄρ᾽ ἄτερ σπουδῆς τάνυσεν μέγα τόξον Ὀδυσσεύς.
δεξιτερῇ δ᾽ ἄρα χειρὶ λαβὼν πειρήσατο νευρῆς·
ἡ δ᾽ ὑπὸ καλὸν ἄεισε, χελιδόνι εἰκέλη αὐδήν.

(21.406–11)

Just as a man skilled in the lyre and song easily stretches a string around a new peg, fastening it well-twisted on both sides, the gut of a sheep, so without haste did Odysseus stretch the great bow, and taking it in his right hand he tested the string, and it sang out beautifully, like a swallow in its voice.

Tried by Odysseus, the bow "sang out beautifully, like a swallow"— or, as the verb ἄεισε (sung) also suggests, like a bard.[32] The aesthetic and social order implied by song once more approximates the moral and political order reestablished by the return of the king. Disorder in Mycenae, we recall, included the banishment of the bard when Agamemnon left to guard his queen (3.267–72).[33]

Among the Phaeacians, Odysseus could re-create his heroic past and its *kleos* only in song. Here on Ithaca he is a warrior who brings back to the palace the joy and rightful celebration of heroic deeds that earlier could be evoked solely by bards whose tales made the listeners weep. The joyful songs of Phemius and of Demodocus on Scheria caused private grief to Penelope and Odysseus but gave public "joy" (*terpsis*) to the rest of the audience.[34] The "song" of the bow gives public "grief" (*achos*) to the audience at large (21.412) but private "rejoicing" to Odysseus (γήθησέν τ᾽ ἄρ᾽ ἔπειτα πολύτλας δῖος Ὀδυσσεύς, "and then did much-enduring Odysseus rejoice," 21.414). This inversion of joy and grief now refers not merely to the quiet, interior bardic situation when Odysseus was isolated in the house of strangers but also to the heroic situation on the battlefield, where the bow brings a living *kleos* to one and "grief" (*penthos*) to the other in actual deeds, not their reflection in song. We may compare the wounding of Menelaus in the *Iliad*:

ὅν τις ὀϊστεύσας ἔβαλεν τόξων ἐῢ εἰδώς,
Τρώων ἢ Λυκίων, τῷ μὲν κλέος, ἄμμι δὲ πένθος.

(4.196–97 = 4.206–7)[35]

---

[32] For other aspects of the simile of the bow as lyre, see Chapter 3, above; also Austin (1975) 247–51 and Stewart (1976) 158–59.

[33] For the importance of the bard in book 3, see Rüter (1969) 234n.12.

[34] See 1.342, 347; 8.91f., 536–43; 9.3–15.

[35] For the contrast of "joy" and "grief" in the bardic tradition as reflected in Homer, see Nagy (1974) 255–61 and Nagy (1979) chapter 5.

[Menelaus] whom some one of the Trojans or Lycians shot plying his
bow, well-experienced in archery, to him glory but to us grief.

When Odysseus sang like a bard on Scheria, heroic *kleos* was a fossilized
vestige in the amber of the Phaeacians' hedonism (cf. 8.246–55). In this
unheroic setting it was incongruous to declare *kleos* as it appears in
Odysseus' self-proclamation in 9.19–20 or in his reaction to a taunt
about a more trivial *kleos* in an athletic, not a martial, competition
(8.152–57; see 8.146–47). Now, at the brink of heroic battle once more,
the hero uses a bardic metaphor not merely to state in words but to enact
in deeds as well what it meant to win *kleos* at Troy.

This perspective on heroic song also casts fresh light on the episode
of the Sirens. They are described in the vocabulary of the bard: their
song casts a spell (θέλγουσι, 12.40; λιγυρῇ θέλγουσιν ἀοιδῇ, 12.44),
like that of Phemius (θελκτήρια, 1.337; cf. 11.334). This vocabulary
links them with the ambiguous and seductive magic of Circe (10.291,
317). Their power depends emphatically on hearing. Their "voice" is
itself a "song" (*aoidē*, 12.44, 183, 198), which is "clear-sounding" (*ligurē*,
12.44, 183) or "honey-voiced" (*meligērus*, 12.187): hence the homoeo-
pathic magic of the "honey-sweet wax," *meliēdēs*, as an antidote to its
danger (12.49). It also brings the "joy" or "delight" associated with
bardic song.[36]

The content of the Sirens' song is the epic tradition, the heroes' efforts
at Troy, as well as "what passes on the wide-nurturing earth" (12.189–
91). The rendering of the heroic tradition that the Sirens practice,
however, is akin to the bardic song of Scheria: it shows heroic adventure
as something frozen and crystallized into lifeless, static form, something dead and past, a subject for song and nothing more. For this
reason, perhaps, they are the first adventure of Odysseus after Hades:
"First you will come to the Sirens," Circe tells him (Σειρῆνας μὲν
πρῶτον ἀφίξεαι, 12.39); and they stand in close proximity to that dead
world of purely retrospective heroism, where the only existence is in
song. Yet when Odysseus had related his adventure among the dead—
with the Siren-like "spell" and the art of a bard, to be sure (11.334,
368)—those shades were still a living part of his past, directly related to

---

[36] So *terpomenos*, 12.52, and *terpsamenos*, 12.188; cf. 1.342, 347. For the Sirens' attributes of epic song, see Fränkel (1962) 10 and Reinhardt (1948) 60–62. See Pucci (1979)
121–32, especially 126ff., and Segal (1989) 332. On "hearing" in the Siren episode see
12.41, 48, 49, 52, 185, 187, 193, and 198.

his *nostos,* or return (see 11.100 and 196).[37] What he hears in the Underworld stirs grief or arouses indignation (11.435–39, 465f.) and thus reinforces that longing for mother, father, and wife which is essential to his return (cf. 11.152–334). What the Sirens sing is remote from any experience. The magical charm of their sweet voice on the windless sea is epic *kleos* in the abstract, lovely but somehow dehumanized: hence the vagueness and generality of their form of *kleos* (ὄσσα γένηται ἐπὶ χθονὶ πουλυβοτείρῃ, "all things that arise on the most fertile earth," 12.191).

As the past of which the Sirens sing has the deathly vacuity of what is long dead and without flesh (cf. 12.45f.), so they themselves are characterized by motionlessness. As Odysseus and his men draw near, a windless calm forces them to take to the oars (12.167–72). These Sirens, unlike their later descendants in Greek art, do not fly[38] but "sit in their meadow" (ἥμεναι ἐν λειμῶνι, 12.45) and ask Odysseus to "stop the ship" (νῆα κατάστησον, 12.185) in order to hear their voice. They claim that no one "has ever yet passed by [παρήλασε] in black ship before hearing the honey-voiced speech from our mouths" (12.186f.). Escape from them, therefore, consists in keeping active, moving, passing by (παρὲξ ἐλάαν, 12.47; παρήλασαν, 12.197).

Not only do the Sirens know of the exploits at Troy, but they also address Odysseus by the heroic epithet "great war-glory of the Achaeans" (μέγα κῦδος Ἀχαιῶν, 12.184), the only place in the poem where he is so titled. This epithet occurs seven times in the *Iliad.* The only other occurrences in the *Odyssey* are the formulaic lines by which Telemachus twice addresses the aged Nestor in book 3 (79 = 202). Well might the inexperienced youth at his first direct contact with the glories of Troy speak to the oldest of the Achaean warriors in these terms, for Nestor, more than any other Homeric character, lives in the past and has virtually his entire existence defined by his memories of the Iliadic world.

Odysseus, however, will continue his journey and effect a return to

----

[37] See J. Finley (1978): "His [Odysseus'] curiosity might have been thought satisfied in the Underworld. But that revelation surrounded or concerned his own past and future; the Siren song has no tie with him. . . . He will reach home by what he learned in the Underworld; this other, complete, impersonal song ends a man's hope of wife and children. . . . The famous song expresses one side of a myth of which homecoming expresses the other; the two sides are not quite compatible" (130–31).

[38] See Pollard (1965) 137–45. On the change from the flowery meadow of Homer to the cliffs of later painters and writers, see also Reinhardt (1948) 61.

the living past and the living *kleos* that await him on Ithaca, not at Troy. He must therefore resist the blandishments of a heroic tradition that is frozen into spellbinding but lifeless song. What the Sirens know is too general and too remote to help him in his quest to recover Ithaca. To remain and listen to their song would be to yield to the seduction of a heroic tradition rendered in its most elegant, attractive, and deadly form, devoid of reality for the tasks that await this hero of *dolos*. The *Nekyia* and, in a different way, the lives of Nestor and Menelaus have shown this danger in lived example. The Sirens cast that danger of entrapment by the past specifically into the form of poetic song and the fascination it exercises. Were he to heed it, he, too, would be frozen into a sterile past, one of those rotting skeletons on the island. Thus his task is not to listen but to "pass by."

Rather than preserving fame by the remembering Muse of true epic song ("Muse," after all, is probably etymologically related to "memory"),[39] the Sirens bring forgetfulness of home and loved ones (12.42f.). Pindar told how golden "Charmers" (*Kēlēdones*), akin to these Sirens, perched atop a mythical temple of Apollo at Delphi and sang so sweetly that the visitors "perished there apart from wives and children, their souls suspended by the honeyed voice" (*Paean* 8.75–79 in Snell and Maehler).[40] For Odysseus thus to perish obscurely on the rock to which the magic of the Sirens' song draws him would be to forget the return on which in fact his *kleos* rests.

In this temptation of "forgetting the return," the Sirens' magical spell has affinities not only with Circe but also with the Lotos-eaters. There too a man "forgets his return" (νόστοιο λάθηται, 9.97 and 102; cf. οἴκαδε νοστήσαντι, 12.43). The victims of the Lotos, like Odysseus in book 12, have to be bound forcibly in the ship (9.99 and 12.196). The Sirens inhabit a "flowery meadow" (λειμῶν' ἀνθεμόεντα, 12.159); the Lotos is a "flowerlike food" (ἄνθινον εἶδαρ, 9.84).

The Sirens' flowery meadow, however, is characterized by a literal death and decay that are only implicit in the Lotos-eaters' temptation to forget the return. Circe describes the bones of "rotting men" near their meadow (ἀνδρῶν πυθομένων, 12.46), and Odysseus warns his men of the danger in terms of dying or avoiding death (ἀλλ' ἐρέω μὲν ἐγών,

---

[39] For the Muse and "memory," see Lanata (1963) 3, with the references there cited; Pucci (1977) 22–24; and Detienne (1973) 13ff.

[40] Athenaeus 8.36 (p. 290E), cited by Snell and Maehler (1975) fragment 52i, points out the affinity between these "charmers" and the Sirens in this "forgetting" of home and loved ones.

ἵνα εἰδότες ἤ κε θάνωμεν / ἤ κεν ἀλευάμενοι θάνατον καὶ κῆρα φύγοιμεν, "But I shall tell you [Circe's prophecies], in order that we may die knowing them, or else avoiding death and doom we might escape," 12.156f.). That forgetting of *nostos* may be even more intimately associated with the decay in the Sirens' flowery meadow if, as Douglas Frame suggests, the root of *nostos* implies a return of consciousness (*noos*) in a "coming back" (*neomai*) from Hades. *Lēthē*, forgetting, also has associations with darkness and the obscurity of death.[41]

Epic song and the memory that it preserves, however, confer a victory over death. Its "imperishable fame," *kleos aphthiton*, is the exact antithesis of the Sirens' rot and decay. As Nagy has shown, *aphthiton*, whose root, *phthi-*, often describes the "withering" or "decay" of plant life (cf. the "imperishable vines," ἄφθιτοι ἄμπελοι, of the golden age fertility of Goat Island across from the Cyclopes, 9.133), has associations with the vital liquids or substances that overcome death: "From the present survey of all the Greek epic nouns (except *kleos*) which are described by *aphthito-*, we may posit a least common denominator in context: *an unfailing stream* of water, fire, semen, vegetal extract (wine). By extension, the gods representing these entities may also have the epithet *aphthito-*, as well as the things that they own or make."[42] True epic song counters the decay to which mortal things are subject with a *kleos* seen as close to the very essence of life, akin to the vital fluids that sustain human life and the natural world.

In the Siren episode, song not only is a ghostly imitation of epic but even becomes its own negation. This song brings death, not life. It does not go out over the broad earth among mortals. Those who succumb to it remain closed off from men, becalmed on a nameless sea, their bodies rotting in a flowery meadow. The Sirens know the secrets of the past, but it is a past that has no future life in the "remembering" of successive generations. Here the hero forgets his loved ones among whom his *kleos* might live on after his death (cf. 12.42f.). The epic bard, aided by the goddess of memory, makes the past live in the present and bridges the void between the sunless realm of the dead and the bright world of the living,[43] as Odysseus himself does in the *Nekyia* of book 11; the

---

[41] On *nostos* and the return to consciousness, see Frame (1978) chapter 3. On the semantic field of *lēthē*, see Hesiod *Theog.* 211–32 and Detienne (1973) 22–24.

[42] See Nagy (1974) 244 and Nagy (1979) chapter 10.

[43] See Vernant (1959) = (1974) 1:82–87, especially 87: "En faisant tomber la barrière qui sépare le présent du passé, [la mémoire] jette un pont entre le mondes des vivants et cet au-delà auquel retourne tout ce qui a quitté la lumière du soleil. . . . Le privilège que

Sirens' song entraps the living in the putrefaction of their own hopelessly mortal remains.

Though fundamentally different in many ways, the Sirens have certain resemblances to the Harpies, *Seelenvogel,* "snatchers" of the soul from life to death.[44] In the case of Homer's Sirens, the song that should immortalize ironically brings oblivion. Where the *Odyssey* mentions these "Snatchers" in relation to Odysseus, there is an interesting overlap with the Sirens, for *harpuiai* negate his *kleos:*

> ἠδέ κε καὶ ᾧ παιδὶ μέγα κλέος ἦρατ' ὀπίσσω.
> νῦν δέ μιν ἀκλειῶς ″Αρπυιαι ἀνηρέψαντο.
>
> (1.240f. = 14.370f.)

And he would have won great fame for his son after him; but now the Snatchers [Harpies] carried him off without fame.

Closely related to this negation of Odysseus' *kleos* is Penelope's lament as she imagines the death not only of a husband, but also of a son, the latter also "snatched" away:

> ἢ πρὶν μὲν πόσιν ἐσθλὸν ἀπώλεσα θυμολέοντα
> παντοίης ἀρετῆσι κεκασμένον ἐν Δαναοῖσιν
> ἐσθλόν, τοῦ κλέος εὐρὺ καθ' Ἑλλάδα καὶ μέσον ″Αργος.
> νῦν αὖ παῖδ' ἀγαπητὸν ἀνηρέψαντο θύελλαι
> ἀκλέα ἐκ μεγάρων, οὐδ' ὁρμηθέντος ἄκουσα.
>
> (4.724–28)

I who have lost a noble husband, fine-spirited, endowed with all the virtues among the Greeks, noble, whose fame is widespread in Greece and the middle of Argos. But now the storm winds have snatched up my beloved son without fame [report] from the halls, and I did not hear of his setting forth.

Mnemosune confère à l'aède est celui d'un contact avec l'autre monde, la possibilité d'y entrer et d'en revenir librement. Le passé apparaît comme une dimension de l'au-delà" ("In removing the barrier that separates the present from the past [memory] makes a bridge between the world of the living and that world beyond to which everything that has left the light of the sun must return. . . . The privilege that Mnemosune confers on the singer is that of a contact with the other world, the possibility of freely entering it and freely returning from it. The past appears as a dimension of the Beyond"). See also Detienne (1973) chapter 2, especially 20ff.

[44] For similarities and differences between Sirens and Harpies, see Wilamowitz-Moellendorff (1959) 1:263–64, with 264n. 1; Sittig (1912) 2422; and Zwicker (1927) 293–94.

Such a death is analogous to the doom of the Sirens' island in book 12. The Harpies who snatch a man away "without *fame*" to the remote corners of the world on the winds of storm deprive him of the *kleos* that would be "heard" as men in a civilized community sing of a death by glorious deeds, witnessed by his comrades and commemorated by a funeral monument (τῷ κέν οἱ τύμβον μὲν ἐποίησαν Παναχαιοί, "all the Achaeans would have made a tomb for him," 1.239 = 14.369). Lost in the obscure reaches of the wild, he would necessarily perish *akleōs,* without report of his end, without the song or story in the "hearing" of men that could keep his memory alive. He would be lost in the anonymity of nature's violence, just as the victims of the Sirens in book 12 rot in nameless heaps in a remote, mysterious ocean, reclaimed entirely by nature's elemental processes of putrefaction and decay.

The Sirens have the *terpsis* of the epic bard but no contact with the *kleos* through which the bard conquers death. The verb that repeatedly describes the "hearing" of their song is *akouein* (purely acoustic hearing, used eight times), never *kluein,* the social hearing of fame.[45] As their voice does not go beyond the nameless "island" (12.201) where they sit, so the "hearing" (*akouein*) of their song is entirely material, not the transcendent "imperishable *fame*" (*kleos*) that leads from death to life. As their victims succumb to the decay of their physical remains and are reduced to the rotting flesh of mere body, so a purely physical blocking of the ears as the corporeal organ of hearing suffices to defeat them. Indeed, Homer dwells concretely on the physical details of placing wax, a substance also used to preserve, in the ears (12.47f., 177).

Like Hesiod's Muses, the Sirens speak the language of "knowing" (ἴδμεν . . . ἴδμεν, 12.189, 191; cf. *Theog.* 27f., *Il.* 2.485f.), but no word of "memory" or "remembering" characterizes their song. All the basic elements of this song—its knowledge, pleasure, and "hearing"—are a perversion of true heroic song. Whoever heeds it is caught by the fatal "spell" of empty "delight" in a purely physical "hearing" that will isolate him far from the living memory of future men. Here he will rot away obscurely, his remains indistinguishable in a heap of rotting skin and bones, not the whole forms of the active figures of heroes who breathe and move in their deeds when the epic bard awakens the *klea andrōn.* Seen in this perspective, the episode of the Sirens is not just

---

[45] *Akouein* is also the verb that Odysseus uses about "hearing" the Sirens when he relates this episode to Penelope in 23.326: Σειρήνων ἀδινάων φθόγγον ἄκουσεν, "He heard the trilling voice of the Sirens."

another fantastic adventure of Odysseus' wanderings. Through his characteristic form of mythic image, the traditional singer here finds poetic expression for the implicit values and poetics of epic song and epic *kleos*.

Odysseus' last words in book 21 are an ironical invocation of the nonheroic scenes of feasting and song that have occurred throughout the poem. With grim humor he suggests that it is now the time to make merry "with song and the lyre, for these are the accompaniments of the feast":

> νῦν δ᾽ ὥρη καὶ δόρπον Ἀχαιοῖσιν τετυκέσθαι
> ἐν φάει, αὐτὰρ ἔπειτα καὶ ἄλλως ἐψιάασθαι
> μολπῇ καὶ φόρμιγγι· τὰ γάρ τ᾽ ἀναθήματα δαιτός.
>
> (428–30)

We recall the first feast and the first song in book 1, when Odysseus seemed hopelessly far away and the suitors controlled the palace and forced the bard to sing (1.145–55, especially 152; cf. 21.430, 22.351f.).[46] But now, as the equation of lyre to bow in the similes of 1.405 and 1.411 changes from trope to action, so the ironical invitation to feasting and song in 21.428–30 changes to heroic combat in the military formula that closes the book:

> ἀμφὶ δὲ χεῖρα φίλην βάλεν ἔγχεϊ, ἄγχι δ᾽ ἄρ᾽ αὐτοῦ
> πὰρ θρόνον ἑστήκει κεκορυθμένος αἴθοπι χαλκῷ.
>
> (21.433f.)

And Telemachus threw his own hand around his spear, and stood near him [Odysseus], by the stool, armored in flashing bronze.

Now, too, the "contests" that accompanied those feasts as part of Phaeacian levity (cf. the *aethloi* and *kleos* of 8.145–48) have higher stakes as Odysseus opens a "destructive contest" (22.5, οὗτος μὲν δὴ ἄεθλος ἄατος; cf. 21.91)[47] and aims "at a target that no one ever yet hit" (22.6). Odysseus no longer has to use the bardlike "magic" (*thelxis*) of his lies to

---

[46] Stanford (1958–61) on 21.428–30 notes the parallelism between the *anathēmata daitos* of 21.430 and 1.52; see also Saïd (1977) 25 and below, Chapter 6, note 26.

[47] If ἄατος means "blameless," as some have thought (see Stanford [1958–61], on 21.91 and 22.5), then the phrase will be ironic. For the special nature of this contest and its possible ritual associations, see Germain (1954) chapter 1.

win his way into the palace, as he does through the tales that Eumaeus praises when he introduces him to Penelope for the first time (17.518–21). Making good his rightful place within the palace by a "song" of a very different kind, Odysseus performs a final bardlike act that both completes and supersedes all his previous skillful manipulation of words.

The image of the bard at the end of book 21 resonates in still a different register when the great deed is really accomplished and Odysseus has purged the enemies from his halls. Still reflecting on the practical exigencies of the situation, Odysseus orders a bath and fresh clothes and then gives instructions that "the divine singer, holding the clear-sounding lyre, lead us in the playful dance, so that one hearing it outside may say that it is a wedding" (133–35). His commands are promptly obeyed: soon "the divine singer took up the smooth lyre and stirred up in them desire for sweet song and blameless dance" (143–45); and afterward, Odysseus and Penelope are led into the bedchamber like a newly married couple (293–96). Now, Odysseus, not the suitors, commands song. He is indeed celebrating a wedding, for he and Penelope, the obstacles removed, are on the verge of their reunion, the next major event in the poem (152–288). The motif of the wedding celebration, however, appears with a twist of bitter irony: the "suitors" of the new "bride" are lying dead, and the festivity is the extension of the deed of killing them and part of the guile characteristic of Odyssean action. The situation is just the opposite of Agamemnon's betrayal by his wife at a banquet; and it is part of the sustained contrast between the two returns that Agamemnon, describing to Odysseus the slaughter of his men at his failed *nostos,* compares them to swine being slaughtered at a great man's house in preparation for a wedding (*gamos,* 11.415).

The occasion for the song here in 23.133–35 contrasts both with Phemius' singing in book 1 and, more immediate, with his anxious holding of his lyre in the fear of death in 22.330–39 (22.332b = 23.133b). Phemius' song here also contrasts with the song of Demodocus in book 8. The stated aim of song in book 23 is not *terpsis* per se, though Phemius' patronymic is Terpiades, "Joy-son" (22.330), but rather the dangerous circumstances of battle and the prospect of facing still more uneven odds (23.118–22). Not a scene of happy conviviality but a speech about the martial virtues of valor and loyalty introduces the command that the "divine bard" play on his lyre (23.124–28). The purpose of this song, finally, is not to proclaim and perpetuate *kleos* but the opposite, to *prevent* the "wide fame" of a great deed from going out into the world:

μὴ πρόσθε κλέος εὐρὺ φόνου κατὰ ἄστυ γένηται
ἀνδρῶν μνηστήρων. . . .

(23.173f.)

Let not the wide fame of the suitors' slaughter arise around town before
[we go to the country].

Thus even when Odysseus accomplishes his great exploit, the usual
terms of heroic *kleos* are inverted.

The comparison of the bow to the bard's lyre just before the battle
(21.404–9) not only introduces the long-anticipated scene of heroic
combat and heroic *kleos* but also brings together the two sides of Odysseus' role in the poem. By subordinating song to action (for in book 21
the bardic associations are figurative only), the similes implicitly reas-
sert Odysseus' full return to the heroic world and to the *kleos* that is
rightfully his and that has been so problematical in the poem. He may
owe that *kleos* to trickery, as his announcement of his identity to the
Phaeacians suggests (9.19f.); yet this hero of guile, device, and craft
(*mētis, mēchanē,* and *polukerdeiai*) is also capable of heroic battle against
great odds.

An important ambiguity still remains, one parallel to the ambiguities
of Odysseus' *kleos*. The slaughter of the suitors has, to be sure, some of
the appurtenances of heroic battle: Athena-Mentor is there to exhort
Odysseus by his valor at Troy (22.226–30). Yet this deed is hardly a
heroic exploit on the Iliadic scale. From the suitors' point of view, given
a full hearing in the second *Nekyia,* it is guile and murder. When the
slain suitor Amphimedon describes the deed, he begins with the deceit
of a woman (24.125–49), stresses the craftiness of Odysseus (24.167),
and implies that he and his companions never had a fair chance. The
heroic detail of "lovely armor" (περικαλλέα τεύχεα, 24.165) figures
only as part of the hopeless odds against which he and his companions
had to contend. Like Agamemnon in book 11, he views his death not as
a proud heroic end on the field of battle but as "a wretched doom"
(κακὸν τέλος, 24.124) that resembles the "death most pitiful" of a king
in his own palace (οἰκτίστῳ θανάτῳ, 11.412). As we have already
noted, however, this scene in the second *Nekyia* completes the symmetries and contrasts between Odysseus and Agamemnon, Penelope and
Clytaemnestra. In Odysseus' case the murderous *dolos* is on the side of
the male, and it assures his *kleos*. It also complements the many years of
the *dolos* of Penelope and so reaffirms her good fame in contrast with the
"disgrace" and "harsh report" of Clytaemnestra.

The peculiarities in the language of *kleos* that we have studied here suggest that the poet of the *Odyssey* was aware of the ambiguities attaching to his hero "of many turns." He deliberately plays off against one another different perspectives on the heroic tradition. Composing, probably, at a time when the heroic ideal is itself undergoing change and redefinition and when, possibly, epic language is becoming more fluid, he uses traditional elements in new ways and refashions a hero and a style where nonheroic values and fresh social, ethical, and aesthetic currents make themselves felt.

From distanced, self-conscious, and ironic reflection on *kleos,* Homer returns us in the last three books of the epic to full participation in the *making* of *kleos.* Odysseus' reassertion of his heroic persona and his restoration to wife, house, and kingship consist precisely in this movement from singer to actor. He (re-)creates *kleos* in song when he recites the *apologoi* to Alcinous' court skillfully like a professional bard, but he finally wins *kleos* in deeds when he makes the warrior's bow sing like the poet's lyre. Both in song and in action, Odysseus' task is to restore domestic, civic, and cosmic order. He reestablishes song and feasting as a sign of that order in his palace when the bard, spared from death by the grim warrior-king (22.330–57), can once more play the accompaniment to joyful dancing and merriment as king and queen are about to be united (23.143–45; 22.332b = 23.133b).

With its characteristic openness toward what is new, changing, and dangerous as well as what is firm and traditional in life, the poem's last scene is not the songful feast of a reunited house in a celebratory *hieros gamos* (sacred marriage), as one might have expected, but a scene of battle. Odysseus' last address to his son is an admonition (24.506–9): "Telemachus, you yourself, stepping forth [to battle] where men fight and the best are separated out, shall learn not to shame [*kataischunein*] the race of your fathers, for in valor and in manliness we are distinguished over the whole earth." Is this a final realism beneath the poet's apparently happy ending? What the wily and much-enduring hero bequeaths to his son for the future is not only the visible proof of his own *kleos* (here defined by its opposite, non-*aischos*), but also the necessary experience of war.

PART TWO

POETICS: SINGERS, LIARS, AND BEGGARS

CHAPTER 6

Bard and Audience
in Homer

The attempt to make Homer know everything, from farming to fighting, is like trying to make the sacred olive bough known as the *eiresionē* hold apples and pears and other things too heavy for it. Such is the comparison of Hipparchus, quoted by Strabo in defending Homer against Eratosthenes' attacks on his poems as merely frivolous, fanciful entertainment (*psuchagōgia*, Strabo 1.2.3). One sort of knowledge, however, the ancient readers almost unanimously grant Homer: knowledge about words and song, the arts of speech and persuasion, or what Strabo calls *rhētorikē phronēsis*, "rhetorical skill," best exemplified by Odysseus in the *Iliad*.[1] Homer shows the same knowledge of the other side of making songs and speeches, not just their creation but also their reception. This chapter is a study, then, of what Homer thinks, or might think, of his audiences, actual and possible.

The Homeric poems repeatedly depict audiences listening to singers. The gods banqueting on Olympus are entertained by Apollo and the Muses (*Il.* 1.602f); grape pickers lighten their toil by joining the young boy who sings the "Linus song" in the vineyard (*Il.* 18.561–72). In the former passage, "banquet," Apollo's "lovely lyre," and "Muses" with their "beautiful voice" are joined in a coordinate construction as simultaneous attributes of divine happiness:

ὣς τότε μὲν πρόπαν ἦμαρ ἐς ἠέλιον καταδύντα
δαίνυντ', οὐδέ τι θυμὸς ἐδεύετο δαιτὸς ἐίσης

[1] For Odysseus' rhetorical skill in the *Iliad*, see especially books 2, 3, and 9; also Strabo 1.2.5, ad init.

οὐ μὲν φόρμιγγος περικαλλέος, ἣν ἔχ Ἀπόλλων,
Μουσάων θ', αἳ ἄειδον ἀμειβόμεναι ὀπὶ καλῇ.

(1.601–4)

Thus they feasted the entire day to the setting of the sun, nor did their
spirit lack the equal *feasting*, nor the very lovely *lyre* which Apollo held,
nor the *Muses*, who sang in responsion with their *beautiful voice*.

Like the Muses who inspire him, the poet of early Greece is a singer.
His aim is to produce songs performed at more or less public occasions
ranging from a large Panhellenic festival, such as those at Delos or
Mycale, to an affair of state, such as Hieron's inauguration of his newly
founded city of Aetnaea with Pindar's first *Pythian Ode,* to local family
gatherings, feasts, and symposia in the houses of the rich. While the
Hellenistic Callimachus holds his writing tablet on his knees and doubtless a pen (or stylus) in his hand (Callimachus *Aetia* 1.21f.), the Homeric
poet holds a lyre.

Our first detailed account of song in Homer, and therefore in Western
literature, depicts a scene of group festivity in the open air. On the shield
of Achilles girls and boys dance together, a lad plays a clear-sounding
lyre in their midst, and the dancers sing as they follow the tune and
"skip with their feet" (*Il.* 18.567–72). There is also dancing accompanied by flute and lyre at a wedding feast, doubtless also outdoors, as
women are watching from the forecourt. Later, a large crowd watches a
dance "like that at broad Cnossus" (18.603), and two whirling acrobats
"lead off the singing" (18.604f.).

As such passages indicate, poetry is envisaged as part of a performance, as the living voice of song (what John Herington calls "the song
culture").[2] Whether secular or ritual, whether public or private, poetry
belongs to a social occasion. The spectators who "stand about" admiring or enjoying on the shield of Achilles are an inconspicuous but
essential element of the scene (18.496, 603).

All the more significant, therefore, is the private context of song, as
Achilles, in his tent, sings the "glorious deeds of heroes," the κλέα
ἀνδρῶν (*Il.* 9.185–91). He is playing on a lyre with a silver bridge that
he took when he destroyed Eetion's city—a reminder of his own *klea*
and prowess as a warrior. More important, he is singing only for
himself, "giving pleasure to his heart" (φρένα τερπόμενον, 9.186; τῇ ὅ

---

[2] Herington (1985) part 1, passim. On the importance of song in the world of the
Homeric poems, see Schadewaldt (1965) 54–86, especially 62–65, 67–68.

γε θυμὸν ἔτερπεν, 9.189). Note what Homer does *not* say: Patroclus is not listening or paying attention to the song; he is only "waiting for Achilles to leave off singing" (δέγμενος Αἰακίδην, ὁπότε λήξειεν ἀείδων, 9.191). We are not to confuse the singing of this great warrior with that of a bard; he gives pleasure only to himself, not to others (note φρένα τερπόμενον, in the middle voice, 9.186). The hero of the *Odyssey* is very different, as we shall see.

Private song figures at the opposite end of the social scale, too, though with more pathos, in the two shepherds on the shield. Innocently they "take joy in their pipes," τερπόμενοι σύριγξι (18.525f.)—remote ancestors of Theocritus' Daphnis and Milton's Lycidas, save that in this violent world they "did not foresee the ambush," whose members carry off the cattle and "kill the herdsmen besides" (18.529).

Alcinous' palace in *Odyssey* 8 is the setting for Homer's fullest account of bardic performance. The scene has the richness, ease, and splendor that one would expect in this happy, comfort-loving land of the Phaeacians. The palace and court gradually fill with the king's followers, young and old (57f.). Alcinous makes an elaborate sacrifice for the coming feast: twelve sheep, eight boars, and two oxen. The meat is prepared, and "they fashioned the lovely banquet" (τετύκοντό τε δαῖτ' ἐρατεινήν, 61). As the crowning touch, the herald leads in the bard, the blind Demodocus. A silver-studded stool is set for him in the midst of the banqueters; his lyre is carefully hung within reach, above his head; and bread, meat, and wine are placed before him (65–70). This bard, like Phemius on Ithaca, is no wandering minstrel, and is not to be classed with the "craftsmen" (*dēmioergoi*, "workers for the people") who come and go from the palace (17.383–85).[3] He is a permanent fixture in the royal establishment and has a respected place and regular duties there.

Later, in book 13, Odysseus has finished his long tale in the palace of Alcinous, and a charmed silence descends over the hall. The king, who has already congratulated the speaker on his grace as a raconteur (11.367f.), urges his guests to add more gifts: "To each one of you I speak enjoining this, you who always drink the aged bright wine in my halls and hear the bard" (αἴθοπα οἶνον / αἰεὶ πίνετ' ἐμοῖσιν, ἀκουάζεσθε δ' ἀοιδοῦ 13.7–9). The implication is that the bard is a prized accoutrement of a rich and generous house. Hearing him is like drink-

---

[3] On this passage see Schadewaldt (1965) 69, 70; Walsh (1984) 15–16; and Bertolini (1988) 145–64, with further bibliography. See also below, Chapter 7.

ing the good wine of his patron, a privilege that puts the guests under an obligation.

The Demodocus scene probably reflects the ideal rather than the actual, and the wish fulfillment may be as much for the poet as for his audience. Nevertheless, the basic situation may not be beyond the possibilities of an eighth-century B.C. aristocrat. As the princes of the Italian Renaissance collected sculptures or paintings to display their culture, affluence, and power and adorned their palaces with memorials of great men of the past in the form of busts, frescoes, and statues, so the nobles of the Greek renaissance, twenty-two hundred years earlier, may well have adorned their houses with poets who could monumentalize in song the great deeds of the past and thereby provide models of heroic excellence and grandeur. At this period, material culture in Greece is still relatively modest; and a resident bard, for long or short term, probably represents an inexpensive investment.

The luxuries of the time are social and (fortunately for posterity) artistic. A good bard enhances a good feast. It is tempting, of course, to think that Homer actually sang at or after banquets (though perhaps not "for small earnings and good cheer," in Richard Bentley's notorious formulation); and bards like him may well have sung at the courts of nobles and prices. If, as Anthony Snodgrass argues, great scarcity and poverty lay in the not so distant past, his audience would appreciate images of a time when there was always an extra ox or hog to be sacrificed and the wine flowed endlessly.[4] Through such regal settings as those of Demodocus' songs, Homer can transport his eighth-century audience into the wealth and abundance of the heroic age.

One of the *Odyssey*'s most insistent messages is that eating properly and listening properly go closely together.[5] Only the rude, cannibalistic Cyclops asks his guest for a story before feeding him. The hospitable Eumaeus, who admiringly compares his disguised guest's narrative ability to that of a professional bard (17.518–21), feeds him two dinners (14.80–120 and 414–45). The best audience in the poem, the Phaeacians, permits the after-dinner tale to go on for the length of four books (9–12) as Odysseus tells his story with the skill of a bard (cf. 11.363–69).[6]

---

[4] On the economic duress of the tenth and ninth centuries B.C. in Greece, see Snodgrass (1980) 15ff.; also Snodgrass (1971) 413–14.

[5] See, for instance, Stewart (1976) 68–69; Saïd (1977) 9–49, especially 13; and Thalmann (1984) 158ff.

[6] The relevance of 11.363–69 to Homeric conceptions of bardic performative aspects of this scene has often been noted: see Schadewaldt (1965) 81, Walsh (1984) 7ff., and Stewart (1976) 157.

When Eumaeus describes to Penelope the disguised beggar's "charm" with words, he begins with a wish that the suitors would be quiet so that Penelope, too, might feel the spell of his guest's tales, which he enjoyed for three nights and three days on his farm (17.513–21). Those noisy suitors, however, are the most disrespectful audience we see, and they eventually get arrows from the bowstring instead of music from the lyre, as Athena/Mentes had hinted and as Telemachus had warned at the first feast of the poem (1.225–29, 253–59).

The close relation between song and feasting is crystallized into the formulaic phrase ἀναθήματα δαιτός, song as "the accompaniment of the feasting." With intentional irony, the formula's first occurrence in the *Odyssey* describes an occasion when that "accompaniment" is reluctant: Phemius sings "by necessity" to Telemachus' unwelcome guests, the suitors who arrogantly appropriate the good things of the palace, bard included (see 1.154). The only other occurrence of the phrase in the Homeric corpus comes after Odysseus has accomplished the trial of the bow and is about to make the singing of the bowstring into an "accompaniment of the feasting"—a feast that is the suitors' last meal (21.430).[7]

But, to return from the bow to the lyre, even "good" audiences do not sit in the rapt silence of the Phaeacian nobles around Odysseus (11.333f.). Menelaus, for example, whose tastes incline slightly toward the grosser side, has acrobats (along with the "divine singer" and his lyre) to entertain his guests (4.17–19). This detail may be as much a commentary on Menelaus as a reflection on the taste of Homeric audiences. It may be significant, then, that tumblers appear in the *Odyssey* only in Menelaus' palace and not, for example, in Alcinous' entertainment, even though the Phaeacians are expert dancers and Odysseus himself "admired the flashing movement of feet" (8.265). In fairness to Menelaus, however, it must be said that these tumblers are also part of the vocal entertainment, since they "lead off the song" (4.19). Dance, moreover, regularly accompanies song in Homer;[8] and Homer's audiences doubtless enjoyed these tumblers, for geometric vases show dancers or acrobats performing to the lyre.[9]

---

[7] On the repetition of *anathēmata daitos* (accompaniment of the feasting), see above, Chapter 5, note 46, and below, Chapter 7, note 37. In 8.99 Homer uses the similar expression ἤ δαιτὶ συνήορός ἐστι θαλείῃ ("which accompanies the flourishing feast") of the lyre (*phorminx*), which he does not repeat elsewhere.

[8] Note the formulaic combination of "dance" and "song," *orchēstus* and *aoidē,* in *Od.* 1.421, 8.253, 17.605, and 18.304; cf. also 23.133–35. See in general Wegner (1968) 41–44.

[9] See Wegner (1968) 65–67, with the figures in plates III a (Athens, National Museum Catalogue no. 43), VI a (Copenhagen, National Museum Catalogue no. 43), and VI d (Athens, National Museum Catalogue no. 53).

The Homeric singer clearly functioned as accompanist as well as soloist, but there still seems to be a distinction between his solo performance of narrative songs (what we would call epic) and his accompaniment of choral dance as it appears in Menelaus' palace in *Odyssey* 4 and in the wedding celebration on the shield of Achilles (*Il.* 18.490–95, where, however, there is "shouting," *boē,* but not necessarily song). Despite the importance of music and singing, there is good reason to think that when an *aoidos* performs what we call epic narrative, people are expected to listen to what he says and not just enjoy a catchy tune. Homer's own accounts of performance situations clearly privilege the singing of epic. Thus, when Demodocus performs among the Phaeacians, he plays to accompany choral dancing only once, and nothing is said of words or song (8.254–62, in contrast to 8.266), whereas in his three other appearances his words are obviously the primary focus of interest.

But things in Homer, and especially in the *Odyssey,* are always a little more complicated than they seem. Consider the most frivolous and risqué story in the epic corpus, Demodocus' song of the adultery of Ares and Aphrodite, the beautiful gods who are caught in bed by the cunning net of Hephaestus. This song offers the delight, or *terpsis,* that is ideally suited to the brittle hedonism of the Phaeacians. Such was essentially the judgment of Plutarch, some two millennia ago, in his delightful essay "How a Young Man Should Listen to Poetry." Yet this piece of apparently frothy entertainment proves, in fact, to be the model for Odysseus' own story: the grimy, hardworking little man of soot and sweat defeats the big, gorgeous hunk—a prefiguration of Odysseus combating the Cyclops but also perhaps a hint of that anti-aristocratic sentiment that seems to creep in here and there.[10] But there is contrast as well as parallelism. The woman whom Odysseus will win back is not the goddess of love or the embodiment of sex appeal as is Helen but the soul of domestic virtue, patience, and prudence. And Homer gives us a further surprise: the trickery practiced around the bed will be not the husband's but the wife's (the test of the living olive tree). This singing, then, exemplifies the multiple functions of the poet in his society: pure entertainment at one level, concern with the central values and conflicts in the world of the poem at another.

[10] For the thematic relevance of the song of Ares and Aphrodite to the poem, see Olson (1989) 135–45, especially 137, 141, with further bibliography; also Newton (1987) 12–20, especially 14–16. For the question of anti-aristocratic sentiment in the poem, see Farron (1979–80) 59–101. For a less extreme and more balanced view, see Raaflaub (1988) 208–11; also Morris (1986) 123ff.

The song of Aphrodite's adultery is a revealing scene for differences in audience response.[11] Both Odysseus and the Phaeacians "took pleasure in hearing" it (8.367–69). Yet it is not this tale of the gods but rather the song about the sufferings of the Achaeans that wins from Odysseus the most extravagant praise that a bard receives in Homer (8.474–83). Odysseus not only honors Demodocus with a choice cut of meat but also suggests that he has been taught by the Muse or even by Apollo himself (8.487). Earlier, Odysseus had praised Demodocus' skill as derived merely from "a god" or "the Muse" (8.44, 8.63). What Odysseus prizes is the ability to evoke not the carefree realm of the remote Olympians but the human woe that stirs the heart, told, he says, "as if you were present yourself or heard from someone else" (8.491).[12] So the Muses themselves, in the poet's invocation to the Catalogue of Ships in the *Iliad,* "are present and know everything," whereas we mortals have only hearsay (*Il.* 2.485f.).

The differences in response between the Greek warrior and the hedonistic Phaeacians are already encoded into Demodocus' tale itself in the contrasts among the divine spectators of the narrated events. The female divinities stay away (8.324), while Hermes makes a locker-room joke to Apollo. This releases the tension among the other (male) gods in "laughter unquenchable," like Hephaestus' clumsy wine service in the *Iliad* that breaks the tension of this first feast on Olympus (*Il.* 1.597–600). But even this male response is divided: Poseidon is not amused and remains concerned, serious, and legalistic (8.344–58). This narrative of Olympian frivolity becomes itself a spectacle of audience response within a performance, like the wedding song on the shield of Achilles (cf. 8.321 and 325 and *Il.* 18.495–97), revealing major divisions in the mood of the spectators.

Odysseus goes on to request a third song of Demodocus, the story of the wooden horse and the capture of Troy. Again he weeps, and again Alcinous observes him. This time, however, Alcinous does not hold his peace (as he had in the case of the first song, 8.90–103) but delivers a long speech that ends with some generalizations on mortal suffering and the request for Odysseus' identity. The gods, he says, "have spun out doom for men so that there may be song for those to come" (ἵνα ἦσι καὶ ἐσσομένοισιν ἀοιδή, 8.580). Helen makes a very similar reflection

---

[11] For some of these differences, see Walsh (1984) 4ff., 6ff.; also Thalmann (1984) 16off. and Monsacré (1984) 151ff.

[12] On this valuing of a vivid "presence" at the event in the bard as a poet of truth, see Schadewaldt (1965) 82 and Puelma (1989) 68ff., with further bibliography.

in her scene with Paris, but the differences are important. She speaks in the first person, and her concern is about men, whereas Alcinous' is about song. The gods have set upon *us* an evil doom, she says, "so that *we* may be a subject of song for men to come" (ὡς καὶ ὀπίσσω / ἀνθρώποισι πελώμεθ᾽ ἀοίδιμοι ἐσσομένοισι, *Il.* 6.357f.).

The distance that Alcinous here implies between the pleasurable effect (*terpsis*) of song on its hearers and the pain of its subject matter becomes even clearer as he goes on to ask if Odysseus has lost a kinsman or dear companion in the war (8.581–86). He thus acknowledges that an audience could feel a specific personal involvement in the subject of song, but he still does not envisage the more radical possibility that the song could lead Odysseus to the broader identification with the suffering that it describes, in this case the suffering of the victims of his own glorious conquest. Such is the effect of the simile that compares Odysseus' weeping at Demodocus' song to that of a woman in a captured city as she is led off to slavery—a city very much like the Troy of Demodocus' song:

> ταῦτ᾽ ἄρ᾽ ἀοιδὸς ἄειδε περικλυτός· αὐτὰρ Ὀδυσσεὺς
> τήκετο, δάκρυ δ᾽ ἔδευεν ὑπὸ βλεφάροισι παρειάς.
> ὡς δὲ γυνὴ κλαίῃσι φίλον πόσιν ἀμφιπεσοῦσα,
> ὅς τε ἑῆς πρόσθεν πόλιος λαῶν τε πέσῃσιν,
> ἄστεϊ καὶ τεκέεσσιν ἀμύνων νηλεὲς ἦμαρ·
> ἡ μὲν τὸν θνῄσκοντα καὶ ἀσπαίροντα ἰδοῦσα
> ἀμφ᾽ αὐτῷ χυμένη λίγα κωκύει· οἱ δέ τ᾽ ὄπισθε
> κόπτοντες δούρεσσι μετάφρενον ἠδὲ καὶ ὤμους
> εἴρερον εἰσανάγουσι, πόνον τ᾽ ἐχέμεν καὶ ὀϊζύν·
> τῆς δ᾽ ἐλεεινοτάτῳ ἄχεϊ φθινύθουσι παρειαί·
> ὡς Ὀδυσεὺς ἐλεεινὸν ὑπ᾽ ὀφρύσι δάκρυον εἶβεν.
>
> (8.521–31)

These things the far-famed bard sang, but Odysseus melted and wet his cheeks with tears beneath his lids. And just as a woman laments falling about her dear husband who falls before his city and his people as he wards off from city and children the pitiless day, and she seeing him dying and gasping pours herself around him and shrieks shrilly, but [the soldiers] behind her strike her back and shoulders with their spears and lead her off as a slave to have toil and woe, and her cheeks wither in grief most pitiable: so pitiful a tear did Odysseus let drip beneath his brows.[13]

[13] Euripides also draws on this simile in his re-creation of the sufferings of the Trojan captive women in *Hecuba* 936–42, but he transforms it into first-person lyrics for greater intensity. See Segal (1993) 174.

Odysseus might, of course, be weeping only for himself and his old glory and prowess, now so far in the past. Yet the simile associates his grief with the victims, not the victors. It in fact evokes exactly the situation that is a reality for the war victims in the tragic world of the *Iliad,* as in Briseis' personal memories when she laments over Patroclus:

ἄνδρα μὲν ᾧ ἔδοσάν με πατὴρ καὶ πότνια μήτηρ
εἶδον πρὸ πτόλιος δεδαϊγμένον ὀξέϊ χαλκῷ,
τρεῖς τε κασιγνήτους, τούς μοι μία γείνατο μήτηρ,
κηδείους, οἵ πάντες ὀλέθριον ἦμαρ ἐπέσπον.

(*Il.* 19.291-94)

I saw torn by the keen bronze before the city the husband to whom my father and lady mother gave me, and three brothers, my dear kin, whom one mother bore, who all came upon their day of destruction.

The *Iliad,* in fact, underlines the perspective of the helpless captive woman by the poet's remarkable editorial comment:

ὣς ἔφατο κλαίουσ', ἐπὶ δὲ στενάχοντο γυναῖκες
Πάτροκλον πρόφασιν, σφῶν δ' αὐτῶν κήδε' ἑκάστη.

(19.301f.)

So [Briseis] spoke lamenting, and the women groaned in response: the occasion was for Patroclus, but each one grieved for her own sufferings.

The scene of Odysseus' weeping, then, articulates two very different modes of response: the aesthetic distance of Alcinous that can treat poetry (fiction) as a source of pure pleasure (*terpsis*), and the intense, painful involvement of Odysseus as he participates, through memory, in the sufferings that are the subject matter of the song. The comparison of Odysseus' tearful response to a weeping captive woman suggests the possibility that this identification with the subject matter of the song applies not just to the memory of an actual participant but also to vicarious, imaginary participation. The Odysseus of the *Iliad* never so identifies with the victims on the Trojan side; and, with the exception of the extraordinary scene between Priam and Achilles in *Iliad* 24, there is little in the heroic code that would encourage him to identify with his conquered enemy, especially one of the opposite sex.

Through these contrasting responses Homer reveals the paradox (of which Hesiod, too, is aware) between the pleasure that mimetic art affords its audience and the pain of its contents. For the hedonistic Phaeacians, war itself is absorbed into *aoidē*, "song" (*Od.* 8.580); for Odysseus, the sufferings of war, even in song, are still sufferings and bring tears. The simile that compares him to a captive woman, however, creates a deliberate slippage between the two positions and at least raises the possibility that the division may not always be so sharp. Menelaus, like Alcinous, regards weeping as an undesirable response to an after-dinner song, the reverse of the *terpsis* that song should bring or enhance (4.193–95 and cf. 220–26; 8.538–43). Menelaus' court, however, having been touched directly by the sufferings of the narrator as that of Alcinous has not, joins in the weeping (4.183–88).

A further detail complicates the contrast between Odysseus and the Phaeacians. In the long speech in which Alcinous makes his formal request for Odysseus' identity and asks the reasons for his weeping, he tells of a prophecy that Poseidon will one day destroy one of his ships as it returns from escorting a passenger to his homeland (8.564–69). Characteristically, he dismisses the prophecy as something that the god may or may not accomplish (8.570f.). Alcinous' lack of concern, as we learn later, is mistaken, for the angry god does fulfill the prophecy (13.170–83). In fact we see the Phaeacians for the last time when they gather in fear about Poseidon's altar as they attempt to appease his wrath (13.183–87). These events have some bearing on poet and audience, for in Demodocus' second song, about Ares and Aphrodite, it was Poseidon who resolved the embarrassment. His solemn pledge assuages Hephaestus' anger and secures Ares' release (8.344–58). This is a Poseidon suited to Phaeacian aestheticism. He intervenes to keep the violation of marriage in the realm of play, without the consequences, for example, that it has on Ithaca. Odysseus' Poseidon, however, is not a god who soothes anger or intervenes in the name of peace. This wrathful, dangerous Poseidon lay beyond the frame of Phaeacian song; but he is the god that Alcinous now begins to know, if only as a remote possibility (8.570f.; cf. 13.125–64).[14]

From the point of view of "real" life, of course, the tales of Odysseus at Troy and of Ares and Aphrodite on Olympus are equally "mythical," and so are both Poseidons too. But, for a moment, Homer allows the two modes of "mythical" narration to cross over into each other. The Phaeacian king relates a kind of story (albeit in the future rather than the past) that thematically resembles Odysseus' life story in its divine

---

[14] On the different images of Poseidon, see below, Chapter 10.

blocking-figure as the central antagonist. This story, moreover, will be fulfilled as fact for the Phaeacians themselves in book 13. Homer thus brings together story as pleasurable entertainment (Demodocus' Poseidon) and story as emotionally involving exemplar of human suffering (the tale of Poseidon who punishes the Phaeacians in book 13).

The effect of sympathetic involvement can also apply to us, the mortal listeners, vulnerable to the wrath and power of the gods. And this possibility, as we have suggested, is envisaged in the simile of the weeping captive woman in *Odyssey* 8, where the song that celebrates the hero's triumph arouses a response that identifies him with the vanquished and helpless rather than with the victorious. A song, in other words, not only has an unforeseen emotional impact but may also lead the hearer imaginatively to reach beyond the limits of self-identity and to experience vicariously an inversion of role, status, and gender. Homer's most powerful use of this crossing of boundaries through empathetic identification with the other is, of course, Priam's appeal to Achilles to think of his own father as he looks on his enemy in supplication (*Il.* 24.486–89, 503–7).

The *Odyssey*'s embedding of narratives that have different relations of closeness to or removal from a "mythical" world forces the hearer to become aware of the work's construction of its fictionality or mythicalness and thus of the disjunction between different levels of "reality." It is an effect analogous to the self-consciousness and plot construction that emerges in the retrospective narrative of the second *Nekyia*. There the slain suitor Amphimedon tells a version of Odysseus' success that includes the conscious collusion of Odysseus and Penelope in setting up the contest of the bow. "Odysseus in his multifaceted craftiness [πολυ-κερδείῃσιν]," Amphimedon says, "*ordered* his wife to set up for the suitors the bow and the hoary iron [of the axes]"; and this event, he adds, proved to be "the beginning of the slaughter" (24.167–69). Odysseus, of course, gave no such orders; but Homer thus shows his audience an alternative dénouement, a version that he might have used but chose not to. The "multifaceted craftiness" is in this case as much the poet's as his hero's.[15] This bard has the same kind of flexibility to reshape his tale as his chief character has to reshape his life narrative.

Homer shows his control of the narrative in another way at one of the poem's major transitions, the shift from Telemachus back to Odysseus

---

[15] On this episode see Goldhill (1988) 6–7, who stresses how Homer here plays with his audience's expectations.

at the beginning of book 5. In book 1, when Athena formally introduces Odysseus by winning Zeus' sympathy for his sufferings, Zeus replies, "My child, what is this saying that has escaped the barrier of your teeth? How then would I forget [*lathoimēn*] divine Odysseus, who surpasses mortals in intelligence?" (63–65). In the corresponding scene in book 5, Zeus repeats his formulaic first line (5.22 = 1.64) but omits the second line about forgetting Odysseus. Instead, Athena, as in book 1, initiates the mention of Odysseus, absent from the narrative now for four books, by "making mention" of him and his many sufferings (λέγε κήδεα πόλλ᾽ Ὀδυσσῆος / μνησαμένη, 5.5f.). She then continues with the complaint that "no one remembers divine Odysseus among the people over whom he ruled" (ὡς οὔ τις μέμνηται Ὀδυσσῆος θείοιο / λαῶν οἷσιν ἄνασσε, 5.11f.). She is here recalling Zeus' verse about "forgetting divine Odysseus" in book 1 (1.65) but has put "memory" in place of "forgetting" (*memnētai*, 5.11; *lathoimēn*, 1.65). This change comes just at the point when many of the people (*laoi*, 5.12) in the audience may well be asking themselves whether their bard has "forgotten divine Odysseus"; and he reassures them by "reminding/relating" and "remembering" that he has forgotten neither the main hero nor his own plot line. Indeed, he brings back the "memory" of his hero with a foretaste of his most spectacular and also most disastrous triumph in the repeated *mē tis/ou tis* (nobody) of 5.8 and 11, a reference to Odysseus' "guile" (*mētis*) of giving his name as Nobody (*Outis*) to deceive the Cyclops in book 9. As both "relating" and "remembering" are characteristic activities of the oral bard, Homer is here delicately signaling to his audience that he anticipates their possible malaise at the postponement of the main narrative concern and also asserting his own overall command of the story's direction that should alleviate that concern.

It is a commonplace of classical criticism that whereas the *Odyssey* loves to talk about poetry and song, the *Iliad* is very reticent about them.[16] True, the *Iliad* shows very few bards in action. Yet Achilles can take up his lyre in the privacy of his tent to sing of the "glorious deeds of heroes," the *klea andrōn*, a phrase that could describe the events of the *Iliad*. In fact, the very withdrawal that by its enforced leisure makes this song possible is now shaping the story of Achilles which will have a conspicuous place, thanks to the bard of the *Iliad*, among these *klea andrōn*.[17] This paradox is in turn part of the deeper paradox that Achilles'

<hr>

[16] See, for instance, Stewart (1976) 148ff.
[17] See Frontisi-Ducroux (1986) 53.

rejection of the heroic code in the ninth book leads to the deeper, more powerful, and more thoughtful formulation of that code that is the *Iliad*. The paradoxes of Achilles' song of heroes thus reflect his simultaneous rejection and affirmation of the heroic world. More generally, they anticipate the paradoxical relations between distance and involvement, pleasure and participation in the bardic narrative of war, killing, and suffering—paradoxes that the *Odyssey* explores more directly and in greater detail.

Helen, too, reflects on the future of the war as a subject of song for those to come (*Il.* 6.357f.). And parallel to this explicit verbal reflection on her future fame in song is her weaving the present conflict in book 3, the age-old women's way of telling stories in the wordless medium of their work: "Iris found Helen in her chamber, and she was weaving a great work of the loom, double-folded, deep red, and upon it she wove the many struggles of the horse-taming Trojans and the bronze-armored Achaeans" (3.125–28). But whereas Achilles sings the deeds of heroes in general as the living fame of past exploits, the *klea andrōn,* Helen's focus is entirely on the present events, either as the subject of song "for men to come" or as the actual subject of her weaving. Even when she envisages the war as eventually part of a total heroic tradition, her primary interest is in what she is actually undergoing.

The poem presents another woman whose life is also bound to the events of the war and who, like Helen, climbs to the wall to take a long view. But whereas Helen's weaving in her chamber in book 3 contains the "many struggles of the horse-taming Trojans and bronze-armored Achaeans," Andromache's weaving is only of "many-colored flowers" (*Il.* 22.441f.).[18] Andromache cannot make an artwork of the war raging around her. The two kinds of weaving enable Homer to objectify his literary self-consciousness. He can thus crystallize his own narrative reflexivity into clear, external actions, just as in the *Odyssey* he can suggest different modes of responding to song in the different responses of Odysseus and the Phaeacians.

The differences between Helen and Andromache also raise the issue of narrative perspective or point of view. Helen's distanced weaving of the battle scenes comes to an end when the goddess Iris calls her from

---

[18] For the contrasts between the two scenes, see Segal (1971) 40–41. It is among these differences that Andromache is inside the house, fully engrossed in the domestic tasks of her wifely role, including the preparations for her weary husband's return, whereas Helen is out on the wall, being admired for her beauty by the elders of Thebes.

her quiet chamber to the scene of action, the walls of Troy from which we see, with her, the Greek army and its leaders (*Il*. 3.121–233). Whereas Helen thinks of her absent brothers, "far away in lovely Lacedaemon" (3.234–44), Andromache's view from the wall is not of distant events, nor are her thoughts for those far away; she takes in the present scene only, the death of Hector that completes her tragedy. Although the *Iliad* rarely takes advantage of this kind of distancing of events through the aesthetic frame in the way that the *Odyssey* does, it has its own kind of literary self-consciousness.

Or consider the famous scene between Glaucus and Diomedes in book 6. At this moment of intense fighting, the action, surprisingly, comes to a halt. The telling of tales replaces fighting. Without breaking the illusion, Homer momentarily lets the act of narration step into the foreground, as if he is gently reminding us that we are *listening* to a story of battle, not fighting one.[19] But the content of this narrative also makes us appreciate the specific nature of Homer's song. The Lycian Glaucus tells the story of his ancestor, Bellerophon, a story of illicit love and palace intrigue, secret signs, fire-breathing monsters, and flying horses. Does Homer want us to perceive this as a typical Near Eastern tale— one of those many bizarre tales that the Greeks had been eagerly absorbing from their Eastern neighbors for at least the past century? To push the point, does Homer also mean us to appreciate the contrast with the more sober, more austere story of human conflict to which he has held himself in the severe masterpiece that is the *Iliad*?[20] Whether or not the *Iliad* was composed with the aid of writing, it is certainly not without artistic self-awareness. It is not the naïve or primitive voice of *Volk*, nature, or the pure warrior spirit in the way that eighteenth- and nineteenth-century critics, from Giambattista Vico and F. A. Wolf to John Ruskin and even Gilbert Murray, could claim.

In the *Odyssey*, to be sure, the contrast between aesthetic distance and emotional involvement is not displaced from poetry into weaving or into the contrasts that exist between Achilles and Helen or Helen and Andromache in the *Iliad* but is developed with much stronger and more

[19] On this scene see Frontisi-Ducroux (1986) 37.

[20] Although the probably orientalizing motifs of the Chimaera and the Lycian setting point to Near Eastern connections, Homer has also removed the fabulous detail of the flying horse (Pegasus) and has Bellerophon kill the Chimaera only by "obeying the portents of the gods" (*Il*. 6.183). In the background, too, of course, is folktale, which has likewise been transformed into the very different register of epic narrative: see Bertolini (1989) 131–52, especially 138–40.

explicit focus on poetry per se. To put it differently, the *Odyssey* has a language of overt poetic reflexivity that the *Iliad* lacks. It even takes a playful delight in making a display of its own inventiveness.[21] It is perhaps not accidental that the *Odyssey* is the first poem of European literature to tell the myth of Proteus. Teiresias' prophecy that Odysseus must again take off after his return to Ithaca and the effort with which Zeus and Athena have to hold him back from further fighting are the hallmarks of a poet who can keep his many-turning hero and his own many-turning story going interminably, with ever new adventures and ever-continuing battles.[22]

In contrast to the fluency and eagerness of Demodocus' song, the first mention of song or singing in the *Odyssey* depicts a bard who sings "by necessity" (*anankē*, 1.154). On this occasion, our introduction to the palace on Ithaca, Telemachus confides to the stranger (Athena in disguise) that the suitors think only of "the lyre and singing, since they are eating another man's substance without payment" (1.159f.; cf. 151f.). The sequence of ideas suggests that the suitors may like poetry well enough, but they like it particularly when it accompanies a good meal, that is, as Telemachus says in line 152, when it is *anathēmata daitos*, an accompaniment of the feasting. We soon learn the title of Phemius' song: "The Grim Return of the Greeks." This is the only song in the palace whose actual subject is specified (1.325f.). Otherwise, very little is said of what the bard sings on Ithaca, nor are the suitors ever shown as reacting to or caring about the quality or the material of the songs they hear.

Characteristically, this first song brings a *terpsis* that sharply divides its hearers. As in the case of Demodocus' song of "Odysseus and the Wooden Horse," one member of the audience weeps while the rest "take pleasure." The teenager, rather careless of mother's feelings, approves of the bard's recital of what is newest in fashion. Penelope, looking back to the past and the losses of which this song reminds her, withdraws after her ineffectual protest and weeps with her maids upstairs (1.360–64).

Despite her departure, her appearance has created a disturbance that Telemachus, in his first assertion of budding manly authority, has to quiet (1.368–71): "Suitors of my mother, you who practice insult most violent [*huperbion hubrin*], now let us take joy in the feasting, and let

---

[21] See, for instance, Stewart (1976) 146–95 and Goldhill (1988) 1–31, *passim*.
[22] See Chapter 10, below, *ad fin.*

there be no shouting, since it is a lovely thing [*kalon*] to listen to a bard such as is this one, godlike in his voice." The strange collocations reveal how anomalous singing is in this setting: insult and feasting, violence and pleasure, shouting and a godlike voice. In fact, this scene shows the suitors at their best; they never again behave even this well. After Telemachus' call for orderly listening, Antinous, the first of the suitors to speak, is the most shameless, complaining of Telemachus' "lofty address and bold speaking" (ὑψαγόρην τ' ἔμεναι καὶ θαρσαλέως ἀγορεύειν, 1.385), while the others bite their lips. At the suitors' last feast, he meets his end in silence, with Odysseus' first arrow in his throat, kicking away the table and scattering the food on the ground (22.15–21).

Phemius' song of the "Grim Return of the Achaeans" is the only song to which the suitors listen "in silence." Otherwise, song is for them only "the accompaniment to the feasting," a kind of Mycenaean Muzak, to deaden the clatter of the cups. The bard is merely the physical background to their eating and drinking, as Telemachus perhaps implies when he describes the suitors to his father in book 16 and lists the bard along with the herald and the two carvers of meat (16.252f.). The suitors would just as soon throw the javelin, the discus, or for that matter the odd ox hoof or footstool. Their idea of real fun is to see the two beggars slug it out. At their last banquet there is no mention of song or bard at all. But instead of a bard, they have the prophet Theoclymenus, with his ominous vision of darkness and bloody meats (20.345–57). The suitor's last song is performed by Odysseus himself as he finally throws off his rags, handles the great bow as a bard handles the lyre, makes it sing like a swallow, and then with triumphant irony shouts that it is time "for singing and the lyre, accompaniments of the feasting"—with the irony in the formula that I mentioned above.

The *Odyssey*'s first scene of bardic performance gets special prominence from the suspense created by postponing the song of Phemius for nearly two hundred lines after his introduction. He enters with his lovely lyre and beautiful song in 1.153–55; but we have to wait until the end of the interview between Telemachus and Athena/Mentes (1.158–324) for the song (τοῖσι δ' ἀοιδὸς ἄειδε, "the bard sang to them," 1.325, takes up ἦ τοι ὁ φορμίζων ἀνεβάλλετο καλὸν ἀείδειν, "then, playing the lyre, he struck up the tune to begin his lovely song," 1.155). And, as we have observed, this song then becomes the focus of a three-way conflict between Telemachus, Penelope, and the suitors (1.336–61).

Demodocus' entrance receives an even fuller description than does that of Phemius. Homer tells us no less than six times that this bard's skill has a divine origin,[23] with the culminating praise that it comes from "either the Muse or Zeus' son Apollo" (8.488). Here, too, there is a steady progression of honors for the poet, from the initial epithet "divine bard" (8.43, repeated at the end by Alcinous in 8.539) to Odysseus' honorific speech and gift of meat when he asks for the Song of the Wooden Horse (8.474–91). Homer even suggests an etymological play on Demodocus' name as "honored among the people" (Δημόδοκον λαοῖσι τετιμένον, 8.472). He also introduces a number of unique personal details: the Muses' gift of song in compensation for blindness (8.63f., the reverse of their punishment of Thamyris in *Il.* 2.594–600); the combination of singing tales of gods and heroes and serving as an accompanist for the dance (8.256–65); Odysseus' reflection that bards receive honor and reverence from all men because of the Muse's love and teaching (8.479–81); and Alcinous' generalization, like Helen's in the *Iliad,* that "the gods weave doom for mortals so that there may be song for men of the future" (8.579f.).

The Phaeacians fully appreciate their bard, but their score in audience attentiveness may even be a little too high, for when Arete and then Alcinous compliment Odysseus on his bardlike skill, they urge him to delay his return and thus present him with a delicate problem out of which he tactfully maneuvers (11.335–61).[24] He finds a better balance in audience response among the eager, attentive listeners who constitute his true friends on Ithaca, especially Eumaeus and Penelope. The trusty swineherd Eumaeus would gladly while away the long night with the tales of his guest, listening to the woes that he has endured (14.191–98). Later, Eumaeus praises this guest to Penelope, telling how he "enchanted" him with his tales, like a bard (17.513–22), unknowingly repeating the terms of the Phaeacian praise of Odysseus in book 11: silence, "enchantment," and bardlike skill. But the respectful silence that is reality on Scheria is only a wish among the noisy suitors on Ithaca (cf. 17.513 and 11.333). "Wine is the mirror of a man," said the lyric poet Alcaeus early in the archaic period; but in the *Odyssey,* song, or how one listens to song, is also such a mirror.

These scenes of telling one's life story show us another appeal of bardic song and one that runs throughout all archaic and classical Greek

---

[23] *Od.* 8.44f., 63f., 73, 480f., 488, 498.

[24] For an interesting analysis of this tension from the point of view of the oral performer, see Wyatt (1989) 235–53, especially 240–47.

culture. For Eumaeus, the telling of tales—and, by implication, the singing of songs—is a sharing of the woes of life that bind together all men as "miserable mortals," *deiloisi brotoisi*. Hence the two men, Odysseus the beggar and the swineherd Eumaeus, exchange their experiences of *kēdea*, "griefs," with sympathy on both sides (cf. 14.185). Eumaeus' comment is characteristic: "Wretched among strangers, much did you stir my heart telling each of these things that you suffered and all your wanderings" (14.361f.). In the next book, Odysseus, on hearing Eumaeus' tale, echoes Eumaeus' sympathy: "Alas, how, small as you were, swineherd Eumaeus, were you tossed far from your native land and your parents" (15.381f.). This is the kind of involvement that a good story creates. Men weep over such tales, as Odysseus did over Demodocus' song of Troy; and this emotional response of tears, though concealed out of politeness to the host, is not regarded as remarkable or shameful. Alcinous' reflection on seeing Odysseus weep over Demodocus' song of Troy is the complement to this affective view of song: "The gods have spun out doom for men so that there may be song for those of the future" (8.579f.). But the Phaeacian king, characteristically, looks at the song (ἀοιδή) from the outside, as an aesthetic object, rather than at the sufferings that make up its contents.

There is a direct line between this function of song as a celebration of human solidarity in the face of suffering and the development of Attic drama, which in so many other respects owes much to Homer. Drama, among other things, creates the community of the theater as a community of shared grief and compassion. We may think of plays such as Euripides' *Andromache, Suppliants, Hecuba,* or *Trojan Women.* Here, for example, is the chorus's closing song in the *Hippolytus:*

> κοινὸν τόδ' ἄχος πᾶσι πολίταις
> ἦλθεν ἀέλπτως.
> πολλῶν δακρύων ἔσται πίτυλος·
> τῶν γὰρ μεγάλων ἀξιοπενθεῖς
> φῆμαι μᾶλλον κατέχουσιν.
>
> (1482–58)

This woe came without expectation as common to all the citizens. There will be an oar-beat of many tears; for the tales of the great that are worthy of grieving do more prevail.

Through the experience of this "common woe" in the tragic performance, the individual spectator participates in the "community" of suffering mortality and thereby experiences the unifying solace of grief contained in the poetic tradition.[25] The epic equivalent is the ever present generality of the *deiloi brotoi* (wretched mortals) in the background of the poems, the suffering, ephemeral mortals whose "wretchedness" of all times and places is reflected in the innumerable victims, named and unnamed, of war and its aftermath.

If we leap ahead about a thousand years, we see this community of shared suffering established as a regular topos of consolation literature. Plutarch, writing, not speaking, to a friend who has lost a son, begins his *Consolatio ad Apollonium* thus: "I had long since been sharing in your pain and your grief, Apollonius, when I heard of your dearest son's departure from life" (1.102 E). And he concludes:

> Resume, therefore, the spirit of a brave-hearted and high-minded man and set free from all this wretchedness both yourself and the mother of the youth, and your relatives and friends, as you may do by pursuing a more tranquil form of life, which will be most gratifying both to your son and to all of us who are concerned for you, as rightly we should be [καὶ πᾶσιν ἡμῖν τοῖς κηδομένοις σου κατὰ τὸ προσῆκον].
>
> (36.122 A)

It is as if the letter effects the consolation itself by including Apollonius within the community of "all" the kin and friends who share in his suffering.

In terms of audience response, the most sympathetic and attentive audience that we see in Homer is the longed-for wife to whom Odysseus tells the tale of his wandering in book 23 (248–341). Even more than the Phaeacians, Penelope, in her fascinated and involved hearing, provides a clue to what might be the bard's ideal audience: there is a quiet, attentive, personally engaged, and patient listening, with "joy in the hearing." There is no postprandial or postcoital dozing; she stays awake "until he had related everything" (23.306–9). Here, as in the meeting of (disguised) husband and wife in book 19, we also catch a glimpse of the privileged circumstances in which a bard might try out new songs or improve old ones: a quiet setting; a single, well-disposed auditor; all the time he needs; and the opportunity to sing of something he loves. If Homer did in fact at some point dictate the "monumental composition" he finally achieved, might he have done it in an atmo-

---

[25] On this feature of tragedy, see Segal (1988a) 52–74, especially 62ff., and Segal (1993) 24–25, 120–29.

sphere of friendly calm analogous to that between Odysseus and Eumaeus or Odysseus and Penelope?

Making songs and telling tales, however, are always integral parts of
the plot of the poem; and so is this scene between husband and wife.
Their joy in listening and telling re-creates and exemplifies that mutual
trust and concern which belong to the ideal of *homophrosunē* (like-
mindedness) that Odysseus singles out as the greatest happiness in
marriage at the point when he has overcome the biggest obstacles to his
return (23.301–9; cf. 6.181–85).[26] Indeed, Penelope enacts this special
involvement in the teller's story when she insists that, before they bed
down for the full account of his wanderings (23.306–43), Odysseus
recount the prophecy of Teiresias, even though this is a tale that will
definitely not give "joy to the heart" (23.256–67).

This telling gives a momentary flash of an anti-*Odyssey*: a tale received without the "pleasure" that aesthetic distance makes possible. It
is a narrative of a long voyage to the "towns" of strange men, one that
recalls the poem's opening statement of its theme (ἐπεὶ μάλα πολλὰ
βροτῶν ἐπὶ ἄστε' / ἄνωγεν ἐλθεῖν, "When he bade me go to very many
towns of mortal men," 23.267f.; cf. 1.1–4). In the manner of Odysseus
hearing Demodocus' song of Troy, it is also a tale that its audience (i.e.,
Penelope) receives with intimate personal concern and therefore without "joy" or "pleasure" in the woes about to be rehearsed.

> αὐτὰρ ἐγὼ μυθήσομαι οὐδ' ἐπικεύσω.
> οὐ μέν τοι θυμὸς κεχαρήσεται· οὐδὲ γὰρ αὐτὸς
> χαίρω, ἐπεὶ μάλα πολλὰ βροτῶν ἐπὶ ἄστε' ἄνωγεν
> ἐλθεῖν.
>
> (23.265–68)

Well, I will tell you the tale and not conceal it. Yet your spirit will take no
joy in it; for I myself have no joy, since [Teiresias] bade me to go to very
many towns of mortal men.

This reluctant exchange of personal fortunes between husband and
wife also re-creates an analogous situation between a differently reunited couple, Helen and Menelaus in book 4. But their exchange of life
stories contains implicit accusation, distrust, and guilt; and their talk of
the past brings them no delight or forgetfulness of woes (4.235–89).[27]

---

[26] For *homophrosunē*, see above, Chapter 5, note 25.
[27] See Thalmann (1984) 166; also Bergren (1981) 200–214, especially 205ff., and
Goldhill (1988) 21–24.

To resolve their conflict and bring them peace in their household, they need the Circe-like drug that Helen puts in the wine (4.220–32), something external to the tales themselves. Odysseus' telling, by contrast, has a magic "spell" of its own (*kēlēthmos* or *thelxis;* cf. 11.334, 17.514, 17.521).

The poets obviously had a practical interest in suggesting that their presence at banquets sets a seal of approval on the host's good behavior and upright character. From the *Odyssey* to the *Oresteia,* the harmonious banquet song gets a deeper meaning, perhaps most programmatically in Pindar. One need only think of his first *Pythian Ode,* the richest elaboration of the situation of the performance itself as a microcosm of the social and political order:

> Golden Lyre, jointly shared possession of Apollo and the violet-tressed Muses: this the dance step, beginning of radiance, hears; and the singers obey the signals whenever you, quivering in song, fashion the preludes of hymns that lead the choruses. And you quench the spear-pointed lightning of [Zeus'] ever-flowing fire.
>
> (1–6)

Through Apollo and the Muses, Pindar lifts the power of the joyfully resounding instrument at the festive performance from earth to the heavens, where it embodies both the order of art and the moral order of the gods working among humans.

Homer does not use the more abstractive mental operations of metaphor to separate poetry from the actual conditions of performance. Unlike Pindar, he never treats song as a symbol of something other than itself. Such a step may go along with the movement toward an increasingly literate culture that Pindar's poetry begins to reflect.[28] Yet the *Odyssey's* self-consciousness about poetry also hints at the poet's moral authority. This emerges at its clearest in the comparison of Odysseus to a bard stringing his lyre at the moment when he bends his great bow and makes it sing like a swallow for the shot that restores order, kingship, and marriage on Ithaca (21.406f., 411). And, as I have noted, how an audience in this poem listens to a bard or a bardlike narrator is a touchstone of its moral character.

If the poet of the *Odyssey* is explicit about the analogy between bard and hero, the poet of the *Iliad* is not so very far away. Although the *Iliad* does not take the final step of assimilating bard and hero, it too ennobles

---

[28] See Segal (1986) 153ff.

art by presenting the best of the Achaeans in a bardic role, singing the *klea andrōn* in the solitude of his tent. Hesiod suggests that poetry, by evoking the memory of past events, brings a pleasurable forgetting of sorrows (*Theog.* 54f., 98–103).[29] Are we to see this therapeutic function of poetry put into practice by Homer's Achilles? In the *Odyssey,* song and narratives of the past belong to pleasure, not grief, and tears are not the appropriate response to an after-dinner story or song.

Giving pleasure to his audience is obviously the Homeric bard's first concern, but it is not his only one. By the very fact of creating a tearful response of sadness, as we have seen, the *Odyssey*-poet calls attention as well to the paradoxical pleasure that its tales of woe create.[30] In a culture where knowledge of the past is preserved largely through oral transmission, the bard also preserves the memory of earlier generations and the names of those who would otherwise be "invisible" in Hades (ἄφαντοι or ἄϊστοι). What is alive is what is heard on the lips of men, that is, what the bards preserve in song.[31] Hence Homer can count on his audience's interest in the catalogue of the Achaean princes and the cities they rule (*Il.* 2.494–759). The generations of men are as fleeting as the seasonal growth of leaves, but Homer can give the generations of the Lycian Glaucus a more than seasonal life by incorporating them into his song (*Il.* 6.145–211).

In the *Odyssey* the first threat to the hero's return is the destruction of memory: the Lotos-eaters, the first people to be encountered beyond the familiar limits of Troy and the heroic world, would keep Odysseus and his men stranded in never-never land through the amnesiac drug that would make them "forget their return" (*nostou lathesthai, Od.* 9.97). The loss of the memory of his homeland in Circe's bed will deprive him of his humanness just as surely as her drugs deprive his comrades of their human form. The other side of that loss of human identity is to be forgotten in the homeland that waits for him, to be carried off to some unknown place "without fame [*akleiōs*], unseen, unknown," leaving no trace in the "hearing" of men (1.241f.; cf. 4.727f.).[32]

The Sirens' song holds a subtle form of this self-obliteration. It is a

[29] This paradoxical connection of the memory of the Muse's song and the forgetfulness it brings has often been noted. For discussion and bibliography, see Walsh (1984) 22–23, Thalmann (1984) 136, and Bertolini (1988) 155–56.

[30] See *Od.* 1.340–55, 4.183–95, and 8.536–43 and 572–78; also above, note 11.

[31] See Havelock (1963) passim, especially chapter 4; also Havelock (1982) 122ff. This "presentness" of what oral communication keeps alive in the "hearing" of men in a preliterate society produces what anthropologists refer to as the homeostasis of oral cultures: see Morris (1986) 87, with the references there cited, and Ong (1982) 46ff.

[32] See above, Chapter 5.

deadly alternative to being remembered among the living generations who define and continue one's human identity. Although their song of Troy promises both "knowledge" and "pleasure" (12.188), these effects are entirely detached from a human community. Sitting in the watery waste somewhere between Circe's island and the Clashing Rocks, these singers are surrounded not by a living, eager audience of men and women in a palace or a place of assembly but by the skin and bones of rotting corpses (12.45f.), the horrid truth behind the "flowery meadow" of their island (12.159) and the sweet seduction of their voice (12.44).[33] This decay and putrefaction are the complete antithesis of the "non-perishable glory" (kleos aphthiton) conferred by song, just as the remoteness of their voice from any human society and the solitariness of Odysseus' listening are the negation of the communal context where life-giving memory has a place.

By keeping alive the memory of noble deeds, the bard also preserves and promulgates the values achieved in heroic action. Tyrtaeus' use of Homeric battle scenes to celebrate the rather un-Homeric solidarity of the Spartan hoplite formation will be a familiar example.[34] The bard's function as the vocal embodiment of the communal values exemplified in his songs is perhaps what leads Agamemnon to the step of putting his bard in charge of watching over Clytaemnestra during his long absence at Troy.[35] The task proves to be beyond the abilities of this anonymous singer, who clearly should have stuck to what he knew best (cf. Od. 3.267–71). Is this bard's anonymity in fact a mark of his failure?[36]

Because the Greeks, at least to the end of the fifth century B.C., envisage poetry as part of a performance and as the living voice of song, they pay special attention to its vocal dimension. Its physical qualities recur again and again in metaphors of sweetness, flowing, abundance, or strength. Invoking the Muse in the proem to the Catalogue of Ships, Homer speaks enviously of a "voice unbroken" and "a heart of bronze"—reminders of the physical effort that sustained recitation demands of the oral poet.

A voice that "flows tirelessly sweet from the mouth" is the magical

---

[33] On the Sirens see above, Chapter 5; also Walsh (1984) 14–15, Pucci (1979) 121–32, Pucci (1987) 209–13, Vernant (1986) 61ff., and Segal (1989) 332. Schadewaldt (1965) 82 aptly describes the Sirens as "dämonische Gegenbilder der Musen" ("demonic counter-images of the Muses").

[34] Cf., for example, Tyrtaeus 11.31–33, West (1992) and Il. 13.130–33 or Tyrtaeus 10.21–30 and Il. 22.71–77.

[35] See Scully (1981) 74ff.; also Svenbro (1976) 31ff.

[36] Scully (1981) takes a different view of this bard's anonymity, as "generic, that is, characteristic of the singer's craft and appropriate to his art" (74).

possession of Hesiod's Muses as they sing to Zeus on Olympus. In the space of five lines, Hesiod uses three different words for the poet's "voice," each time with a different epithet: ἀκάματος αὐδή, ὄπα λειριόεσσαν, and ἄμβροτον ὄσσαν (tireless voice, delicately clear voice, and voice immortal). Each time, too, the voice participates in an active, energetic movement: it "flows," "spreads forth," or "is sent forth."[37] Nestor, the repository of traditional wisdom codified into tales and legends, has a voice that "flows sweeter than honey" (Il. 1.250). The elders of Troy, past their prime but still good speakers (agorētai esthloi), have a clear, sharp voice, like the cicadas singing in trees (Il. 3.150–52). In thinking of the performance of this poetry, then, we need to keep in mind not just its quality of orality but what Paul Zumthor calls its "vocality," the beauty, strength, and resonance of the voice that sang it (cf. Il. 2.489f.).[38]

This attention to the materiality and tangibility, almost the visibility, of the voice extends to other features of the performance. The poet fills his scenes describing bards with concrete things, much as the painter of ripe geometric vases fills his surface with ornaments, animals, or designs. The moment of the song's beginning is adorned with rich objects that hold good cheer, comfort, and beauty:

> τῷ δ᾽ ἄρα Ποντόνοος θῆκε θρόνον ἀργυρόηλον
> μέσσῳ δαιτυμόνων, πρὸς κίονα μακρὸν ἐρείσας
> κὰδ᾽ δ᾽ ἐκ πασσαλόφι κρέμασεν φόρμιγγα λίγειαν
> αὐτοῦ ὑπὲρ κεφαλῆς καὶ ἐπέφραδε χερσὶν ἑλέσθαι
> κῆρυξ· πὰρ δ᾽ ἐτίθει κάνεον καλήν τε τράπεζαν,
> πὰρ δὲ δέπας οἴνοιο, πιεῖν ὅτε θυμὸς ἀνώγοι.
>
> (Od. 8.65–70)

In the midst of the feasters Pontonoos placed for him [Demodocus] a silver-studded seat and set it against a tall pillar. And the herald took down from its peg the clear-singing lyre above his head and showed him how to take it into his hands. And beside him he set a basket of food and a lovely table and a cup of wine to drink, as his heart bade him.

When the song is done, the herald again "hung the clear-singing lyre from its peg and took the hand of Demodocus and led him forth from the hall" (8.105–7). This handing back and forth of the lyre is repeated three times in Demodocus' second song (8.254f., 257, 261f.).

---

[37] On this passage see Bertolini (1988) 156, 163n. 45.
[38] See Zumthor (1984) 9–36, especially 11–12.

The pattern had already been established, although far more briefly, at the first appearance of a bard, Phemius among the suitors on Ithaca (1.153). The details are omitted from Demodocus' third and last song, perhaps because Homer wants to give special emphasis to Odysseus' response, which takes the form of a signal mark of honor: the herald puts a cut of meat into the singer's hands (8.471–83). Close repetition of the formulas introducing Demodocus early in the book helps show both the continuity with the previous honor and the new, even more distinctive token of respect.[39] In terms of the formulaic structure of the theme "respect for the bard," the chine of roast pork (whatever its effects on Demodocus' digestion and clarity of voice) replaces the lyre. Even here, however, the lyre is not forgotten, for at the end, when King Alcinous notices Odysseus weeping, he orders, "Let Demodocus stay his clear-singing lyre" (8.537).

If we glance ahead some two and a half centuries to Pindar, we can at once appreciate this delight that Homer takes in the sensory pleasures that make song "the accompaniment of the feasting." Where Homer is literal, Pindar makes metaphors. Demodocus gets real wine; Pindar, in the radiant proem of *Olympian* 7, for Diagoras of Rhodes, makes the wine that foams in its golden cup into a symbol of the gift of the song that he is offering to the victor.

Another scene of the *Odyssey* may contain an authentic kernel of physical detail about the performance, in this case the performer's attachment to his instrument as an especially precious possession. In book 22, after Odysseus has dispatched the suitors, the bard Phemius makes his appearance. He crawls out of his hiding place and takes refuge at the altar of Zeus in order to ask for mercy (22.330ff.). He enters the narrative here in the characteristically bardic pose of his first appearance, "holding in his hands the clear-singing lyre."[40] When he decides to approach Odysseus and clasp his knees in supplication, he "first places the smooth lyre on the ground, in between the mixing bowl and the silver-studded stool" (22.340f.). These details are gratuitous. Are they perhaps an indirect reflection of the singer's professionalism? The singer would protect his instrument as a modern violinist might his Stradi-

---

[39] Cf. 8.471 = 8.62: κῆρυξ δ' ἐγγύθεν ἦλθεν ἄγων ἐρίηρον ἀοιδόν, "and the herald drew near, leading the trusty bard," and 8.473 = 8.66: μέσσῳ δαιτυμόνων, πρὸς κίονα μακρὸν ἐρείσας, "in the midst of the banqueters, setting him against a tall pillar"; also 8.483f. = 8.71f., and line 482 closely resembles 68.

[40] *Od.* 22.332; cf. 1.153. Note, too, that 22.331 = 1.154. Cf. also 8.67f. and 105f., of Demodocus.

varius. We may recall, too, Achilles' lyre, precious booty from Eetion's city (*Il.* 9.188).

Homer chooses this setting of bloody corpses and overturned tables for what is probably his fullest account of poetic inspiration. "You will feel grief afterwards if you kill a poet," Phemius tells Odysseus, "as I am, who sing for gods and men. I am self-taught [*autodidaktos*], and a god breathed into my breast songs of every sort."

> αὐτῷ τοι μετόπισθ' ἄχος ἔσσεται, εἴ κεν ἀοιδὸν
> πέφνῃς, ὅς τε θεοῖσι καὶ ἀνθρώποισιν ἀείδω.
> αὐτοδίδακτος δ' εἰμί, θεὸς δέ μοι ἐν φρεσὶν οἴμας
> παντοίας ἐνέφυσεν.
>
> (22.345–48)

For all the abject situation in which he finds himself, the bard manages to assert his privileged position. His songs are "for gods and men," and his inspiration comes from a god. When he calls himself *autodidaktos,* he may mean that he "has learned the songs from himself," that is, he is not just repeating what he has acquired from a specific human teacher or model but is capable of adding to or improving on traditional elements.[41] Yet the word does not exclude divine aid. In fact, his next sentence makes it clear that the poet regards the sources of his inspiration as mysterious and therefore divine. In that contact with divinity lies his claim to a special value for himself. Inspired by "a god," he also sings "for men and gods"—*hominum divumque voluptas,* one might say, with Lucretius.[42] By choosing this unlikely occasion to reflect on the poet's divine inspiration, Homer sets his special value into even higher relief.

When Phemius combines his point about self-learning, *autodidaktos,* with the inspiration of a god, he defines his ability to make songs as not just a personal quality or a mark of genius. The ancient poet views his art as coming *both* from his own power and from a god. He may sing, as does Phemius among the suitors, "by necessity," *anankē* (1.154 = 22.331); but he also sings, as does Demodocus, "in whatever way his impulse [*thumos*] bids him" (ὅππῃ θυμὸς ἐποτρύνῃσιν ἀείδειν, 8.45).

---

[41] The passage continues to be much discussed: see Schadewaldt (1965) 78–79; Walsh (1984) 11–13; Thalmann (1984) 126–27; Pötscher (1986) 12; Puelma (1989) 69, with note 7; Dougherty (1991) passim, especially 98–99; and Brillante (1993) 13–16. There is a growing consensus that being *autodidaktos* and enjoying divine inspiration are not mutually exclusive for the Homeric singer.

[42] Schadewaldt (1965) 67 plausibly suggests that the reference is to festivals in honor of the gods and purely secular occasions such as banquets.

In a variation on this expression, he sings "when the Muse has impelled him to sing the famed deeds of heroes" (Μοῦσ' ἄρ' ἀοιδὸν ἀνῆκεν ἀειδέμεναι κλέα ἀνδρῶν, "The Muse urged on the bard to sing of the glorious fame of heroes," 8.73, also of Demodocus). The bard needs the Muse, or the god, to keep him in touch with the memory of remote events, to provide inspiration, or to complete his limited knowledge (as in the invocation of the Muses in the Catalogue of Ships, Il. 2.485f.). But at the same time he feels the surge of his *thumos,* an intensification of his own energies. At such moments, he is like the warrior into whom the god breathes *menos* (energy) at the height of battle. Homer uses the same term, ἐνέπνευσε, "breathed into," for both.[43] At such times of full concentration, then, the bard, like the warrior, has access to all the strength and power of which he is capable. Conversely, the Muses, like the gods of the *Iliad,* can deprive their favorite of his special strength. Thus they deprive Thamyris of his bardic memory, that most necessary of all the singer's capacities (Il. 2.600: ἐκλέλαθον κιθαριστύν, "they made him forget his lyre-playing").

The Homeric bard is a singer rather than a maker, an *aoidos* rather than *poiētēs,* because he is the voice and the vehicle of an ancient wisdom. But if the poet's powers are divine, they are not irrational. There is no trace here of the ideas of the divine madness or Dionysiac frenzy that Plato connects with poetry, or certain kinds of poetry, in the *Ion* or *Phaedrus.* Though the poet's art bears the sign of its divine origin, it is nonetheless still a social art: he sings "for men" as well as for gods (θεοῖσι καὶ ἀνθρώποισιν ἀείδω, Od. 22.346).

Phemius and Demodocus may regard their songs as the result of what a later age will call divine inspiration, but the lyre remains solidly rooted in its physical world of sound, sight, and touch, and the poet remains a vulnerable human being who needs food and drink and has to watch out so as not to get himself stabbed. Hesiod takes a momentous step away from this attitude in the famous proem to his *Theogony.* As a visible objectification of his music power, the scepter that he receives on Mount Helicon parallels the physical "breath" of inspiration that his Muses have "breathed into" him:

> καί μοι σκῆπτρον ἔδον δάφνης ἐριθηλέος ὄζον
> δρέψασαι, θηητόν· ἐνέπνευσαν δέ μ' ἀοιδήν
> θέσπιν, ἵνα κλείοιμι τά τ' ἐσσόμενα πρό τ' ἐόντα,

---

[43] For such analogies between bard and warrior, see Pötscher (1986) 21–22.

καί μ' ἐκέλονθ' ὑμνεῖν μακάρων γένος αἰὲν ἐόντων
σφᾶς δ' αὐτὰς πρῶτόν τε καὶ ὕστατον αἰὲν ἀείδειν.

(30–34)

> They [the Muses] plucked the staff and gave it to me, wondrous branch of
> blooming laurel, and they breathed into me a voice divine, so that I might
> sing of the things to come and the things that are, and they bade me hymn
> the grace of the blessed gods who are always, and to sing of them
> themselves always, first and last.

This scepter, to be sure, is still a concrete object in the physical world,
stripped from its tree and presented to the poet at a specific moment in
his life. It is not yet Pindar's symbolical Golden Lyre on Olympus,
microcosm of divine and aesthetic order (see *Pythian* 1, above). But it
does point in that direction. Unlike the lyre of Phemius in *Odyssey* 22, it
is bestowed on the poet in a supernatural encounter that he describes in
the first person.

Hesiod's Muses do not give the lyre itself. Their gift has no *necessary*
connection with poetry or song. It is, rather, a symbol of power in a
more general sense, not identical with song, obviously, but a signifying
of the poet's privileged contact with the divine realm of song to which
the Muses belong. Hesiod thus detaches the empowering sign of poetic
craft from the act of singing and from the immediate performative
context. In this respect he is operating in a zone of greater speculative
freedom about his art than did Homer. Scepter instead of lyre also
alludes to the social function of his poetry, for the kings in the Homeric
assemblies hold the scepter to command speech (e.g, *Il.* 2.100–109; cf.
1.234–46). Hesiod can, therefore, address the venal princes, "devourers
of gifts," in the *Works and Days* (βασιλῆες δωροφάγοι, 248, 264; cf.
38f.). Whereas Hesiod confronts the greedy kings in his own voice,
Homer can set up only a fictional attack in a remote period (Achilles
confronting Agamemnon in *Iliad* 1, Odysseus confronting Thersites in
Iliad 2).

The Homeric bard presents himself as more attuned to his audience
than to the situation of composition or creation. His chief concern, one
could say, is pragmatics, not poetics (which is not to say that he lacks a
poetics). His Muses are the repositories of social memory rather than
principles of creativity per se. He identifies with his audience rather than
claiming (as Pindar, for example, will do) that he is different from or
superior to his audience and thus has a right to speak with a special

moral authority on his own account. Homer and even Hesiod, though inspired by Muses, do not call themselves their "prophet" or "spokesman," as does Pindar. Nor do they call attention to their own moralizing revisions of the tales that they tell, as Pindar does with the story of the gods' cannibalistic feasting on Pelops in *Olympian* 1 (48–58). Neither Homer nor Hesiod ever sets himself apart from a large segment of his audience in Pindar's manner when he labels "the crowd of men, in the largest part," as "blind in heart" and "unable to see the truth" (*Nemean* 7.23f.).[44]

The Homeric bard certainly does convey moral judgments and ethical insights (one need only think of the proem of the *Odyssey*, 1.32–43), but he does not define himself in terms of such tasks. This more critical spirit develops only with the more individualizing, independent, and self-assertive poetics of late archaic lyric (especially Simonides and Pindar); and, of course, it culminates in the dialogic presentation of myth and the conflictual situations dramatized in tragedy. However much it owes to epic and lyric song, tragedy also represents a radical break with the archaic view of the poet.

The Homeric bard remains, above all, a "singer of tales" (to use Albert Lord's phrase), a purveyor of pleasure, and a preserver of traditions. But in that role he is indispensable to his memory-hungry and pleasure-loving audience, and he is valued and honored accordingly. The Phaeacians, idealized for many of their political and technological skills, are also idealized for their skills as an audience. They are the most eager for song and story, both about the gods and about mortals, take the most pleasure in hearing the bard, and accord him more honor than we see anywhere else in the poem. Telling his story in this privileged setting (whatever the risks and dangers in the background), even the habitually lying Odysseus exercises the magical spell of an inspired singer (11.333f.); and for all we know he may even be telling them the truth.

---

[44] For the importance of the context of performance and audience awareness in Homer generally, see Martin (1989) 4–10, 89–95, 231–35.

CHAPTER 7

Bard, Hero, Beggar:
Poetics and Exchange

Greek literature has been subjected, with more or less success, to various critical divisions and periodizations: oral and literate, mythic and conceptualizing, pre- and post-Socratic, and so on. Among the least contested of such cuts in the continuum of Greek culture is that between a pre- and postmonetary economy. As Jean-Pierre Vernant has suggested, there is an impassable gulf between the premonetary view of man and Aristotle's definition of the liberal man in terms of money in the *Nicomachean Ethics*.[1] A premonetary economy defines achievement and status in terms of honor rather than payment in cash or kind. In the *Odyssey* it is a sign of lower status to do something for a specific reward (*misthos*); and even in the *Iliad*, where Poseidon and Apollo have built the walls of Troy ἐπὶ μισθῷ (for reward), it is in the negative context of anger at having been cheated.[2]

In an important essay, Louis Gernet pointed out that notions of value in archaic Greece are not the abstract, numerical relations created by

---

[1] Vernant (1989) 308, citing *Nicomachean Ethics* 4.1119b26.

[2] Benveniste (1969) 1:163ff., especially 165, has proposed the widely accepted view that Homeric *misthos* originally meant not "payement régulier" (ordinary payment) but "le prix que remporte le gagnant d'un concours, le héros d'une action difficile" ("the prize that is carried off by the winner of a contest, the hero of a difficult action") (165). Benveniste's etymological evidence for this meaning in other early Indo-European cultures is impressive; but it must be pointed out that his Homeric interpretation rests essentially on one passage and a rather slippery passage at that. This passage, the sole example that Benveniste cites from Homer, is *Il.* 10.304, where Hector offers a reward to anyone who can penetrate the Greek lines. But, given the greed and cowardly nature of the one who accepts, Dolon, one cannot rule out an ironical undertone in the episode. Note the very humble use of the phrase in *Od.* 18.357f.

money but inhere in concrete, precious objects (*agalmata*) that are often endowed with magical or religious significance, like the golden scepter handed down from Zeus to Agamemnon in the second book of the *Iliad*.[3] The exchange and accumulation of such precious objects are characteristic markers of heroic or noble status. In the *Odyssey* in particular, travel to collect such guest-gifts is a normal activity for a hero. It is not only the gift itself, however, that confers honor and status but also the ceremony attending its giving.[4] This ceremonial accompaniment to the bestowal of guest-gifts constitutes in effect a code of ritual gestures which helps to distinguish the status of the participants.

To take a prominent example, in the embassy scene of *Iliad* 9, Achilles refuses the extravagant gifts of Agamemnon because the accompanying ceremony is deficient in the public gestures that Achilles considers appropriate recompense for the insult to his honor. That ceremony is in fact performed when Achilles and Agamemnon are reconciled in book 19. Achilles is now quite indifferent to the gifts (19.145–51); but Odysseus, characteristically, insists on their being displayed publicly and conspicuously to the whole army "so that all the Achaeans may behold them with their eyes" (19.172–74). Parallel to this scene of the *Iliad* but at the opposite end of the scale is Tyrtaeus 12.39–42 (West 1992), in which the public honor is offered to the warrior who has fought for his city. He receives a visible, public display of honor from young and old embodied in gestures of respect in civic space. Not only is he "conspicuous among the citizens" as he grows old, but both young and old also deliberately yield their places to him when he comes among them.

I am using "ritual" in a broad sense, to mean a socially recognized set of words and/or actions, distinguished by stylized, formal features, whose conventional nature affirms, reinforces, or explores the hierarchies and values of the society. In Homer, formulaic language and thematic composition are additional markers for the regularity of such actions and emphasize their place in a system of familiar, stylized behaviors. Such scenes in the Homeric poems may reflect actual rituals of the time, as is probably the case with sacrifice.[5] My concern here is not

---

[3] Gernet (1968) passim, especially 100–101, 136.

[4] M. Finley (1965) 132–33. See also Snell (1953) 158–59 and Francis (1983) 84–86 on the possible semantic connection between *aretē* (excellence) and the root of the verb *arnumai*, to "win" prizes. For further discussion and bibliography, see Kurke (1991) 92–98.

[5] See, for instance, Burkert (1985) 56–57 and Seaford (1989).

to reconstruct the rituals themselves but to examine their expressive nature and the way in which they function in a premodern society to articulate values and indicate modes of social interaction.

Viewed in this perspective, the bestowal and the acceptance of gifts belong to a set of visible, enacted rituals, a miniature drama of sorts whose ultimate aim is the assertion of status or the conferral of honor rather than the accumulation of wealth for its own sake. In a famous scene in the *Iliad*, Diomedes' dramatic gesture of planting the spear in the ground initiates the exchange of armor between himself and Glaucus. The two warriors exchange narratives before they exchange armor, and these tales form an essential part of the ceremonial occasion that confirms the status of both participants. Glaucus' recitation of his ancestry proves that his *geneē* (family line), far from being the nameless sprouting and withering of leaves from spring to fall (6.146–49), is in fact known to many (6.151) and will remain so in the heroic tradition.[6]

This whole scene validates and simultaneously enacts the process whereby a heroic tradition creates and memorializes itself as the embodiment of a social practice. Diomedes' narrative of how his ancestor Oeneus once entertained Glaucus' ancestor Bellerophon in his palace for twenty days and how they exchanged gifts thus becomes the paradigm for his own exchange of armor with Glaucus, getting golden armor worth a hundred oxen for his own of bronze, worth nine. Diomedes thus translates narrative into the performative terms of exchanging the armor, thereby creating the possibility for further narrations, one of which is this very account in the *Iliad*. The tale-within-a-tale has a self-reflexive function and contains an implicit account of the origins of epic song in stories embedded in the ritual exchanges of gifts. From a functional point of view, the poem uses such exchanges to deepen the aura of its own monumentality and authority.[7]

Like the *Iliad*, the *Odyssey* relies heavily on ritual exchanges of gifts and their attendant ceremonies to confer honor and mark differences in status. In early Greece, the banquet is often the traditional place for bestowing special marks of honor and for displaying differences in status; and this is particularly the case in the treatment of bard, beggar, and hero in the *Odyssey*.[8] Alcinous' request that the Phaeacian chiefs give

---

[6] On *geneē* as the expanded narrative of a man's basic *genos* (place of origin or father), see Muellner (1976) 68–99, especially 72–78.

[7] For such self-reflexive markers of monumentality and their problems, see Ford (1992) 138ff., 157ff.

[8] See Gernet (1968) 101. Note, too, the etymological connection of δαίς, "banquet," with δαίω, δατέομαι, "divide," "distribute" the spoils that mark the different degrees of honor.

Odysseus gifts (8.387ff.) publicly reasserts the honor that had been
impugned when Euryalus called the stranger a trader concerned for
profit (8.159–64). He makes amends by giving Odysseus a bronze
sword and scabbard immediately after Alcinous' gift, and the gesture
has the formal, ritualized structure that seals this acknowledgment of
Odysseus' heroic status (8.398–415).

This ceremonial giving is also marked as the possible source of later
tales. When Alcinous diplomatically tries to mitigate the insult, he sums
up the Phaeacians' softer pursuits and says that Odysseus will tell of this
"to another of the heroes, when you feast in your own halls, beside your
wife and your children, remembering our excellence" (aretē, 8.241–44).
Later the gift giving that Arete requests in book 11 and that Alcinous
officially bestows in book 13, on the eve of Odysseus' departure, constitutes the ritual gestures that give the final stamp of confirmation to
his restored honor (11.336–41, 13.4–15). In the former passage, as
Odysseus politely declines the Phaeacian invitation for a longer stay, he
states explicitly that staying and receiving those "brilliant gifts" would
be "of greater profit" (kerdion), for thus he would "arrive with fuller
hand at my dear native land" and so would have greater status, as "more
respected and more dear [aidoioteros kai philteros] to all the men who
would look upon me as I return to Ithaca" (11.355–61).

How does a premonetary society find an appropriate medium of
exchange for the elusive, god-inspired ability of the bard to sing songs
and tell stories? These questions recur in the Odyssey, which is so much
concerned with the bard and his place in society, and they are answered
in part through the poem's depiction of ritualized ceremonies of gift
exchange.

The Odyssey presents a curious contradiction in its view of the bard's
livelihood. In one place it depicts a relatively low status by associating
him with craft (17.381–86).[9] Even lower, as we shall see, is the association of the bard with the dependency of the wandering beggar. Yet the
poem elevates the bard far above these workaday necessities not only
through the recurrent language of divinity and inspiration but also, in
the scenes of Demodocus in the Phaeacian palace, by allowing him to
participate in heroic feasting and an equivalent of gift exchange. Indeed,
the poem never shows the bard working for hire like a wandering
craftsman. In fact, the singer has a far loftier model, namely, the god of

---

[9] On a diachronic level, however, the association of the bard with craftsmanship may
belong to traditional Indo-European terminology for poetic creation: see Nagy (1989)
18–24.

the lyre, Apollo, playing to enhance the festivity at Zeus' banquets on Olympus (*Il.* 1.602–4; cf. Homeric *Hymn to Apollo* 182ff.). In his enthusiasm for Demodocus' song of the Trojan horse, for example, Odysseus says that the bard has been taught by the Muse and Apollo (8.488); and Hesiod says that singers are from Apollo (*Theog.* 94).

There are many possible explanations for these contradictions. On the diachronic level, the palace-attached bard of Ithaca and Scheria may reflect Mycenaean or Dark Age practice, whereas the bard as traveling *dēmiourgos* (craftsman) may correspond more closely to the poet's contemporary circumstances in the late eighth or early seventh century, where we should understand the nascent polis in place of the palace. Synchronically, however, the different degrees of bardic honor depict different levels of social and moral order and different paradigms of acceptable and unacceptable behavior. The obvious contrast is between the happy and orderly Phaeacians who give food, gifts, and free travel and the unruly suitors who take someone else's food for their own banquets. It is a touch of brilliant self-advertisement (as it were) that in the happiest society the bard gets the highest honor.[10]

The status and freedom of the bard are major indicators of the level of general culture. In book 1 the impulse for singing comes from the suitors: when they have had enough of food and drink, their thoughts turn to song and dance, "the accompaniments of the feasting." The herald hands Phemius his "most lovely lyre," and he "sang among the suitors by necessity" (1.148–54). Here the bard is merely a useful appendage to the banquet, a menial whose unwilling service increases the pleasure of his superiors. Among the Phaeacians, however, the bard, led in by the herald, is described as beloved by the Muses, who gave him sweet song in recompense for his blindness (8.63f.). He is seated "in the midst of the banqueters" ($\mu\acute{\epsilon}\sigma\sigma\omega$ $\delta\alpha\iota\tau\nu\mu\acute{o}\nu\omega\nu$, 8.66) and provided with a basket of viands, "a lovely table," and "a goblet of wine to drink whenever his spirit bids him" (8.69f.). He is thus set on an equal footing with the other diners, and the eating described in the formulaic lines that follow includes him too (8.71f. = 1.149f.).[11] In contrast to Phemius, the urge to song comes from within himself or from the Muse, not from the other banqueters ("The Muse bade the singer to sing of the famed tales of heroes," 8.73).[12]

---

[10] The repetition of a number of formulaic lines between the Phemius episode in book 1 and Demodocus' singing in book 8 makes the comparisons even sharper (e.g., 1.149f. = 8.71f., 1.325 = 8.83). See above, Chapter 6.

[11] On this passage see above, Chapter 6.

[12] In 1.347, however, Telemachus, defending the song of the *nostoi* (Returns) that

Demodocus' third and final song follows the same procedures for including the bard "in the midst of the banqueters" (8.470ff.); but Homer significantly adds an etymological play on his name: *Dēmodokos*, literally "received by the people," is glossed as "Demodocus, honored by the people" (Δημόδοκον, λαοῖσι τετιμένον, 8.472).[13] The honorific treatment now reaches its height as Odysseus not only has the herald present him with a cut from the chine of the boar but also makes a speech that establishes "honor and respect [*timē* and *aidōs*] for bards among all men on the earth, because the Muse has taught them their songs and loves the race of singers" (8.471–81, especially 479–81). As the herald places the meat in the bard's hands, he is raised to the level of "hero" in the phrase ἥρῳ Δημοδόκῳ (hero Demodocus). The rank thus accorded Demodocus is underlined by another honorific play on his name as he "receives [*dexato = dokos*] the gift and rejoices in his heart" (8.483). Once more the feasting that follows includes the bard (8.484f. = 8.71f. = 1.149f.). Although the bard now sings at Odysseus' request, not at his spirit's bidding, as was the case for the first song, the situation is still very different from the suitors' request for song on Ithaca in book 1. The signal marks of honor bestowed on the bard make him virtually equal in status to any of the guests; and Odysseus prefaces his request with still higher praise, namely, that not just the Muse but also Apollo, son of Zeus, has taught him (8.488).[14]

The poem employs a loose gradation in the honor of the singer at the feast that corresponds to the general level of morality in the society at large. In this scale, the Phaeacians are obviously at the top and the Ithacan suitors at the bottom. But an even lower place seems to be reserved for Agamemnon's Argos, where the anonymous bard left in charge of Clytaemnestra is set out on a desert island—the worst possible fate for a bard—where instead of being given food and drink he is feasted on, "to be a prey and spoil for birds" (3.267–71). The anonymity of this bard is thus parallel to his end: his personal identity is blotted out along with the destruction of his proper place in a human society and before a human audience.[15]

The particular relation of Phemius to the feast when he again appears

---

Phemius sings, claims this bard's right "to give pleasure wherever his mind urges" (τέρπειν ὅππῃ οἱ νόος ὄρνυται).

[13] On the significance of Demodocus' name, see Nagy (1979) 17, with note 1, and 149, with note 6.

[14] On this detail see above, Chapter 6.

[15] For Aegisthus' maltreatment of the bard see Scully (1981) and Andersen (1992); also above, Chapter 6.

in book 22 constitutes almost the exact antithesis of the honorific position of Demodocus in book 8. Whereas the Phaeacian herald "set a silver-studded stool beside [Demodocus] in the midst of the banqueters" and hangs the lyre on a peg above his head (8.65–68), Phemius, fearing for his life in the midst of the carnage, "set down his lyre on the ground between the mixing bowl and the silver-studded stool" (22.340f.). Instead of receiving special cuts of meat, he wonders whether he should make a run for the altar of Zeus outside where Odysseus and Laertes used to burn the thighs of oxen, the preliminaries to a big feast (22.333–36). Instead of receiving from Odysseus godlike honor as a "hero," he grovels at his knees as a suppliant (22.342ff.). Instead of having his skill praised by another as a teaching from the Muses (8.488f.; cf. 8.63), he praises his own art, with a rather ambiguous combination of human and divine teaching, and speaks only of a general "god" (*theos*) rather than of the Muse and Apollo (22.346–48).[16] Instead of saying that he is honored among all men, as Odysseus had said of Demodocus, he says only, "I sing for gods and men" (22.346; cf. 8.479; cf. also 9.19f.).

Even in this inglorious situation, however, Phemius takes care to separate his dependent status among the suitors from that of the beggar. He closes his plea with the word, "I did not come of my own accord into your house nor asking in need did I wander among the suitors [οὐδὲ χατίζων πωλεύμην] to sing at the banquets, but they being more and stronger led me by necessity" (22.351–53; cf. 331). Thus, even in this position of humiliation and self-abasement, he disclaims the total subservience and shameless, indiscriminate "need" (*khatizōn*) of the beggar. Odysseus respects his plea and restores his honor by referring to him as "much-famed singer" (*poluphēmos aoidos*, 22.376); and in the next book, after the slaughter, he refers to the bard as "divine singer" (*theios aoidos*) in telling him to play dancing songs to conceal the deed temporarily (23.133).

As these contrasts between Demodocus and Phemius imply, the *Odyssey* explores the anomaly of the bard's social position by placing his activity between the heroic exchange of gifts and the dependency of the needy, wandering beggar. Phemius himself, as we have just observed, implies the comparison (see especially 22.351–53, just above), and it recurs indirectly, as we shall see, in other contexts that describe the bard's status.

[16] For other aspects of this much-discussed passage, with further bibliography, see above, Chapter 6, with note 41. One may add that the bard seems to be a little more dignified than the herald. He stands by the door to the passage, whereas the herald, covered by the skin of a newly flayed ox, crouches under a stool (22.332f. and 362f.).

More specifically, a three-way parallel between bardic song, heroic gift giving, and wandering for the collection of wealth or food forms a network of analogies that help define (and perhaps idealize) the bard's place in the heroic world. The profit motive that is suppressed for the bard can surface shamelessly in his humbler alter ego, the storytelling beggar, as we shall see in Odysseus' role as beggar/narrator in Eumaeus' hut in book 14. On the other hand, the bard's participation in the feast and its honorific gestures helps bridge the gap between the poet's dependent status and his role as the repository of heroic values or, as Peter Rose suggests, between his role "as the bearer of the elite culture" and his "status as a wandering craftsman and his proximity to the discontented peasants and marginal elements in society."[17] These gifts of honor at the feast suggest a certain permeability of the barrier between bard and hero on the one hand, but they insist on and clarify the reality of that barrier on the other hand. The bard stands in an intermediate, but not necessarily mediated, relation between the hero and the beggar. He can, on occasion, partake of the high status of the hero, but he may also have the needy, inferior, and precarious life of the beggar.

The two extended comparisons of Odysseus to a bard in the *Odyssey* present the two extremes of beggar and bard, and both cases use the ritual gestures of gift giving. Arete and Alcinous, admiring Odysseus' bardlike skill, call for more gifts, which are duly bestowed (11.333–69, 13.13ff.). But if Alcinous' honorific gestures treat Odysseus qua bard as a hero, he also glances at the alternative, namely, that Odysseus might be one of those "deceivers and thieves and fashioners of lies" such as the earth feeds in large numbers (11.364–66, especially ἠπεροπῆα . . . καὶ ἐπίκλοπον . . . ψεύδεα τ' ἀρτύνοντας). His word ἠπεροπῆα (deceiver), here, describes the unflattering side of the beggar, soon to be evoked explicitly by Odysseus in that role as he defends his prophecy to Eumaeus in 14.398–400: "And if the lord does not come just as I say, urging on the servants, hurl me down from a great rock, in order that another beggar too may avoid being a deceiver" (ὄφρα καὶ ἄλλος πτωχὸς ἀλεύεται ἠπεροπεύειν).[18] Alcinous' verb, "feeds" (*boskei*) in 11.365 also associates the lying traveler with the beggar, whose main concern is to "feed the belly" (see p. 155 below). Every "stranger" is in a sense a beggar, as suggested by the formulaic collocation *xeinoi te*

---

[17] P. Rose (1992) 139; cf. also 113.

[18] Note the wordplays on ἀλήτης, "wanderer," and ἀληθής, "true," in 14.124–26, on which see Chapter 8, below. The verb ἠπεροπεύειν, "deceive," is used of the untrustworthy Phoenicians as well, people also on the margins of Greek society and also men of travel, trade, and deceit: see 15.419–22.

ptōkhoi te (strangers and beggars).[19] And even as a recognized hero among the Phaeacians, Odysseus is still, as he confesses, very much "in need" of their aid for his return (*nostoio khatizōn*, 8.156; cf. 11.350).

In 17.512–27, on the other hand, where Odysseus has in fact been playing the role of beggar, not hero, Eumaeus prefaces his praise of his guest's bardic talent with the explanation, "For three nights I kept him, and for three days I detained him in my hut" (515f.). These words are a scaled-down version of the ideal type of heroic gift exchange as we see it in the scene between Glaucus and Diomedes: the latter tells how his grandfather "divine Oeneus" entertained "blameless Bellerophon" in his palace and kept him for twenty days (*Il.* 6.216–17). This exchange is remembered over many generations and recalled and reenacted in conspicuous, extravagant gestures by mighty heroes engaged in feats of war. Eumaeus' entertainment is more modest: "For three nights I kept him, and for three days I detained him in my hut" (τρεῖς γὰρ δή μιν νύκτας ἔχον, τρία δ' ἤματ' ἔρυξα / ἐν κλισίῃ, 17.515f.; cf. *Iliad* 6.217, ξείνισ' ἐνὶ μεγάροισιν ἐείκοσιν ἤματ' ἔρυξας, "[Bellerophon] entertained him in his halls, detaining him for twenty days").

Whereas Alcinous' heroic gift giving to Odysseus as bard/hero keeps the lying and deceitful beggar in the background, the humble beggar/bard of Eumaeus has a heroic gift exchange in the background. The "divine" warriors, however, exchange tripods and goblets of precious metals (or, when carried away, gold armor for bronze), whereas a beggar and a swineherd have only the tales of their woes to exchange, their life stories and attendant griefs (*kēdea*). What the host gives his guest is a cloak and perishable food, both to be used in the immediate present, not admired by descendants in a storeroom some generations in the future. Eumaeus in fact stipulates that the beggar will have to put his rags back on at dawn, because each man has only one cloak apiece (14.512–14).[20] This is hardly the world of aristocratic abundance where cloaks and coverlets are folded one upon another in seemingly bottomless chests, like the one from which Helen takes out the beautifully embroidered robe, shining like a star, as her parting guest-gift to Telemachus (15.104–8).

If the scene in the swineherd's hut illustrates that even a lowly slave may give to a beggar, the treatment of a beggar by the aristocrat

---

[19] For the formula *xeinoi te ptōkhoi te*, see *Od.* 6.208 = 14.58; cf. also 17.10f., 18.106, 21.292.

[20] See Nagy (1979) 235ff., who suggests that Odysseus/beggar's tale of the cloak is a humble version of motifs in praise poetry such as appear in the Pindaric epinicia.

Antinous goes in the opposite direction. Antinous threatens the beggar Irus in book 18 and then the disguised Odysseus in 21, saying he will send them each to King Echetus, "harmer of all mortals," for mutilation (18.82–87, 21.306–10). Instead of being received by a king who loads his guest down with gold and bronze that would sustain his household for ten generations, the beggar would be horribly disfigured or killed. In both cases, Antinous' threat occurs in the context of an unruly or violent banquet, the bloody boxing match that replaces song as the suitors' festive entertainment in book 18 and his own myth of the Lapiths and Centaurs in book 21, just before Odysseus turns this paradigm back on the suitors in an unexpected way (21.295–304). Antinous' picture of what a king gives to poor strangers, then, is totally in keeping with the kind of banquet that he enjoys and in which he meets his end (22.8–21).

The bard resembles a beggar; but then even great heroes undertake wandering tours to collect gifts.[21] The gifts that the hero seeks, however, are "objets de valeurs," in Gernet's sense, precious crafted items that endure in the *oikos* (house), endowed with symbolical meanings and expressing cultural values such as power or kingship. The ultimate reversal of the heroic exchange is, of course, in the Cyclops episode, in which Odysseus' expedition to acquire guest-gifts (9.229) nearly reduces him to being nothing more than perishable flesh, entrails, and marrow that will disappear into a monster's belly. Odysseus escapes only by abandoning both his heroic name and normal heroic battle (9.299–306). His return guest-gift is, appropriately, not a lasting *agalma* (precious object) or *keimēlion* (guest-gift) but the wine that the Cyclops consumes on the spot and then belches out in a grisly disfigurement of a heroic banquet (9.372–74).

The scenes in the palace on Ithaca enact both the differences and the resemblances between hero, bard, and beggar. When Eumaeus escorts Odysseus disguised as a beggar into the palace, the treacherous goatherd Melanthius, using the language of blame, insults the beggar by saying that he is after scraps of food and not the heroic gifts of "swords or caldrons" (17.222). Instead of working, Melanthius continues, Eumaeus' companion will prefer "to go slinking around the town begging to feed his insatiate belly" (ἀλλὰ πτώσσων κατὰ δῆμον / βούλεται αἰτίζων βόσκειν ἣν γαστέρ' ἄναλτον, 17.226f.). When Odysseus/beggar then enters the palace, he admires not only the architecture but

---

[21] See *Od.* 15.80–85; cf. 19.273 and 15.558, 19.203, 11.358–61; in general Redfield (1983) 234 and M. Finley (1965) 131.

also the feasting and its musical accompaniment: "Inside resounds the lyre, which the gods made as the companion to the banquet" (ἐν δέ τε φόρμιγξ / ἠπύει, ἥν ἄρα δαιτὶ θεοὶ ποίησαν ἑταίρην, 17.270f. = 18.363f.).

One cannot exclude the possibility that Odysseus is here playing his role to the full and so contemplates the bard's proximity to the food with a certain degree of professional envy. If so, the remark is no less revealing for the juxtaposition of bard and beggar. In contrast to Odysseus' view of the lyre (and by extension the bard) as "the companion to the feast," we may compare Melanthius' and Antinous' insulting descriptions of the beggar a little later as "ruiner of feasts" (daitōn apolumantēra, 17.220 and 317) or an "annoyance to the feast" (daitos aniēn, 17.446).

In reply to Eumaeus' warning about possible ill treatment, Odysseus/beggar replies that he "cannot hide [his] raging belly, destructive, which gives many woes to men" (17.286f.). The passage indirectly places bard and beggar at the opposite ends of the social spectrum. The bard belongs inside the feast, with the lyre "which the god made as the companion to the feast," whereas the beggar, entering from outside, is bound to the needs of his belly (gastēr), for which he will have to endure blows and missiles (17.283ff.). The bard gives pleasure (cf. also 17.385, just below); the beggar, as Antinous says later, is an annoyance.

Soon after, inside the hall, Eumaeus defends the beggar against Antinous by introducing the fourfold list of nonresident specialists (dēmiourgoi) who have to be summoned to the palace when needed (17.381–86). These include healer, prophet, carpenter, and the "divine-speaking bard who gives pleasure in his singing" (θέσπις ἀοιδός, ὅ κεν τέρπῃσιν ἀείδων, 17.385). This linking of bard and craftsman may reflect Eumaeus' view of the bard as that of the lower rather than the upper class, that is, he views singing as a profession that earns a wage, as do other workers.[22] By contrast, Odysseus associates the bard with something divine: "the god," he says, "made the lyre as the companion to the feast" (17.270f.). Much as Eumaeus enjoys stories and values the pleasure that the bard gives (17.385), he seems to have a more practical and prosaic view of his economic situation. In any case, his view of the bard as a wandering craftsman does not correspond to the situation that we see anywhere else in the Odyssey, for in Mycenae, Scheria, and Ithaca

---

[22] For other aspects of class status reflected in the dramatic situation, see Nagy (1979) 233–34.

the bard seems closely attached to the palace. Indeed, Alcinous brings together his fine wine and his fine bard as joint amenities that he can offer to his guests (13.8–9). The exceptional situation that Eumaeus describes may reflect a situation closer to the historical reality. It may also indicate that the poem's overall perspective on the bard, in contrast to Eumaeus' individual perspective reflected in 17.381–86, is primarily that of the noble class, a fact that may have some implications for the audience that the poem is addressing. As we shall see later, however, this contradiction may be an inevitable concomitant of employing non-aristocratic singers to ennoble aristocratic pursuits. Aristocrats could also look down on bards as merely hired "craftsmen," but the poem seems to prefer a different view.[23]

Unlike such "craftsmen," the bard enters into regular association with kings and nobles, whose food he shares. This perspective, along with the studied differentiation of bard and beggar, clearly works to the bard's advantage, as it exalts his status and separates him from other "craftsmen." At the same time, the class lines are firmly drawn. When the best of the Achaeans, Achilles, sings the *klea andrōn* (famous songs of heroes) like a bard, he is differentiated from that bardic status as strongly as possible. He sings only for his own pleasure, not that of others (*Il.* 9.187–89), ignores his "audience" (190f.), and is in the position of receiving guests but refusing gifts. His lack of an audience and his refusal to enter fully into a relation of reciprocal exchange (however justified his motives) distinguish him from the bardic role into which he is momentarily cast. He gives, not receives, hospitality (202ff.), and he even refuses an elaborate offer of gifts out of a conviction of an even higher level of personal honor, "in the portion of Zeus" (607–10). And that honor is further enhanced, as Diomedes observes when Odysseus reports Achilles' refusal (697–700), by the suppliant status of the ambassadors.

The bard who is the repository of heroic deeds is totally incapable of performing them, being either blind (like Demodocus) or helpless (like Agamemnon's hapless bard left to guard Clytaemnestra) or rather cow-

---

[23] See P. Rose (1992) 112–14 for a different interpretation of the relation between bard and social structure. He suggests that the different levels of society embodied in the poem are reflected in the "composite character of Odysseus, who both selectively appropriates and challenges the values of the ruling elite" (121). Rose and I agree, I think, on the ambiguities of the bard's social status but take complementary approaches. My emphasis is on the unifying vision and shaping direction within the poem, his on the social realities reflected through the poem.

ardly (like Phemius). Although Odysseus begins his bardlike narrative with an elaborate proem on the pleasure of hearing a bard at dinner (9.2–11), he makes a strong distinction between such bardic song and the contents of his own telling, which are his personal sufferings, soon to be told in the first person (12–15). He begins, furthermore, not with bardic anonymity but with the proud declaration of his own name and his "fame that mounts to the heavens" (19ff.). Thus he is in the anomalous position of being the singer of his own *kleos* (fame).[24]

The bard may receive honor for his song, like Demodocus in book 8; but in contrast to the gifts of the heroic *xenos* (guest), these are not to be carried away and stored as *keimēlia* (guest-gifts). Like the verses or tales of the bard, they must be consumed on the spot. In receiving these conspicuous tokens of honor at a feast, then, the bard approaches the status of a hero or noble (cf. 8.471–83, p. 147 above); but in the wholly alimentary nature of this token, he approaches the beggar.

There is thus complete symmetry between the form of honorific gifts that the bard receives and the skill for which he receives them. This is the mode of honor appropriate to the bard. Whether he is a wandering *dēmiourgos* or a dependent attached to a great king, he has no *oikos* of his own for the thesaurization of the precious objects, nor does he have the material wealth with which to make the necessary return gift. A noble's house, however, will endure over many generations and so can eventually return the countergift to a descendant of the original giver. These heroic gifts, moreover, often become a source of song, of the *kleos aphthiton* that the great heroes can claim. As Diomedes' response to Glaucus in *Iliad* 6 shows, the exchange of *keimēlia* is the starting point for casting the hero into the role of bardlike narrator. Sophocles is being quite Homeric when he has Ajax himself relate the story of exchanging guest-gifts with Hector (*Ajax* 66off.). In Homeric terms, these are just the details that should survive in the memory of later generations.

When Odysseus, in his role as beggar, tells of Odysseus' generous reception by the Thesprotian king Pheidon, he emphasizes only the material side of the guest-gifts' duration: these *keimēlia* of iron and bronze "would feed [*boskoi*] another man up to the tenth generation: so many guest-gifts lay in the halls of the lord" (*Od.* 14.325f.). Odysseus' disguise is perfect, for as a beggar he emphasizes the consumption, not the durability, of the gifts. His (supposed) thoughts are of food, not of storage, as such. Alcinous used this same verb, *boskein,* of earth's "nur-

[24] See above, Chapter 5.

turing" deceivers and liars in a context when he is differentiating his guest from the wandering beggars who are looking only for their own profit (11.364–66, cited p. 149 above). And Eumaeus uses *boskein* again when he congratulates the beggar on obtaining an interview with Penelope, for thus he will obtain the cloak and chiton that he so extremely needs and "by begging for food around the town [he] will *feed* his belly" (τῶν σὺ μάλιστα / χρηΐζεις· σῖτον δὲ καὶ αἰτίζων κατὰ δῆμον / γαστέρα βοσκήσεις, 17.556–58).

The beggar's word "feed" in these two passages may also cast some light on the Muses' scornful address of the shepherds as "base reproaches, only bellies" just before giving Hesiod his staff of bardic authority. The gesture in effect separates the belly-shepherds from the singer that Hesiod is to become. To be devoted to the *gastēr* is to be a beggar rather than a bard and thus to be unable to transcend the biological imperative of day-to-day survival.[25] These belly-shepherds, then, remain in the realm of insult rather than of honorific gifts. Their lives follow the pattern of the *ephēmeroi*, subject to uncertainty and abrupt change of status, as Odysseus warns Amphinomus in 18.125–50 and Melantho in 19.71–88, rather than the heroic model of the genealogy of Glaucus that endures throughout time and is memorialized in song and story. The bard, on the other hand, has a face-to-face meeting with the Muses, and he receives from them the *skēptron*, the sign of inspiration and authority among men.

In the tale of the cloak that the disguised Odysseus tells at the end of book 14, bard and beggar again come together and diverge in interesting ways. The disguised hero is in effect begging, but he introduces his story by saying that the wine is making him sing (*aeisai*, 14.464). His tale is memorable in itself as an example of Odyssean *mētis* (guile), but it soon becomes performative as a clever way of getting a cloak. In other words, it moves from "pure," disinterested bardic narration to begging and so serves as a link between the bard and the beggar.

[25] On the *gastēr* and the realm of perishable mortality and the human separation from the divine, see Vernant (1990) 194, apropos of the Prometheus and Pandora myths in Hesiod; also Arthur (1982) 72–75. Svenbro (1976) 46–59 has a detailed and helpful semantic study of *gastēr* in *Theog.* 26–28, which he shows to be associated with the situation of dependency and marginality that would make the bard say anything, including falsehood, to the one who will feed him. He seems to me, however, to neglect the connection of *gastēr* and mortality, to overrate the connections with the sacrificial system and meat eating, and thus to exaggerate his criticism of the "dualist" view (spirit or intellect versus materialism), which in fact is implicit in his view of the passage. His impressive demonstration of the links with the motif of the beggar in the *Odyssey*, however, is a valuable contribution. See also Thalmann (1984) 143–47.

The bard earns a dinner at a feast of kings and nobles by telling a tale of great heroes of past times whose deeds could not otherwise be preserved. The beggar, in the lowly setting of a swineherd's hut, wins a cloak by telling of a memorable and characteristic deed of the master of the house. This tale of war, however, illustrates the subject's rather ambiguous virtue of *mētis* or *dolos* and is itself a literal actualization in the present of that alleged request in the past (cf. 14.488 and 504). In both cases, need rather than honor is the motive.[26]

Both the bard and the beggar tell tales; but when the bard receives the material reward for his song, he follows the model of honorific gift giving between heroes, and there is no direct relation between the subject of the song and the personal situation of the bard. In the case of the beggar, however, the request for the reward is explicit, and the subject of the song is but a thinly disguised version of the teller's situation. He wishes that he were young and strong, and then "someone of the swineherds would give me a cloak in the steading" (14.504). But as it is, "they dishonor [me] because I wear base clothing on my body" (506). He virtually enacts his lack of honor by calling attention to his ugly clothes.[27] Eumaeus, even though he responds generously, recognizes the "profit" in his motivation ("Not inappropriate is the word you spoke, nor profitless," οὐδέ τί πω παρὰ μοῖραν ἔπος νηκερδὲς ἔειπες, 509).[28] The needs of the body erode the aesthetic distance that the abundance and munificence of the heroic setting afford to the bard (cf. 9.5–11). Maintaining this difference is crucial for the bard's status. Hence (once more) the insult involved in Hesiod's Muses calling the shepherds "merely bellies," *gasteres oion.* From the divine singers' point of view, mortals subject to the needs of the belly risk the degeneration of their art and its truth.

Whereas the hero/bard among the Phaeacians is sheltered from want by his noble patrons and so is able to listen to his divine teachers, the Muses and Apollo, the shepherd-bellies, like the traveling beggar, will

[26] On the beggar's tale of the cloak and the *mētis* of Odysseus in *Iliad* 10, see Muellner (1976) 96–97, with note 43; also Edwards (1985) 27–41 and Haft (1983–84) 298.

[27] Cf. Odysseus' warning to Melantho not to be disrespectful just because of his ugly clothes, 19.71–84; cf. also 24.154–61.

[28] The distance from the heroic world is all the greater because Eumaeus' phrase about the lack of changes of cloaks (14.513) harks back to Alcinous' words about the Phaeacians' fondness for just such luxuries (8.249). It is a further irony, however, that Eumaeus' generosity enacts a truer nobility here in the lowly hut than at the feasts of the suitors. Eumaeus will be suitably rewarded for this at the end; and we learn in the next book that he was born the son of a king.

say anything to fill their "shameless," "raging," or "destructive" bellies and so will tell lies that please.[29] "Truth," therefore, is an impossibility on Ithaca, where the social order has been destroyed and the palace is without its king. This situation in itself implies an ideology in which poetry as a Muse-inspired art of truth can exist only under a good king and in a stable, Phaeacian-like kingdom. By juxtaposing the status of poet and wandering beggar, the *Odyssey* validates the social organization that provides the order, respect, and civilized setting that we see for bardic performance among the Phaeacians. On the other hand, the beggar also reflects the other side, the less honorific reality of the poet's status, namely, the fact that he is, after all, dependent on the rich and powerful who feed him, that he too may feel constrained to tell what will please, and that like the wandering *dēmiourgoi* he may also be a traveler "summoned" from an itinerant life for a precarious, temporary employment when he is needed. If Demodocus is the ideal, then, the bard's actual status may lie somewhere between the "compulsion" (*ananke*) felt by Phemius and the marginality of the traveling craftsman evoked by Eumaeus.

The bard/beggar's dependence on his belly, like the "bellies" castigated by Hesiod's Muses, thus points not only to economic dependency in its most basic form but also to the mortal side of the poet's song and the mortal limitations of bardic truth. As Hesiod's Muses say, they can tell falsehoods as well as truth (*Theog.* 27f.). In the Catalogue of Ships, Homer reminds us that we mortals have only the tale that we hear, the *kleos,* and "do not know anything [οὐδέ τι ἴδμεν]," whereas the goddesses, themselves immortal and present at all past events, "know everything" (ὑμεῖς γὰρ θεαί ἐστε, πάρεστέ τε, ἴστέ τε πάντα, "for you are goddesses, and you are present, and you know all things," *Il.* 2.485f.). The knowledge and skill vouchsafed the bard by the Muses, like all the gifts of the gods, are precarious.[30] The "beggarly" side of the bard, then, points to this contingent, mortal side of the bardic craft, its participation in the mortal condition denoted by the *gastēr.* The singer's art stands between divine gifts and human needs, between the access to god-given "truth" and the human requirement that "bellies" must be filled if song is to come forth at all.

In his juxtaposition to the divine singer, the beggar, belly and all, has another set of associations, namely, a connection with the resourceful-

---

[29] *Od.* 7.216, 17.286f. and 473f. See Svenbro (1976) 54ff. and above, note 25.
[30] See Thalmann (1984) 149.

ness, inventiveness, and flexibility of the bard, his ability to adapt to many different social situations and levels of society, from the swineherd's hut to the Phaeacian palace. The bard is the wandering beggar/ liar/belly who, even as "wanderer" (ἀλήτης), can be "true" (ἀληθής, cf. 14.124–26);[31] but he can also be the companion of kings and nobles, a "hero," and one whom the Muses and Apollo have taught. If the hero/bard honored at the Phaeacian feasts is the vehicle of a divinely authored truth among men, the beggar/bard is a figure for the adaptability of the poetic art, its multiplicity and variety and therewith its capacity for reaching men and women of different types and classes with tales of endlessly varied moods and registers. The other side of this adaptability, however, is the capacity for telling lies.

These skills are, of course, reflected most prominently in Odysseus' prodigious narrative fluency. In one way or another, all those to whom the hero tells his tales in his bardlike fashion are susceptible to the "spell" of his infinitely plastic art. The "polytropy" of the *Odyssey*'s hero is symmetrical with the polytropic range and versatility of its bard's artistry.[32] This polytropic figure, as hero, bard, and beggar (sometimes all at the same time), not only recounts his own adventures but also embodies the artistry that can hold them together in a complex, shifting, and variable unity. The interweaving of disguise, lying, and bardic self-referentiality in the second half of the poem produces a *mise-en-abîme* effect in which the bard (Homer) sings of a hero who disguises himself as a beggar but who is also a hero.

Odysseus, one could say, is his own poetics. Through the equivalencies and analogies among bard, hero, and beggar, the bard to whom the audience is listening takes as many shapes as his narrative demands. The wandering, needy beggar, willing to say and seem anything, is wrapped in the rags of the mortal contingency and ephemerality that will lead him to seize the occasion of the moment. This figure also embodies the open, carnivalesque space of disguise, inventiveness, and opportunity, which constitute the earthy side of inspiration. Seen in this perspective, he is also a figure for the poem's power of mimetic representation, its ability to render the multiple (dis)guises of reality in the changing, precarious world that this poem shows us. The beggar, then, is the prosaic, Ithacan equivalent to Proteus in the mysterious sea world of the post-Trojan adventures. Like Proteus, he embodies the power of this

---

[31] On the wordplay see below, Chapter 8.
[32] On this feature of the poem and its hero, see Pucci (1987) 16–17, 24–25, and passim and Thalmann (1992) 11–12.

narrative to render the manifold shapes of a reality that is always ready to elude our grasp.

The hero can be compared to a bard, as Odysseus is a number of times, but he is not actually a bard. Odysseus can shoot his bow as a bard handles the lyre, but the comparison is not reversible. Phemius is an utter coward. Hence both the *Iliad* and the *Odyssey* insist on the differences between bard and hero, the *Odyssey* rather less vehemently than the *Iliad*. If the bardlike stranger receives gifts like a hero from the Phaeacians (book 11), he is a beggar on Ithaca (book 17). If Demodocus is honored as "hero," Phemius is disgraced as a coward. The contrast between the Phaeacian and the Ithacan status of the bard stands out even more sharply because, as we noted earlier, the language of Eumaeus' entertainment of his bardlike guest evokes scenes of heroic hospitality, like that of Bellerophon and Oeneus in Diomedes' story in *Iliad* 6 (cf. *Od.* 17.515 and *Il.* 6.516).

The *Odyssey*'s sustained triangular comparisons of beggar, bard, and hero may also point to some real conditions in this world. Reinhold Merkelbach has collected beggars' songs, some from Archaic to Hellenistic Greece and some from other cultures as well. In these songs the singing beggar promises blessings to the one who gives and threatens curses on the one who refuses.[33] Merkelbach concludes, "The travelling and begging poet is a familiar, indeed characteristic phenomenon in the early period of the Greeks, Indians, Germans, and of course many other peoples."[34] Thus there may well have been a historical connection between the roles of singer and beggar reaching back to Homeric times. For what it may be worth, Hesiod juxtaposes the bard and the beggar in describing the two forms of strife in *Works and Days* 26: καὶ πτωχὸς πτωχῷ φθονέει καὶ ἀοιδὸς ἀοιδῷ ("And a beggar is envious toward a beggar and a bard toward a bard"). More generally, the fluid passage between beggar, bard, and hero in the poem suggests the uncertainty of life in this world of sudden reversals. A hero who is shipwrecked is in fact reduced to beggary; and the various lies that Odysseus relates in this disguise are examples of what might happen to a man, even a hero or king, in these changing times. This is a point on which Odysseus reads a lesson to one of the suitors in a context that emphasizes the everyday realities of labor (18.125ff.).

---

[33] Merkelbach (1952) passim, especially 320–23. Striking examples are the potters' song in the Herodotean *Vita Homeri* lines 433–61 in Allen (1912) and the adaptation in Theocritus 16.

[34] Merkelbach (1952) 327.

The comparison works the other way around when Odysseus throws off his disguise at the end of book 21 and reveals through his bardlike expertise with the bow that the beggar is in fact a heroic warrior (21.401–12). The bow sings like a swallow; the more ominous sound of Zeus' thunder gives an omen; and Odysseus shoots the arrow through the axes. As he does so, he shouts, "Telemachus, your guest does not reproach you sitting in your hall" (21.426f.). Invoking the issue of class and status, Odysseus here answers the suitors' scorn of the beggar and their insult of Telemachus as most unfortunate in his guests (literally, "base-guested," οὔ τις σεῖο κακοξεινώτερος ἄλλος, 20.376). What the guest can give his host in exchange is his own worthiness and status, which reflect back on the host; and Odysseus can now make this return to the young man whom he also implicitly recognizes as the true host in the palace.

Odysseus' words and gestures also answer the insults and violation of table rituals when Ctesippus mocks the language of honoring guests at the feast as he hurls an ox hoof at the pseudobeggar as his guest-gift (20.292–98). His last words in particular are a deliberate parody of honorific gift exchange which recalls Polyphemus' loutish humor:

> ἀλλ᾽ ἄγε οἱ καὶ ἐγὼ δῶ ξείνιον, ὄφρα καὶ αὐτὸς
> ἠὲ λοετροχόῳ δώῃ γέρας ἠέ τῳ ἄλλῳ
> δμώων, οἳ κατὰ δώματ᾽ Ὀδυσσῆος θείοιο.
>
> (20.296–98)[35]

Come, let me give him a guest-gift so that he may give it as an honor [geras] to a water pourer or some other of the servants in the halls of divine Odysseus.

There is still a further level of incongruity with heroic behavior, for Odysseus' avoiding the ox hoof evokes a scene of heroic battle (20.209–301), which threatens to become grim reality as Telemachus warns Ctesippus that he will run him through with his spear (20.305f.). When Penelope encourages the beggar in 21.312f. and reproaches Antinous, she also repeats the words that Ctesippus had used ironically to insult the beggar in the previous book (20.294f.). And immediately before Penelope's speech, Antinous threatens the beggar, using the paradigm of the unruly wedding feast of the Lapiths and Centaurs (21.295–304), a

---

[35] Cf. Od. 9.365–70. For other ironies in the xenos theme in connection with Ctesippus, see Nagy (1979) 261.

paradigm of whose true appropriateness to the situation he is totally unaware. At the end of book 21, however, the bard/beggar/hero, in "not reproaching his host," harks back to the coincidence of those three roles at the proper handling of such guest rituals in the palace of Alcinous. There, as we have observed, he is compared to both bard and beggar, but he is also honored as a hero and in fact tells of his heroic exploits (11.326ff.).

The parallels between the Phaeacian and Ithacan scenes go even further, for at the beginning of that scene in book 11, Queen Arete vindicates the honor of her guest: "He is my guest, and each one has a share of the honor" (338).[36] The little gesture of pride in her guest is the equivalent of Odysseus/beggar asserting in book 21 that he does not dishonor his host. Arete then requests that gifts be given him in his need (khrēzonti, 11.340), a word that also belongs to the semantic field of the beggar (cf. also 363ff.). Alcinous praises her for speaking "not off the mark" (344), as Odysseus here claims not to be "off the mark" in his shooting (21.425).

Odysseus with his next words in book 21 also evokes the proper role of song and the lyre at the banquet, calling them the "accompaniments of the feast" (anathēmata daitos, 430). In this way the disguised Odysseus reestablishes his place of honor at the feast in his own house, looks toward an image of an orderly banquet, implicitly also brings honor to the queen (cf. 311ff.), and cancels out the dishonor done to him via his bard, Phemius, whom the suitors compelled, by necessity, to sing "as the accompaniment of the feast" (1.152; cf. 21.430).[37]

The relations between bard, beggar, and hero in the Odyssey, rather than unambiguously reflecting the actual condition of bardic performance, seem to reflect, at least in part, a more or less conscious ideology of an aristocratic, premonetary world view. I have already noted the contradictions between three different views of the bard: attached to the palace but in a menial, subordinate relation on Ithaca; attached to the palace but honored almost as a peer among the Phaeacians; and a wandering craftsman equated with carpenter, doctor, and seer by Eumaeus. It may be possible to reconcile these views in a consistent

---

[36] I take the second half of 11.338 to mean that the honor of such a guest extends to everyone else in the party. So Van Leeuwen and Mendes da Costa (1897) on 11.338. This sense seems to suit best the context and the implicit contrast between "my guest" and the others adding more gifts. See also Heubeck in Heubeck and Hoekstra (1989) on 11.338.

[37] These are the only two occurrences of the phrase in the Homeric corpus. On the significance see above, Chapter 5, note 47, and Chapter 6, note 7.

historical picture; but I would suggest, rather, that the three-way relation between hero, bard, and beggar belongs to a systematic attempt in
the poem to dignify the poet's status while at the same time leaving
intact the impenetrable barrier between aristocratic princes and their
subjects. The contradictions, then, result from a delicate double strategy: to ennoble the bard but also to protect the privileged status of the
heroes.

I want to end by glancing briefly at the way in which writers in a
later, monetary economy translate into their own terms the ritualized
acts that express the honorific status of the poet. Leslie Kurke has shown
how Pindar adapts the heroic traditions to a more complex monetary
society, where the aristocratic patrons of the odes are often caught
between conflicting views of wealth and expenditure. Although the
poet must praise wealth and its uses, especially for epinician display,
Pindar deliberately avoids attributing "pay" or "profit" (misthos, kerdos)
to the poet and instead stresses the poet's relation of friendship or
kinship to his patron.[38] In terms of the issues that I have discussed in
Homer, Pindar, like an aristocrat, can present his ode as a kind of agalma,
a precious guest-gift, to the patron who commissions and pays for it,[39]
whereas in Homer the exchange of precious guest-gifts is reserved for
hero or king, and Homer never uses such objects as metaphors for his
poetry.[40] Many issues are involved in such a transference of the precious
object from exchange between nobles to the poet's work. The later,
literate poet, for instance, exhibits a greater consciousness of the tex-
tuality of his work. But the situation of honorific exchange also reflects
a heightened awareness of the poet's special status and a deliberate claim
to a worth and value that the Homeric bard claims only indirectly,
within the limits of the barrier separating aristocrat and commoners and
in the privileged, fairy-tale kingdom of the Phaeacians.

The Herodotean Life of Homer, dating perhaps from the fourth century B.C.E., is informative for the way in which it transposes the social
constructions of the Odyssey into literal terms and into the civic institutions of a later time.[41] The Life of Homer makes the poet literally a beggar
who wanders in need and earns his bread only with difficulty (123ff.).[42]

---

[38] See Kurke (1991) 225ff. and 240ff. on Isthmian 2.

[39] See ibid., 95ff. and 135ff.

[40] See above, Chapter 6, ad fin.

[41] Dating for the Herodotean Vita has ranged widely, from the fifth to the second
century B.C.E.: see Schmid and Stählin (1929) 1:84, note 7, and Momigliano (1971) 28.
For discussion of the Vita, see Lefkowitz (1981) 19–23, who also provides a translation
(her appendix 1), based on Wilamowitz's text.

[42] References are to the line numbers in Allen (1912) 5:192–218.

Arriving at Cyme, he goes not to a king's palace but to the clubs or gathering places of senior citizens (κατίζων ἐν ταῖς λέσχαις τῶν γερόν-των, 141). He so delights them with his poems that they offer to keep him at public expense so that he may make their city famous (146–48). An assembly is called, a public debate is held, but one member of the council opposes (Is there a hint of the contentious Euryalus in the Phaeacian palace in *Odyssey* 8?), and the plan comes to naught. Here aristocratic entertainment is reframed entirely in terms of the institutions of the polis. The frustrated bard responds to the disappointment with the curse that Cyme shall have no famous poet to assure its fame, a version of Odysseus/beggar's curse on Antinous for his insults (*Od.* 17.475f.) but also an inversion of the Homeric bard's preservation of the fame of heroes. Even this motif, however, is transposed into a civic, polis-oriented form.

The continuing vicissitudes of Homer's life take the form of financial and contractual transactions and civic relationships. In Phocaea he strikes a bargain with a schoolmaster named Thestorides and agrees to assign the authorship of his poems to this man in return for his keep (*Life of Homer*, 194ff.); but when Thestorides moves to Chios and becomes famous for Homer's poems, the latter reclaims his work. He later earns his living as a tutor (*paidagogos*, 327ff.), opens a school on Chios, where he teaches his poems to the children (339ff.), and eventually accumulates enough money (συλλεξάμενος δὲ βίον ἱκανόν) to marry and raise two daughters (343ff.). He stops at Samos on a voyage to Greece during the festival of the Apatouria, and the Samians express their regard for his poetry by entertaining him as a member of their phratry (399–432). Phaeacian appreciation of a good bard is now expressed through a uniquely civic institution: "He enters the phratry hall and reclines with the phratry members; and they honored him and held him in admiration" (430f.).

What seems to animate this amusing little work, in other words, is the systematic translation of the *Odyssey*'s use of aristocratic rituals of gift exchange and hospitality to indicate the status of the bard into terms of a later commercial economy and into the institutions of the polis. Eumaeus' classification of the singer among the traveling craftsmen may be an anomaly for the *Odyssey* itself, but it is here expanded to a scale and a context that would certainly have surprised and perhaps amused the creator of Phemius and Demodocus.

CHAPTER 8

The King and the Swineherd:
Rags, Lies, and Poetry

Books 14 and 15 are probably the most neglected of the *Odyssey*. Nothing particularly important happens, and so they seem to be an earthy pastoral interlude between the fairy-tale world that closes behind Odysseus when he reaches Ithaca (book 13) and the recognitions and plans of revenge that begin when he reveals himself to his son (book 16). Yet these two quiet books create a remarkable poetry of the everyday. The lowly setting in which the swineherd Eumaeus offers his honest but humble entertainment to the beggar who is Odysseus in disguise is all the more striking against the magnificent gifts that Menelaus and Helen bestow on Telemachus, with all the ceremony appropriate to the rituals of regal guest friendship (*xenia*) in book 15. Yet, as we shall see, the humbler character of these books is essential to their meaning for the world of the *Odyssey* and the nature of its poetry.

These books show an Odysseus whose adaptability, skill at storytelling, and improvisatory abilities enable him to establish close ties with a (supposed) stranger and share with him the reflections on the sufferings and uncertainties of life. In the long autumn night, he and Eumaeus sit up alone while the other servants sleep. They exchange the tales of their woes, simply true in Eumaeus' case, elaborate lies that have a more complex kind of truth in that of Odysseus/beggar. The firelight scene and late-night storytelling recall Odysseus' late-night narrative in Alcinous' palace. To be sure, the sojourn with Eumaeus stands at the opposite end of the social scale, and its tales are of humble men who have (supposedly) known servitude and hunger. Eumaeus' hut is a kind of rustic Phaeacia, an island of quiet, if modest, hospitality and the tranquil telling of life stories through which the hero prepares himself for the trials ahead. There are even some striking verbal similarities, as in these two passages:

νὺξ ἥδε μάλα μακρή, ἀθέσφατος, οὐδέ πω ὥρη
εὕδειν ἐν μεγάρῳ· σὺ δέ μοι λέγε θέσκελα ἔργα.

(11.373f.)

This night is very long, endless, nor is it yet the time to sleep in the hall. Do you then tell me your marvelous deeds.

αἵδε δὲ νύκτες ἀθέσφατοι· ἔστι μὲν εὕδειν,
ἔστι δὲ τερπομένοισι ἀκονέμεν· οὐδέ τί σε χρή,
πρὶν ὥρη, καταλέχθαι· ἀνίη καὶ πολὺς ὕπνος.

(15.392–94)

These nights are endless; one may sleep, but one may also take pleasure in listening; nor is there any need to lie down before it is the time, for much sleep is a vexation.

The differences, however, are characteristic of the gulf between fairyland and Ithacan reality. Whereas Odysseus tells his Phaeacian tale among carefree aristocrats wanting a night's entertainment on a charmed island, here he talks to a slave; and the two of them exchange life stories instead of heroic guest-gifts.[1] Each feels compassion for the trials and vicissitudes of the other as an equal. "Drinking and feasting in the hut," Eumaeus urges his guest, "let us take joy in the sorrowful woes [kēdea] of each other as we recall them" (15.399f.).[2] In place of the bronze walls, silver gates, and gold and silver dogs, fashioned by Hephaestus, in Alcinous' palace (7.86–94), there are wooden stakes to enclose the swine, real dogs that threaten Odysseus' life, and the materials of rustic life, from the leather that Eumaeus is carving into shoes at the opening of book 14 (23ff.) to the sheepskins and goatskins that he throws over the beggar at the end of the book (519).

Both the Phaeacians and Eumaeus receive a needy, anonymous trav-

---

[1] Dimock (1989) 191 emphasizes the importance of slavery in books 14 and 15, particularly the ease with which a man who is free may slip into slavery in this world of uncertainties. On the precariousness of status in the poem, see also P. Rose (1992) 106–8; also above, Chapter 7.

[2] Dimock (1989) aptly describes this passage as conveying "a real brotherhood of the woebegone" (204). Note too the reciprocal sympathy for these "woes" (kēdea) in 14.185. On the special bonding between Eumaeus and Odysseus/beggar, see G. Rose (1980) 287ff. and Roisman (1990) 218ff., although I do not think that this sympathy goes as far as her "covert recognition" of Odysseus by Eumaeus.

eler who has just made a mysterious crossing of water at a dangerous transitional moment. Among the Phaeacians this stranger encounters Nausicaa and is led by Athena in the guise of a young girl to the palace guarded by the silent golden dogs of Alcinous. On Ithaca he is met by Athena disguised as a young man, who leads him to the hut of Eumaeus, which is guarded by savage dogs that block his passage to safety and hospitality. Indeed, the detailed account of Alcinous' palace, with its walls of bronze, doors and columns of precious metals, bustle of many servants, rich festivities, and sheltered garden of ever fruitful trees (7.86–132), is echoed in miniature and in the low-mimetic mode in the brief but detailed account of Eumaeus' hut, with its stone walls topped by prickly pears, its enclosure of stakes, and its sties. These crude but effective barriers, of a type still to be seen in the southern Mediterranean, belong to a place designed not for comfort but for the practical work and dangers of herding. Both thematically and geographically, Eumaeus' hut stands between the Phaeacians and the suitors and so is the right place to introduce the hero to the prosaic details of his daily life on Ithaca, the smells, sights, and sounds of his island.

Pervaded by a gentle nostalgia, the recollections of a long-lost past, and in Eumaeus' case by the memories of a long-lost childhood happiness, the swineherd's hut is also the appropriate setting for Odysseus' first recognition of a loved one, the son whom he now sees as a young man (16.164ff.). And it is appropriately in Eumaeus' company that he sees his faithful old dog, Argus, who has just enough strength to wag his tail at the sight of his master before expiring on the dunghill where he has been thrown (17.290ff.). Yet the directness of human feeling that makes the scenes between beggar and swineherd so engaging is only a small part of the episode. These books, as we shall see, also have their share in the poem's recurrent themes of deceptive appearances, multiple identities, and paradoxical interplays of truth and falsehood. They form, therefore, an important link between the central themes of return and renewal and poetics.

Life Stories and Vicissitude

Readers of these books are often struck by the idiosyncratic fondness that they display toward dogs and toward the trusty swineherd himself, often addressed by the poet in the second person as "divine swineherd," δῖε συβῶτα or Εὔμαιε συβῶτα. Striking too is the rapidity with which

Eumaeus exhibits his good qualities of kindness, hospitality, and moral decency (14.33–71). Despite his servile status, he has taken the initiative of adding to his master's property and acquiring a slave of his own, a fact emphasized by the repetition of the line "apart from his mistress and old Laertes" at the two references to this detail (14.9 = 14.451). Dependent on his master for his future happiness and his hopes of a wife and some property (14.62–64), Eumaeus is the ideal servant, the good slave, utterly devoted to his master's welfare. In this role of the happy slave, he justifies and reaffirms the status quo. In his case the existing social order works. It is humane, decent, and just; and under it a good and simple man prospers and finds the rewards of industry, honesty, and fidelity.

The scenes with Eumaeus, then, reveal a part of Odysseus' past that we have not seen before, the loyalty that he can command from his servants in Ithaca. They imply an Odysseus who owns and oversees the lands and herds that the suitors have depleted. Eumaeus, trusty guardian of the slowly diminishing swine, is the appropriate figure to introduce Odysseus to the economic aspect of his past life and to the inroads that the suitors have made on his wealth (14.96–108, 417; 15.328ff.).

Although he is a slave, Eumaeus has the instincts of a nobleman, explained in part by his royal birth (book 15). This nobility, however, also disturbs us by the contrast with his present status. From the very first, he is introduced by the epithet *dios,* "brilliant," which is then applied to Odysseus in the very next verse (14.3f.). His hospitality, piety, and compassion in the lowly hut are a deliberate foil to the violence and outrages of the suitors, heedless devourers of the beasts that the swineherd so faithfully guards and raises for his master. The contrast becomes explicit in the second feast of roast pork (in the same evening) that Eumaeus serves Odysseus/beggar. It is better for them to eat "the best of the boars" themselves, Eumaeus says, before the suitors get them (14.414–17). Unknowingly, he thus gives his disguised master the tribute and entertainment that he deserves and that the suitors so harshly refuse.

This honoring of the master with the festive slaughter of "the best of the boars" is completed in another rustic feast near the end of the poem. After killing off the suitors, Odysseus goes to the house of Laertes in the country for the last of the recognitions. Before approaching his father, he orders the country servants to sacrifice "the best of the boars" (24.215; cf. 14.414). The meal that follows is the last one of the poem, and it celebrates the reintegration of Odysseus' extended household. Old Laertes is freshly bathed and reinvigorated, and Odysseus makes the final set of recognitions with his servants in the country, the aged Dolios and his family (24.386–412). The open feasting here, then, when Odysseus fully reclaims his land and his livestock, harks back to those earlier scenes of marginality and disguise when the swineherd defiantly ordered "the best of the boars" for his unknown guest.

Practical concerns dominate the scenes in Eumaeus' hut too, particularly food, clothing, and shelter. Despite his own humble circumstances, Eumaeus would keep and feed the beggar in his steading; and he proves all too accurate in predicting the harsh treatment that the beggar will receive from the suitors (14.325–39). The homeless beggar's tale about getting a cloak for a similar frosty night at Troy reminds both the swineherd and the audience that having a warm cloak can be a matter of life and death (14.486–88): "Zeus-born son of Laertes, much-devising Odysseus," the beggar quotes in his reminiscence of Troy, "I will not long be among the living, for the cold subdues me, not having a cloak." But the cloak is more than a matter of survival, for it is also the test that Odysseus uses to explore the limits of Eumaeus' hospitality. In addition, it defines the difference between the swineherd's workaday world and Phaeacian luxury. The Phaeacians, Alcinous says, take special delight in "changes of garment," εἵματα ἐξημοιβά (8.249). Odysseus has already enjoyed this abundance of clothing in the loan from Nausicaa which covers his nakedness and which later requires his tact in order to resolve an awkward moment (8.234–39, 295–307). In Eumaeus' world, however, such "changes of clothes" are not easily come by, "for there are not many changes of cloaks and chitons" (οὐ γὰρ πολλαὶ χλαῖναι ἐπημοιβοί τε χιτῶνες, 14.513; cf. 521, ἥ οἱ παρακέσκετ' ἀμοιβάς / ἕννυσθαι, "a cloak which lay there as a change of clothing"). Whereas the Phaeacians enjoy baths and bed (8.249), there is no mention of a bath in Eumaeus' hut; and the swineherd himself rejects a comfortable bed inside for a ruder place among his hogs, which he is reluctant to leave unguarded (οὐδὲ συβώτῃ / ἥνδανε . . . κοιμηθῆναι, "nor did it please the swineherd to sleep" 624f.).

When Eumaeus offers Odysseus his second meal and slaughters "the best of the boars," the preparation and details have a number of unique features that are especially suited to the rustic setting but also underline its generous hospitality.[3] This is the only time in the poem, for example, that we see the sacrifice of a boar, dispatched by a block of oak. He not

---

[3] Dimock (1989) 197 suggests that the more elaborate meal is a sign of greater trust. In one sense, it is also a deliberate defiance of the suitors: cf. 14.81ff.

only does not "forget the immortal gods" (14.420f.) but also, unlike those feasting in the palace, does not forget his master, for whose return he prays "to all the gods" (14.423f.). His following prayer to Hermes and the Nymphs is especially appropriate to the country setting and the swineherd's lowly pursuits (14.425–36), but it also marks Odysseus' renewed ties to the local divinities of his land.[4] Eumaeus honors Odysseus with the long chine in the full heroic manner (14.436f.); but we are still reminded of the slave-master relation in the term *anax*, "lord": "He honored Odysseus with the long chine of the white-toothed boar, and he gratified the heart of his lord" (14.437f.).

However modest his physical circumstances, in spirit Eumaeus resembles his betters. The pity that he expresses for Odysseus and the respect that he shows for Zeus Xenios (14.388f.) echo the pity and respect for the "wrath of Zeus Xenios" that Odysseus/beggar, according to his fictive autobiography, experienced from the Egyptian king (14.388f.; cf. 14.279–84). Even though this is a slave's house, Eumaeus' purchase of Mesaulios provides a servant who bustles about and dispenses the bread (14.449, 455), just as in the grand palaces of Alcinous or Menelaus, and of course, many of the formulas are the same (14.449–56). At the very end of the episode, the swineherd girds himself for the cold night in the sty like a warrior arming himself for battle (14.528–31): "First he threw the sharp sword over his stout shoulders; then he put on a cloak, very thick, defender against wind, and took up the fleece of a huge ram, well-nurtured, and took a sharp javelin, warder off of men and dogs." We may compare the brilliant Paris in *Iliad* 3.330–38, the first occurrence of the arming motif in that poem.[5]

These parallels and discrepancies between lowly herding and heroic life have their center in Eumaeus' personal history, for his slave status is an accident of fortune. He is originally of royal birth. His behavior in the previous book has already hinted at qualities beyond those of the ordinary swineherd. Homer, however, has carefully kept this royal birth hidden until Eumaeus tells his story. When Odysseus/beggar requests Eumaeus' tale, he wonders whether the swineherd had been

[4] Cf. the prayers to the Nymphs by Odysseus and Eumaeus at 13.355–60 and 17.240–46, respectively. See above, Chapter 3.

[5] On the arming motif see Armstrong (1958). There may be overtones of martial formulas here, too, at the entrance of Odysseus/beggar at the start of book 14: σκῆπτρον δέ οἱ ἔκπεσε χειρός, "the staff fell from his hand," in 14.31, and σκῦτος δέ οἱ ἔκπεσε χειρός, "the leather fell from his hand," in 14.34; this formula is often used for martial implements like the bow.

captured when his city was sacked or else kidnapped by pirates when he was out alone with sheep or cattle (15.384–88). The second possibility (386) would imply that Eumaeus had long been a herdsman and so a slave.

Eumaeus' father, however, ruled over a happy island called Syriē; and the place still glows in his memory as the paradise of his lost childhood.

> There is an island, called Syria, you may have heard of it,
> lying above Ortygia, where the sun makes his turnings;
> not so much a populous island, but a good one, good for
> cattle and good for sheep, full of vineyards, and wheat raising.
> No hunger ever comes on these people, nor any other
> hateful sickness, of such as befall wretched humanity;
> but when the generations of men grow old in the city,
> Apollo of the silver bow, and Artemis with him,
> comes with a visitation of painless arrows, and kills them.
>
> (15.403–11: Lattimore's translation)

Yet corruption lurks in this paradise in the form of the deceitful visitors, the Phoenicians, with their beguilements of jewelry and seduction, their lies, and their ready oaths (cf. 15.415–39, 458–63). Eumaeus would even now be king in his blissful homeland were it not for the cruel trick that life played on him when his nurse, seduced by a Phoenician sailor, kidnapped him into a life of slavery (15.415–84).

This kind of "what might have been" reflection, however, is just what this simple and matter-of-fact man does not allow himself. Eumaeus lives in the immediate present, with its tasks and problems, and does not sentimentalize.[6] His lone auditor commiserates (15.486f.): "Eumaeus, strongly did you stir the spirit in my breast relating each of these sufferings that you endured in your heart." This empathy in fact frames the tale, for Odysseus/beggar uttered a similar expression of emotional involvement when he urged Eumaeus to tell his story:

> ὦ πόποι, ὡς ἄρα τυτθὸς ἐών, Εὔμαιε συβῶτα,
> πολλὸν ἀπεπλάγχθης σῆς πατρίδος ἠδὲ τοκήων.
>
> (15.381f.; cf. 14.361f.)

------

[6] There are, however, possible hints of Eumaeus' sense of loss which anticipate his story, e.g., in 14.138–41, where Eumaeus, describing his missing Odysseus, says that he would never find so kindly a master, "not even if I come to the house of my mother and father when I was first born, and they themselves nurtured me."

Alas, how little you were, Eumaeus swineherd, when you were dashed far away from your native land and your parents.

Odysseus' responses perhaps indicate the poet's awareness of the tale's pathos and of the emotions that he knows it would arouse in an audience. But Eumaeus himself draws no such conclusions.

Equally remarkable is Eumaeus' lack of bitterness. He makes no excuses for his nurse's treachery, but he seems to have arrived at a balanced, almost dispassionate evaluation of this woman. Characteristically, Homer does not show us the stages between the childhood past and the mature adult's consciousness; but Eumaeus' straightforward account vividly re-creates the betrayal of the helpless child. The innocent trust and vulnerability are fully apparent in the details. When the nurse offers to take the child Eumaeus along as passage money for the Phoenicians, she describes her young charge as eagerly "running around outside" (15.451). When she carries out the kidnapping a little later, she "takes [him] by the hand" to embark on the Phoenician ship (465).[7]

In recounting this crime, Eumaeus is realistic but not accusatory. The grown man can reflect knowingly on the weakness of women and the power of "bed and love" to win over "even one who is decent" (15.421f.). He even makes allowances for the skill of the nurse's Phoenician seducer, with his clever speech about taking her back to see "the high-roofed hall of her father and mother, and [the parents] themselves, for they are still alive and are said to be wealthy" (432f.). Nevertheless, Eumaeus is clear about her greed and treachery as he recounts her offer of the kidnapped child as passage money (449–52). Reliving the episode through a little child's eyes, he sees her again hiding three goblets from his father's table in her dress as she runs to the ship, "and I followed her in my childish foolishness" (466–70).

Even when he describes the nurse's death on the voyage, Eumaeus is dry and matter-of-fact. He refrains from pointing up a moral or even mentioning justice:

ἑξῆμαρ μὲν ὁμῶς πλέομεν νύκτας τε καὶ ἦμαρ·
ἀλλ᾽ ὅτε δὴ ἕβδομον ἦμαρ ἐπὶ Ζεὺς θῆκε Κρονίων,

---

[7] Dimock (1989) 205 regards this detail of "taking me by the hand" in line 465 as the climax of the story, the first revelation that the small child is Eumaeus himself. That fact, however, is surely implied in Eumaeus' references to the king as his father and his house in 15.413–18.

τὴν μὲν ἔπειτα γυναῖκα βάλ' Ἄρτεμις ἰοχέαιρα,
ἄντλῳ δ' ἐνδούπησε πεσοῦσ' ὡς εἰναλίη κήξ.
καὶ τὴν μὲν φώκῃσι καὶ ἰχθύσι κύρμα γενέσθαι
ἔκβαλον· αὐτὰρ ἐγὼ λιπόμην ἀκαχήμενος ἦτορ.
τοὺς δ' Ἰθάκῃ ἐπέλασσε φέρων ἄνεμός τε καὶ ὕδωρ,
ἔνθα με Λαέρτης πρίατο κτεάτεσσιν ἑοῖσιν.
οὕτω τήνδε τε γαῖαν ἐγὼν ἴδον ὀφθαλμοῖσι.

(15.476–84)

For six days we sailed, night and day. But when Zeus son of Kronos
brought on the seventh day, Artemis who rejoices in her arrows struck
down the woman, and she thudded as she fell into the hold, like the kēx-
bird that dwells in the sea. They tossed her out, a prey to seals and fishes;
but I was left behind, troubled in my heart. Wind and water driving them
on brought them near to Ithaca, where Laertes purchased me for his
possessions. So did I come to look on this land with my eyes.

Artemis' arrow marks an ironic contrast with blissful Syriē, whose
people are never afflicted with disease but die of old age, when "Apollo
of the silver bow comes with Artemis and slays them with his gentle
missiles" (410f.); but it is an irony of which Eumaeus himself seems unaware. His factual, direct account recognizes that in a certain sense the
woman is a victim too, and he is emphatic about the cruelty and callous-
ness of the Phoenicians who throw her overboard. Yet his last memory
of that remote time is the vivid sense of the abandoned child's bewilder-
ment and helplessness: αὐτὰρ ἐγὼ λιπόμην ἀκαχήμενος ἦτορ, "But I
was left behind, troubled in my heart." This is a world where any of us
may be a child set adrift. "Wind and water" (ἄνεμός τε καὶ ὕδωρ) are
the material embodiments of the chance forces of life; and these elements have brought Eumaeus to Ithaca, "where Laertes purchased me
for his possessions."

Eumaeus' one-man audience not only reaffirms his compassion but
also points out that fortune is not always malign:

Εὔμαι', ἦ μάλα δή μοι ἐνὶ φρεσὶ θυμὸν ὄρινας
ταῦτα ἕκαστα λέγων, ὅσα δὴ πάθες ἄλγεα θυμῷ.
ἀλλ' ἦ τοι σοὶ μὲν παρὰ καὶ κακῷ ἐσθλὸν ἔθηκε
Ζεύς, ἐπεὶ ἀνδρὸς δώματ' ἀφίκεο πολλὰ μογήσας
ἠπίου, ὅς δή τοι παρέχει βρῶσίν τε πόσιν τε
ἐνδυκέως, ζώεις δ' ἀγαθὸν βίον.

(15.486–91)

Eumaeus, strongly indeed did you stir the spirit in my breast relating each
of these sufferings that you endured in your heart. And yet for you Zeus
placed evil beside good too, since in your great sufferings you came to the
house of a kindly man who provides food and drink generously, and you
live a good life.

His own life, the beggar notes, is still one of wandering: "But I have
come here wandering over many men's cities" (491f.). This line, which
evokes Odysseus' life as the man of many wanderings from the opening
line of the poem, reminds us that his wandering too, like that of
Eumaeus, has an end; and Zeus will also give him some measure of
happiness to balance the previous suffering.

There is still a further connection between the wandering beggar and
the swineherd, for Eumaeus' double identity as royal child and enslaved
wanderer mirrors the double identity of the disguised Odysseus.[8] Like
the child Eumaeus, Odysseus, according to his fictional autobiography, was twice betrayed by his supposed friends and helpers and nearly
sold into slavery, the first time, like Eumaeus, by Phoenician traders
(14.287–97, 339–59). Odysseus' tale is an adult counterpart of Eumaeus'
story. Even now he could conceivably become a victim of female
vulnerability to seduction should Penelope weaken, so that Eumaeus'
lines about the seduction of a woman of the household holds risks for
him as well (15.421f.; cf. 11.434, 24.202; also 18.164–303, 19.541–43).

More broadly, the life stories of the two men illustrate the chance
incidents of life, the power of fortune (*tuchē*) in this unstable world of
ships and sailors, and the precariousness of identity and status once one
leaves the security of one's *oikos* (house), with its firm bonds of house
and family, its rooted traditions, and its land-based, agrarian economy
(cf. 14.221–28). Odysseus' very presence as a beggar in rags and the
tales he tells to explain them not only illustrate these vicissitudes but
bring that precarious sea world of chance and insecurity into Eumaeus'
hut in his very person. The reality beneath his disguise exhibits the most
extreme form of such change: the king of Ithaca in rags begs his swineherd for food, shelter, and clothing. Yet Eumaeus' situation proves to be
exactly parallel: the settled, loyal swineherd is equally a royal victim of
chance and misfortune.

On the personal level, the tales that the two men exchange are parallel

---

[8] The connection is also reinforced by the repetition of the compassionate response in
each case: 14.361f. and 15.486f.

in function to the exchanges of tales in Menelaus' and Alcinous' palaces. In the *Odyssey* people communicate and establish friendship by telling the griefs of their lives, their *kēdea*. Sharing these *kēdea* creates a bond between human beings, for they thus recognize what can happen to all humans as suffering mortals, *deiloisi brotoisi*. Odysseus and Eumaeus show their reciprocity of feeling by responding to another's tales with almost exactly the same pair of lines. "Ah, wretched among strangers," Eumaeus says, "how very much you stirred my heart relating all the wanderings and sufferings you had" (14.361f.). "Eumaeus, how very much you stirred the heart in my breast," Odysseus/beggar says in his turn, "relating all the sufferings you had in your heart" (15.486f.). This exchange of tales of woe has its highest register in the meeting of Priam and Achilles in *Iliad* 24, the loftiest form in which the motif is played out in epic. *Odyssey* 14 and 15 are in the low-mimetic mode, to use Northrop Frye's terminology, a mode appropriate to the poem's mixture of different levels of society and of the heroic and the georgic.

According to the tale that the "beggar" tells of meeting Odysseus, the king has gone from rags to riches in his fortunate landfall among the Phaeacians (books 6–7) and in his supposed landfall among the Thesprotians and their ambiguous king Pheidon (14.320–26). The "beggar" has himself acquired similar wealth in his travels, this time from the hospitality of an anonymous Egyptian king (14.285f.; cf. also Menelaus in Egypt, 4.81–91). But another turn of the wheel of fortune brings the beggar back to rags again. After seven fat years in Egypt, a Phoenician deceives him and eventually sells him into slavery in Libya (14.288–97). He escapes in a shipwreck (14.301–15), and the cycle begins anew. After receiving generous hospitality from King Pheidon in Thesprotia (14.316–22), he is again betrayed by his supposed escort and stripped of his clothing and so arrives at Eumaeus' hut with only the miserable rags on his back (14.355–59).

Lessons could be drawn from the lives (fictional and real) of both Eumaeus and the "beggar": accept your lot, whatever it is; behave decently, and expect that the gods will reward you with a decent situation and the promise of improvement. Or, even a slave may have a nobleman's spirit. Such lessons could support both an aristocratic and an anti-aristocratic ethos, and it is not easy to choose between them.[9]

Odysseus' lies and Eumaeus' life story also illustrate the dangers of

[9] On the problem of class perspective, see P. Rose (1992) chapter 2, especially 99ff. and 106ff., with the literature there cited.

venturing beyond one's homeland and the traditional occupations of one's house of origin: one may lose one's status, roots, and freedom and become a marginal figure, an outcast dependent on the goodwill of strangers. In the analogous life stories of Phoenix and Patroclus in the *Iliad,* however, the loss of status results from family violence and individual passion rather than from the vicissitudes of travel or encounters with foreign merchants or seamen (see *Il.* 9.447–84 and 23.84–90). The *Odyssey,* on the other hand, allows for the potential windfall that such adventures may bring and thus indirectly implies a new economic awareness, the commercial potential of trade and travel.[10] In the heroic world of the *Iliad,* those who become temporary outcasts, like Phoenix and Patroclus, can find a new life only by being reabsorbed into an aristocratic setting and becoming the companions (*therapontes*) of a king or hero. These proto-novelistic tales of the *Odyssey,* however, reflect an age interested in commerce, wealth, and colonization and in the rewards and the risks of both enterprises.

The *Odyssey* contains one remnant of the Iliadic pattern, the exiled seer, Theoclymenus. When he encounters Telemachus on the beach at Pylos, he asks to be taken on board, for, as he explains, he has killed a man of his tribe and is running away from the avenging kinsmen who are pursuing him (15.272–78). In this post-Iliadic world, such a man can no longer be absorbed into a hero's retinue, there to resume the life of warrior and nobleman. In fact, Theoclymenus proves somewhat of an embarrassment, given the instability in Odysseus' palace. In the absence of the king and the suitors' effective control of the hospitality in the palace, Telemachus is reluctant to receive this guest. He considers sending him to the suitor Eurymachus, changes his mind, and finally has to shunt him off to his friend Peiraeus (cf. 15.508–46). It is almost as if this poem does not quite know what to do with a figure of the old pattern. Once he has performed his narrative function of giving his dire prophetic warnings in 20.350–57, Theoclymenus goes off immediately to the house of Peiraeus and is never heard from again (20.371f.).

The *Odyssey,* however, does suggest a broader range of options for men who leave home, especially if, unlike the outmoded Theoclymenus, they have a commercial bent. In his alleged life story, for instance, Odysseus/beggar gets bored with his settled family life (14.211–28) and joins Idomeneus to fight at Troy (14.235–42). But he can also make his way in a world of trade and shipping, and with a bit of luck

[10] See Redfield (1983) 233ff. and M. Finley (1965) 65ff.; see above, Chapter 7.

and the right contacts (the right Phoenicians), he can accumulate great wealth in a foreign land. Such successes obviously have something of the sailor's yarn about them; they are tall tales of striking it rich beyond one's wildest dreams. But they also reflect the dreams and anxieties of this new world of trade and colonization. Those who leave the traditional agricultural economy and take to their ships and the sea undergo sudden, unpredictable shifts in status, both up and down.

Both Eumaeus and the beggar reflect the two possibilities of this open world of the sea and travel. They are success stories, in a way, but also warning examples. A man may win enormous wealth, easily granted by a lucky landing in a rich and exotic land with a generous king; or he may be reduced to rags, misery, and slavery. The two sides may reflect late Homeric society's ambivalence toward the potential of these wider horizons. We see the doubts, of course, without the hopefulness, in Hesiod's suspicion of the sea and trading in the *Works and Days*.[11] In *Odyssey* 14 the two sides are concretely embodied in complementary ways in the two men whom we first meet in Ithaca. The swineherd is a king fallen from noble birth to slavery; the ragged beggar is in fact the king of the land. But the *Odyssey*, like the romances to which it eventually leads many centuries later, takes a more optimistic view of these vicissitudes than does Hesiod. The slave does not seem to regret his loss of kingship and is content with and devoted to a good master. The real king is a beggar only temporarily, and these very beggar's rags are the magical effect of a divine stratagem to restore him to his palace, his wealth, and his family.

In the Iliadic world such changes of status have a more somber tone and less remediable possibilities. In the *Iliad,* captive women such as Chryseis or Briseis in the present or Andromache in the future face servitude forever (*Il.* 1.29–31, 6.454–65, 19.287–302). The *Odyssey* initiates the picaresque mode, in which abrupt reversals of fortune are integral to the plot. Its world view, unlike the *Iliad*'s, is ultimately nontragic, and so it envisages change, in the comic mode, from misfortune to good fortune (see Aristotle *Poetics* 13.1452b33ff.). When Odysseus is reminded of this tragic world of war by Demodocus' song of his victory at Troy, rendered in the happy palace of Alcinous, he weeps like one of those captive women whose change from freedom to slavery is just beginning and is presumably permanent (8.521–31).[12]

---

[11] Hesiod *Works and Days* 641–53, 667–69, 687–92.
[12] On this passage see above, Chapter 6, with note 13.

The Wanderer's Truth: Punning, Lying, and Truth

If Eumaeus has the transparent simplicity of the completely straight-forward, honest man, Odysseus/beggar has the complexity of the *polutropos* and the *polumētis,* the "man of many turnings" and the "man of many wiles." His physical appearance, status, and language are both double and duplicitous. Despite all the deceptiveness of his clothes and his tales, however, Odysseus is able to elicit some solid truth from those he encounters. As the wandering guest and disguised beggar, he serves as the touchstone that distinguishes the good from the bad in those who receive him. When at the end of book 14 he offers to let Eumaeus put him to death if he is lying about Odysseus' return, Eumaeus imme-diately rejects the proposal as impious and immoral. Yet his life story, fictitious though it is, has a kind of generic truthfulness. It can touch a deep chord in the loyal, decent servant and lead him to reflect on the vicissitudes that have marked his own life.

Odysseus' fictitious tales increasingly demonstrate that the instability of fortune is only one aspect of the deceptiveness of appearances in the world of the *Odyssey.* Because the hero spends the latter half of his poem in the disguise of a traveling, hungry beggar who is also an expert raconteur, clothing, lying, and wandering are closely interconnected in the contrasts of appearance and reality inherent in the disguise plot. And because Odysseus' lies in this disguise are often only a slightly recast version of his actual experiences, the poem insistently develops the irony that lies speak a form of the truth. Both sets of irony also bear on the *Odyssey*'s self-consciousness about its poetics, its exploration of how tales are fabricated, received, and believed or disbelieved.

These ironies accumulate with the growing hints of the disguised wanderer's true status. The pattern develops at an early stage of the Ithacan adventures. The hero tells his first Ithacan lie to his patron goddess, Athena, but she turns the tables on him, deceiving him with a disguise of her own (13.221–351)—the only occasion when his skill at lying does not work.[13] But even here, as his goddess remarks, his lying reveals his "insatiable" love of trickery (cf. δόλων ἆτ[ε], 13.293). In the next book, when the disguised hero, in desperate need of food and clothing, meets his swineherd, Eumaeus, he in effect re-creates the role

---

[13] The scene has been much discussed; for comment and further references, see Pucci (1987) 100–109.

of the heroic Odysseus at Troy by recalling a night exploit that, though never told in the *Iliad,* is fully consistent with the Iliadic Odysseus. In this episode the disguised Odysseus both describes and enacts Odysseus' characteristic mode of success as he tells how the "real" Odysseus showed his famed *mētis* or *dolos* by winning a cloak for the distressed narrator, the beggar/wanderer, thereby saving his life (14.462–506).[14]

The emphasis on the cloak places Odysseus' entrance to the world of the palace under the sign of disguise and concealment foreshadowed in the advice he received from Teiresias and Agamemnon in Hades to return in secret (11.120, 442–44, 455f.). It thus constitutes the first stage of his stratagem for defeating the suitors. This gradual movement toward recovering his kingship is strongly reinforced by the "beggar's" wish of 14.503–6: should someone give him a cloak, he would again feel the vigor of his youth and not be in the dishonored state marked by his present ugly garments.[15] Eumaeus' bestowal of the cloak implies the renewal of Odysseus' strength, as of old, for it not only provides another proof of the skill as narrator, liar, and trickster that Odysseus will need among his enemies but also validates the lie's kernel of truth, that is, the special prowess of Odysseus in his characteristic form of cleverness: deception, a night exploit, and an ambush, or *lochos* (ὑπὸ Τροίην λόχον, 14.469). In effect, through his lies, disguise, and cleverness, Odysseus will convert the banquet hall into the bloody setting of just such an ambush.[16]

The fact that Odysseus proposes a cloak as a reward for the good news of his own return early in the scene with Eumaeus (14.152–56) adds still another irony to the inversions of truth and false appearances, for by his very presence on Ithaca, Odysseus/beggar automatically fulfills his prophecy of the king's return and thus assures his entitlement to the cloak that he will in fact receive, if only temporarily, at the end of the book. As Sheila Murnaghan observes, "By specifying that his reward for telling good news that proves also to be true should be a set of new clothes, Odysseus equates the two roles he plays in disguise—

---

[14] Thus in his tale the "beggar" addresses Odysseus by his heroic epithet, one that is particularly appropriate to the quality of Odysseus that is being both praised and reenacted: διογενὲς Λαερτιάδη, πολυμήχαν' Ὀδυσσεῦ (14.486).

[15] On the importance of clothing in Odysseus' return, see above, Chapters 2 and 4; Block (1985) 1–11; and Murnaghan (1987) chapter 1 and 108–9. On clothing in the Eumaeus episode especially, see G. Rose (1980) 293.

[16] For the close associations between the Iliadic motif of the *lochos* and Odysseus' successful stratagems in the *Odyssey,* see Edwards (1985) 27–41; also Haft (1983–84) 298.

destitute beggar and herald of his own return—and suggests that both will come to an end when his return is revealed."[17]

The "Truth" of the Wanderer

These ironies and paradoxes are reflected in a remarkable set of wordplays early in the scene with Eumaeus, a consistent pattern of puns on the word for "true," ἀληθής, and various forms of the verb ἀλάομαι, "wander," or its agent noun ἀλήτης, "wanderer." Responding to Eumaeus' hints about his master as one who perished at Troy, Odysseus/beggar disingenuously asks who the master is.

> εἰπέ μοι, αἴ κέ ποθι γνώω τοιοῦτον ἐόντα.
> Ζεὺς γάρ που τό γε οἶδε καὶ ἀθάνατοι θεοὶ ἄλλοι,
> εἴ κέ μιν ἀγγέλαιμι ἰδών· ἐπὶ πολλὰ δ' ἀλήθην.
>
> (14.118–20)

Tell me, if perchance I may know him, such as he was; for Zeus and the other immortal gods know somehow whether I have seen him and so might bring news of him, for I have wandered much.

In his reply, the swineherd picks up his last word, ἀλήθην, "I wandered," and intertwines it with its near homophone, ἀληθής, "true."

> ὦ γέρον, οὔ τις κεῖνον ἀνὴρ ἀλαλήμενος ἐλθὼν
> ἀγγέλλων πείσειε γυναῖκά τε καὶ φίλον υἱόν,
> ἀλλ' ἄλλως κομιδῆς κεχρημένοι ἄνδρες ἀλῆται
> ψεύδοντ', οὐδ' ἐθέλουσιν ἀληθέα μυθήσασθαι.
> ὃς δέ κ' ἀλητεύων Ἰθάκης ἐς δῆμον ἵκηται,
> ἐλθὼν ἐς δέσποιναν ἐμὴν ἀπατήλια βάζει.
>
> (14.122–27)

Old man, no man who came here in his *wanderings* and gave report of [Odysseus] would persuade his wife and dear son, but *wanderers [alētai]*, needing provisions, *tell lies* at random, nor do they wish to tell the *truth [alēthea]*. But whoever in his *wandering* comes to the town of Ithaca, he goes to my mistress and *speaks deceptively*.

[17] Murnaghan (1987) 109.

Eumaeus is drawing on a motif that runs all through Odysseus' tales, namely, that the "wanderer" is more likely to tell lies than truths. The special relationship between wandering and truth or falsehood is suggested here in the collocations ἀλῆται ψεύδονται . . . ἀληθέα . . . ἀλητεύων . . . ἀπατήλια, "wanderers tell lies . . . truth . . . wandering . . . deceptively."

Eumaeus has his own reasons for associating "wanderers" with "liars," for he has had experience of another "wanderer over the earth," a man from Aetolia, who accepted his hospitality but deceived him (14.379–81).[18] Odysseus/beggar, however, staunchly holds to the truth of his prophecy of Odysseus' return: if he is lying, he offers, Eumaeus may have him put to death, "so that another beggar too may avoid being a deceiver" (ὄφρα καὶ ἄλλος πτωχὸς ἀλεύεται ἠπεροπεύειν, 14.400). Ithaca in its present state is in many ways more dangerous and less trusting than the land of the Phaeacians, once they have welcomed Odysseus. Their king, Alcinous, more readily accepted the truth of his wandering guest's narrative. When, in Alcinous' palace, Odysseus paused in his long account of his travels, the Phaeacian king congratulated him on his skill as a narrator: he is not one of those "deceivers and thieves and fashioners of lies" such as the earth feeds in large numbers (ἠπεροπῆα . . . καὶ ἐπίκλοπον . . . ψεύδεα τ' ἀρτύνοντας, 11.364–66). All these passages rest on the assumption that the wanderer or beggar is likely to be a liar who will say anything to get food to fill his raging "belly" (gastēr, cf. 17.283–89).[19] These associations give a deeper irony to the wordplays in 14.119–27, for this wanderer, though in one sense a flagrant liar, is actually speaking the truth.

The ironies are especially strong in the phrase ἄνδρες ἀλῆται ψεύδονται (wandering men tell lies, 14.124f.), in which (with a very slight strain on morphology) might be heard the paradoxical relation between "truth" and "lying" that is in fact quite appropriate here.[20] Eumaeus is moved by the beggar's account of Odysseus among the Thesprotians but still maintains his disbelief and his distrust in "wanderers." Once more "wandering" and "lying" are associated:

---

[18] On the wanderer as liar, see Stanford (1958–61) on 14.122.

[19] On the motif of the gastēr, see above, Chapter 7, with note 25.

[20] There is, of course, a difference of accent between ἀληθής (true) and the various forms of ἀλήθην (wandered) and its agent noun ἀλήτης (wanderer), but in the latter case the difference between theta and tau in the original pronunciation would have been only of aspiration. Though Homer rarely pays attention to differences of national language, might we also recall perhaps that the speaker is a Syriē-born swineherd?

ἀ δειλὲ ξείνων, ἦ μοι μάλα θυμὸν ὄρινας
ταῦτα ἕκαστα λέγων, ὅσα δὴ πάθες ἠδ' ὅσ' ἀλήθης.
ἀλλὰ τά γ' οὐ κατὰ κόσμον, ὀίομαι, οὐδέ με πείσεις,
εἰπὼν ἀμφ' Ὀδυσῆϊ. τί σε χρὴ τοῖον ἐόντα
μαψιδίως ψεύδεσθαι;

(14.361-65)

Ah, wretched among strangers how very much you stirred my heart
relating all the *wanderings* and sufferings you had. But these things, I
think, are not in right order, nor will you persuade me when you speak
about Odysseus. Why, being such as you are, should you tell *empty lies?*

This particular "wanderer," however, is not only speaking the truth in
his promise of Odysseus' return but is also indirectly performing that
truth in the present scene through his story of the cloak. That tale of
Odysseus' winning a cloak at Troy is acted out before us in the way in
which this disguised Odysseus wins a cloak on Ithaca. Here, the fictional Odysseus of the beggar's tale wins a cloak for the real Odysseus
before us. He thus displays before our eyes the "device" (*mēchanē*) of
"Odysseus of the many devices" (*polumēchanos Odusseus*, 14.486).

   Eumaeus responds to the performative truth of this tale by the beggar
and grants the cloak, but he does so in terms that continue the paradox
of the wanderer's lying truth. He praises the beggar's tale:

ὦ γέρον, αἶνος μέν τοι ἀμύμων, ὃν κατέλεξας,
οὐδέ τί πω παρὰ μοῖραν ἔπος νηκερδὲς ἔειπες.

(14.508f.)

Old man, blameless is the tale that you have told, nor have you spoken an
account that is against good order and without profit.[21]

By describing this account as "a tale not without profit," οὐδέ . . . ἔπος
νηκερδές, he tips his hat, as it were, to the power of Odyssean *mētis* and
allows himself (knowingly or not) to be taken in by it as were the
soldiers of the "real" Odysseus on that cold night at Troy. *Kerdos*,
"profit," is semantically associated with cleverness, trickery, and lying,

---

[21] Eumaeus' words would convey an even greater sense of solidarity with Odysseus if
ainos here has implications of "marked" speech that has a special meaning for a closed
group: see Nagy (1990) 148ff., 237.

and it is a quality for which Odysseus is particularly distinguished.[22] At his landing on Ithaca, when he refuses to tell the truth (οὐδ' ὅ γ' ἀληθέα εἶπε), he is demonstrating his "mind very wily at profit" (νόος πολυκερδής, 13.254f.) in proper Odyssean fashion. In the same scene, *kerdaleos*, "wily at profit," is Athena's first address to him when she reveals her identity (13.291). His arrival at Eumaeus' hut produced another demonstration of this quality in the *kerdosunē* (wiliness) with which he sat down before the fierce dogs (14.31). Possibly the litotes of 14.509, οὐδέ ... νηκερδές, "not without wiles" (the only occurrence of νηκερδές in the *Odyssey*), hints at the paradoxical interchanges of appearance and truth here at the end of the book. Eumaeus acknowledges the skill of Odyssean *kerdosunē* precisely when it outsmarts or double-crosses him by trapping him through his own supposed cleverness, in this case his certainty that a wanderer cannot speak truth or, in the terms of the wordplays here, that an ἀλήτης (wanderer) cannot be ἀληθής (true).

These paradoxes of a wandering liar who speaks the truth have a further meaning, namely, a self-referential allusion to the mixture of falsehood and truth that constitutes much of the pleasure, or *terpsis*, that the poem as a whole conveys. Like Hesiod, the poet of the *Odyssey* is keenly aware of the special "pleasure" that his tales of the marvelous can produce, tales that seem to go beyond "truth" in their fabulous adventures.[23] It is an aspect of the *Odyssey*'s poetic self-consciousness that the passages that question the truth of the wandering beggar also allude to the art of the poet. Alcinous, shortly after his comment on Odysseus' truth-telling in book 11 cited above, p. 180, does so explicitly ("You told the tale skillfully, like a bard," 11.368). The "beggar," in telling Eumaeus his story of Odysseus at Troy, refers to his narrative as "singing" (ἀεῖσαι, 14.464). Eumaeus, in reporting that encounter to Penelope, compares the "enchantment" of his tales to that of a bard who "having his skill from the gods sings his lovely words to mortals" (17.518f.). Penelope, interested by this report, harks back to the themes

---

[22] On the importance of *kerdos* words in Odysseus' ruses on Ithaca, see Roisman (1990) 219, 225–26, 230.

[23] See Hesiod *Theog.* 27–28, 97–103 and Thalmann (1984) 140ff. On the *Odyssey*'s self-consciousness about its poetics, see above, Chapters 5–7, with the further references there cited; also Walsh (1984) chapter 1, Thalmann (1984) chapter 6, and Segal (1988) 125ff. P. Rose (1992) 139 also suggests that the *Odyssey*'s interest in punning and in significant names may also reflect its specific interest in "text production" at a moment of transition between an oral and a literate culture. On the other hand, oral performance in itself probably sensitizes the poet/singer/reciter to the sounds of words and their possible exploitation.

of deception, disguise, cloaks, and true-speaking in book 14 when she promises to give the beggar a cloak "if I find him speaking everything flawlessly" (νημερτέα πάντ᾽ ἐνέποντα, 17.556).

The references to the "lying" wanderer's narratives in book 14, moreover, suggest the proem's general description of Odysseus as a much tossed and much wandering hero: ἄνδρα . . . πολύτροπον, ὅς μάλα πολλὰ / πλάγχθη . . . / πολλὰ δ᾽ ὅ γ᾽ ἐν πόντῳ πάθεν ἄλγεα, "the man of many turnings, who was much tossed . . . and suffered many woes on the sea" (1.1–4). We may compare the expressions used by or about the "beggar" in book 14: ἐπὶ πολλὰ δ᾽ ἀλήθην, "I wandered much" (14.120); ὅσα δὴ πάθες ἠδ᾽ ὅσ᾽ ἀλήθης, "all the things that you suffered and all your wanderings" (14.362); and ἐπὶ γαῖαν ἀληθείς, "wandering over the earth" (14.380). In book 16 Odysseus takes off his disguise for the first time in Ithaca and reveals his true identity to his son in these terms:

> οὐ μὲν γάρ τοι ἔτ᾽ ἄλλος ἐλεύσεται ἐνθάδ᾽ Ὀδυσσεύς,
> ἀλλ᾽ ὅδ᾽ ἐγὼ τοιόσδε, παθὼν κακά, πολλὰ δ᾽ ἀληθείς,
> ἤλυθον εἰκοστῷ ἔτεϊ ἐς πατρίδα γαῖαν.
>
> (16.204–6)

No other Odysseus will come here, but I, as you see me here, after suffering many woes, after wandering much, have come in the twentieth year to my native land.

In harking back both to the previous passages in book 14 and to the proem of the epic as a whole, he is in effect now assuring Telemachus that this hero is no "other Odysseus" than the Odysseus of this poem, a master of lies and disguise who, like his poet, achieves his ultimate truth through devious paths and through a paradoxical mixture of truth and false appearances.

PART THREE

GODS AND PROPHETS

CHAPTER 9

Teiresias in the Yukon:
On Folktale and Epic

On December 21, 1982, the following entry appeared in the *New York Times:*

> WHITEHORSE, Yukon Territory. Some of the boys in a saloon here the other night were talking about a local woman who had won $1,800 in a lottery. The consensus was that her decision to put the money in the bank showed a sorry lack of ambition. "What I'd do," said one, "is tie a snow shovel to the hood of my car and drive south until nobody had the faintest idea what the damn thing was."

This anecdote is the latest version (so far as I know) of a folklore motif that has its earliest appearance in Teiresias' prophecy about Odysseus and the planting of his oar (*Od.* 11.121–37).[1] It has long been recognized as one of the most tenacious bits of folklore to have survived into modern times. Labeled by the folklorist Richard Dorson as "The Story of the Sailor Who Went Inland," versions of the oar mistaken for a winnowing fan have been collected from the medieval to the modern period, from the Mediterranean to Maine. In Greece the story is most familiar in the tale of Saint Elias, as an etiological account of why his shrines are on the tops of mountains.[2] This example from the Yukon illustrates how widespread and transformable this motif can be.

---

[1] *New York Times,* December 21, 1982, section A, p. 2, column 3. Hansen (1990) 261 noted this article independently and published a part of it in his essay. I wrote this chapter in 1989, before the appearance of Hansen's essay. Our interpretations and concerns are quite different.

[2] See Dorson (1964) 38–39; for further bibliography, see Hansen (1976) 221–30 and Hansen (1977) 27–48, especially 28–30.

This little anecdote gives to the harshness of the Yukon an almost mythical remoteness that corresponds, albeit only approximately, to the spirit of its ancient source, the distant land to which Odysseus will wander after his return to Ithaca. The *New York Times* article continues:

> It is a time-honored sentiment. Robert Service, the gold rush poet, wrote that "some say God was tired" when He made the Yukon, where Service described as "the cussedest land that I know."
>
> Snow can fall almost any month of the year, temperatures of 40 degrees below zero and lower are common and these days the sun is rising after 10 A.M. and setting around 3:30 P.M.
>
> The world's economic tailspin has made things harsher still for a territory that depends on industrialized countries to buy the minerals that run through its rocks like filling in a rich cake. For the first time since the 1893 gold rush, no mines are operating in the Yukon. By next spring more than 5,000 of the 26,000 people who live in the territory are expected to be gone.

To return from Alaska to the Hades more familiar to classicists, we recall that Teiresias foretells that Odysseus must eventually journey to a place where his oar is mistaken for a winnowing fan, so distant is this place from the marine setting of the hero's trials.

> When you have slain the suitors in your halls, either by guile or openly with sharp bronze, then go forth, taking a well-fitted oar, until you come to men who know not the sea or eat food mixed with sea salt or know crimson-cheeked ships or well-fitted oars that are wings for ships. And I shall tell you a sign, very clear, and it will not escape your notice. When another traveler, meeting you, says that you hold a winnowing fan on your bright shoulder, then fixing the well-fitted oar in the earth make lovely sacrifices to lord Poseidon, a ram and a bull and a boar mounter of sows; and then go homeward and make holy hecatombs to the immortal gods who hold the broad heavens, all of them in due succession. And to you yourself death will come from the sea, very mild, which will slay you when you have reached bright old age; and around you your people will be prosperous. I tell you these things without error. (*Od.* 11.119–37)

The episode has been harshly treated by analysts, who have often regarded it as a late interpolation that would harmonize Odysseus' mild death here with the version in the later *Telegonia*.[3] And Odysseus'

---

[3] For discussion and bibliography that is more recent, see Heubeck in Heubeck and Hoekstra (1989) on 11.100–137 (pp. 82–83) and on 11.121–37 (pp. 84–85); also Heubeck

dismissal of the prophecy in 11.139–44, to which we shall turn presently, seemed to be one of those places where the sharp-eyed analyst could most clearly pick out the rough seams of badly stitched together pieces of tradition.[4] There is no need to fight these battles again here; but the present study will, I hope, provide further arguments for the narrative integrity of these passages.

In Homer and in most of the folkloristic examples cited by Dorson and William Hansen, the oar mistaken for another implement belongs to a nautical context; and to the sailor, this mistake is the ultimate sign of otherness, the indication of a way of life totally antithetical to his own. It is, then, the appropriate closure for a hero whose dominant characteristic is "seeing the cities of many men and coming to know their minds" (Od. 1.3).[5] To find a people totally unfamiliar with the sea is the final experience of the alien and unfamiliar. But more important, the journey of this sea-tossed sufferer (ὃς μάλα πολλὰ / πλάγχθη, 1.1f.) finds its peaceful end when he reaches a place where the sea and its ways are unknown. This is the place for him to "fix the well-fitted oar in the earth" (γαίῃ πήξας εὐῆρες ἐρετμόν, 11.129 = 23.276). The gesture is the sign that what awaits him is "death most mild, away from the sea" in peaceful old age (11.134–36), the death of a settled king, not an unlucky hero and wanderer.[6]

Viewed in terms of the return plot as a whole, this movement away from the sea completes the poem's pattern of escape from the sea or a meeting of sea and land that in one way or another closes off the sea. The most striking example is the framing of the return by a shipwrecked sailor's rescue to the land, literally by Odysseus in reaching Scheria (5.390ff.), figuratively by Penelope in the simile that compares her joy in recognizing Odysseus to the sight of land by swimmers whose ship has been wrecked by Poseidon (23.233–40).[7] On the verge of his decisive sea-crossing in the Phaeacians' magical ship, the hero is compared in his impatience to a hungry farmer plowing his fields (13.31–35). When he has left behind his wanderings on the sea, that marine world is

---

in Russo, Fernández-Galiano, and Heubeck (1992) on 23.247–88 (p. 340). See also Hansen (1977) 32ff. and Peradotto (1985) 429–55, especially 438ff.

[4] See Carpenter (1946) 146.

[5] Cf. Peradotto (1985) 445n. 27.

[6] Whether ἐξ ἁλός in 11.134 = 23.281 means "coming from the sea" or "removed from the sea" has been discussed since antiquity. Though one cannot exclude the ambiguity inherent in oracular language, the latter is the more probable: see Hansen (1977) 42–48. For the oar in relation to the life cycle depicted in the Odyssey, see Falkner (1989) 21–67, especially 49ff.

[7] See above, Chapter 3.

closed off forever as Poseidon turns the Phaeacian ship to stone, blocking their harbor and making them cease from conveying men over the sea (13.149–84). Their last action in the poem, as is Odysseus' in his remote future, is to appease the angry Poseidon with sacrifices (13.181–87; cf. 11.130–32).[8] In his first private interview with Penelope, in disguise, Odysseus brings together the fertility of the sea and of the earth as part of her honor as the queen of a fertile land (19.112–14). A ship's cable will fasten the doors of the hall to enable him to take complete vengeance on the suitors (21.391f.); and he will use the "rope of a dark-prowed ship" to hang the delinquent maidservants (22.465).[9]

The unrecognizability of the snow shovel in the Yukon marks a remote place and time of desiderated wealth, here associated with the lucky win of eighteen hundred dollars. In the *Odyssey* the gain implicit in the unknown oar is, of course, not the grossly defined lump sum of money discussed by "the boys in a saloon" but the peaceful end of a life of wandering and seafaring. In both cases, however, the unfamiliarity of the workaday instruments belongs to an escapist mood, a life easier than the present toilsome existence.

It is characteristic of the sacred background and ritual elements in the Homeric poems that Odysseus is told not merely to plant the oar in the ground but also to perform a sacrifice to Poseidon, the hostile god of the sea (11.130f.). Indeed, the oar has sometimes been regarded as a cultic dedication, one marking the tale as an *aition* (cause or origin) for shrines of Poseidon in inland places such as Arcadia.[10] Teiresias, in fact, gives a prominent place to Poseidon in the opening words of his prophecy:

> νόστον δίζηαι μελιηδέα, φαίδιμ' 'Οδυσσεῦ·
> τὸν δέ τοι ἀργαλέον θήσει θεός· οὐ γὰρ ὀίω
> λήσειν ἐννοσίγαιον, ὅ τοι κότον ἔνθετο θυμῷ,
> χωόμενος ὅτι οἱ υἱὸν φίλον ἐξαλάωσας.
>
> (11.100–103)

You seek your honey-sweet return, brilliant Odysseus, but the god will make this hard, for I do not think that you will escape notice of the Earthshaker, who put anger in his heart, wrathful because you blinded his dear son.

The hero's intense desire for the return (*nostos*) is at once qualified by the divine power who has been its chief obstacle.

[8] For the many problems in this scene, see Peradotto (1985) 446ff.
[9] See above, Chapter 3.
[10] See Hansen (1977) 32ff.

This element of divine vengeance, with its theological implications, is one of the features that distinguishes the Homeric motif from its folkloristic transformations.[11] But there is also another important difference. In contrast to the folklore versions, Homer the poet looks beyond the moment when the hero arrives with his unfamiliar implement. This is the point at which most of the folklore examples end, the punchline, as it were, of their anecdotal style.

In the grand, continuous narrative of the epic, the motif of escape from toil signaled by the mistaken oar stands in sharp contrast to the surrounding events. In the prophecy of Teiresias, as we have noted, it forms the final point of the return with which the prophet begins (cf. 11.100, "You seek your honey-sweet return, brilliant Odysseus"). Yet Odysseus himself seems to find little comfort in the remote death of peaceful old age. He seems remarkably indifferent about the end of his life and merely acknowledges his future destiny as "what the gods themselves have spun out" (11.139), a phrase that suggests an attitude of resignation in a cool and distanced perspective.[12] Instead he turns back to the question of his mother, whom he saw but refrained from addressing just before Teiresias' arrival (11.84–89). The contrast between Teiresias' distant vision over the whole course of a mortal life and the hero's immediate wish to address the mother whom he left alive years ago in his homeland belongs to the poem's large concern with the nature of mortality, in this case expressed in the different attitudes of a shade in Hades and a living man from the upper world.

A different but analogous contrast occurs when Odysseus has in fact accomplished his *nostos* and is reunited with Penelope. When the first wave of joy and weeping is past, Odysseus checks Penelope's happiness with a brief allusion to future toils that lie ahead, just as the prophet Teiresias had told him in Hades:

ὦ γύναι, οὐ γάρ πω πάντων ἐπὶ πείρατ' ἀέθλων
ἤλθομεν, ἀλλ' ἔτ' ὄπισθεν ἀμέτρητος πόνος ἔσται,
πολλὸς καὶ χαλεπός, τὸν ἐμὲ χρὴ πάντα τελέσσαι.
ὡς γάρ μοι ψυχὴ μαντεύσατο Τειρεσίαο
ἤματι τῷ ὅτε δὴ κατέβην δόμον Ἄϊδος εἴσω

[11] The relation between Homer and folktale has been much discussed. On this episode see Peradotto (1985) passim, especially 434ff.; Hansen (1976); Hansen (1977) passim; in general, Carpenter (1946), especially 18ff.; Glenn (1971) and (1978); Page (1973); and Hölscher (1978) 51–67.

[12] The tone of distance and generality also characterizes the similar expression that Alcinous uses in the books just preceding: 7.197f. and 8.579f.

νόστον ἑταίροισιν διζήμενος ἠδ' ἐμοὶ αὐτῷ.
ἀλλ' ἔρχευ, λέκτρονδ' ἴομεν, γύναι, ὄφρα καὶ ἤδη
ὕπνῳ ὕπο γλυκερῷ ταρπώμεθα κοιμηθέντε.

(23.248–55)

My wife, we have not yet come to the limit of all our trials, but afterward
will there still be limitless toil, much and harsh, all of which I must
accomplish. For so did the shade of Teiresias prophesy to me on that day
when I went down within the house of Hades seeking the return for my
companions and for myself. But come, let us go to bed, my wife, so that
even now lying together we may take our joy beneath sweet sleep.

Line 253, "seeking return for my companions and myself," is a reference back to the opening of Teiresias' speech in 11.100. Odysseus once
more has the mortal perspective of his initial goal, that of saving his own
life and the lives of his companions, as stated at the opening of the
poem: "He suffered many woes in his heart on the sea, winning his own
life and the return of his companions" (noston hetairōn, 1.5). Teiresias,
however, like the omniscient narrator, knows that Odysseus will
achieve the nostos only for himself (cf. 11.105, 114; also 1.6, "But not
even thus did he save his companions, eager though he was").

Odysseus ends this first account of the prophecy not with the remote
future but with the immediate present. He wants to sleep with the wife
for whom he has longed all these years (23.254f.). In book 11 he had
turned from the prophecy of far-off events to the mother whom he had
only glimpsed; here he turns to the sexual reunion with the wife whom
he has just won back in his full identity as the husband who made the
olive-tree bed. The context surrounding this change in both scenes sets
into relief the abrupt shift from the distant suffering to the immediate,
passionately felt present. In book 11 there is, of course, the gloom of
Hades, where "destructive night" spreads over everything (11.18) and
the countless shades of the dead utter their terrifying sounds as they
approach the blood-filled pit (11.42–50). In book 23 there is the supernatural intervention of Athena, who lengthens the night so that the
dawn does not arise on the reunited as they take their fill of weeping
(23.241–46).

Just as Penelope postponed her initial reunion with Odysseus by
imposing the test of the bed, so here she postpones bed by requesting
that he spell out the prophecy of the "measureless toil" to which he had
alluded (23.256–62). Once more, the folktale motif is framed by the
human concerns, a wife's natural desire to know and share the worst,

especially after the endurance of so much suffering. Odysseus repeats Teiresias' words almost verbatim, changing only the second to the first person where necessary (11.121–37 = 23.268–84). As Odysseus had expressed resignation on hearing the prophecy initially (11.139), so here Penelope expresses acceptance, although in a more hopeful mood than did Odysseus.

εἰ μὲν δὴ γῆράς γε θεοὶ τελέουσιν ἄρειον,
ἐλπωρή τοι ἔπειτα κακῶν ὑπάλυξιν ἔσεσθαι.

(23.286f.)

But if the gods accomplish a better old age, then there is hope that there will be an avoidance of evils.

At this point the dialogue breaks off as Eurynome prepares what is, in essence, a bridal chamber for the reunited couple (23.289ff.).

Odysseus had begun this scene with the foreboding, "But there will be toil limitless afterward" (ἀλλ' ἔτ' ὄπισθεν ἀμέτρητος πόνος ἔσται, 23.249). Penelope, insisting on sharing that suffering, defuses it with a more optimistic, if still resigned, mood, the promised "hope" of "avoiding woes" (23.287).[13] The ray of hope creates the proper mood for the physical reunion; but it also illustrates the full complementarity of husband and wife in marriage, the homophrosunē (concord, harmonious feeling) that Odysseus himself had praised as one of its chief rewards (6.181–84).[14] The much-wanderer looks the future dangers in the face and is ready for still more endurance; the long-waiting wife, whose years of patience have been sustained by just that "hope" (elpōrē) of which she here speaks, takes a more positive view. Once she has accepted the disguised beggar as Odysseus, she resumes her appropriate and characteristic role of the faithful wife, supporting her husband in the face of uncertainty and lightening the burden of the "limitless woe" (23.249) that hitherto he has had to bear alone.

[13] Peradotto (1985) finds "some disappointment, if not bitterness" in Penelope's remark (453). That may be true, but she does speak of "hope" in a way that Odysseus does not; and her dominant tone, especially by contrast with that of Odysseus in 23.266f., is optimism: see Heubeck in Russo, Fernández-Galiano, and Heubeck (1992) on 23.286f.: "Penelope's reply is short and to the point: Odysseus' words have not so much caused her anxiety as inspired her with confidence in the future" (p. 342). It is perhaps worth noting that all such explicit expressions of "hope" (elpōrē) in the poem are made to Odysseus by an encouraging female at a point when he is in uncertainty or crisis: at 2.280 (Athena), 6.314f. (Nausicaa), and 7.76f. (Athena).

[14] On homophrosunē, see above, Chapter 5, note 25.

Odysseus' "limitless woe" here is similar to the "boundless grief" of which Heracles complained in Hades when he commiserated with Odysseus for having to endure, like himself, "a woeful portion" or hard lot in life.

> διογενὲς Λαερτιάδη, πολυμήχαν' Ὀδυσσεῦ,
> ἆ δείλ', ἦ τινὰ καὶ σὺ κακὸν μόρον ἡγηλάζεις,
> ὅν περ ἐγὼν ὀχέεσκον ὑπ' αὐγὰς ἠελίοιο.
> Ζηνὸς μὲν πάϊς ἦα Κρονίονος, αὐτὰρ ὀϊζὺν
> εἶχον ἀπειρεσίην· μάλα γὰρ πολὺ χείρονι φωτὶ
> δεδμήμην, ὁ δέ μοι χαλεποὺς ἐπετέλλετ' ἀέθλους.
>
> (11.617–22)

Zeus-born son of Laertes, much-devising Odysseus, poor man! Truly did you also endure the woeful portion that I myself bore beneath the rays the sun. I was a son of Zeus, but I had boundless grief, for I was made subservient to a much worse man, and he laid harsh trials upon me.

Instead of the unrelieved bleakness described by Heracles' shade, however, Penelope offers something new, a consoling word of "hopefulness" and so leads their conversation to a mood wholly different in spirit from the meetings in the Underworld (23.286f.). She holds out to Odysseus the possibility of a happy life within the limits of mortality, "old age," and an uncertain future. He had already anticipated something of this spirit when he first heard Teiresias' prophecy of his future trials, for he uttered no complaint or cry of lamentation but turned to the shade of his mother whom he had seen among the other ghosts: "Teiresias, the gods themselves have spun these things out for me; but come, tell me this and speak it truly: I see the shade of my dead mother, and she sits in silence near the blood, nor does she dare to look at her son directly or to address him. Tell, O lord, how she would recognize me here before her" (11.139–44). Now his characteristic endurance is shared and affirmed in his own house.

Much more could be said of these scenes, and interpreters from antiquity to the present have said much more. But even this brief comparison of folkloristic anecdote and Homeric narrative makes clear how a great poet transforms folklore and anecdote into those situations of profound human meaning that lead us back to the poem again and again.

CHAPTER 10

Divine Justice:
Poseidon, Cyclops, and Helios

Divine Justice and Human Understanding

The discrepancy between the "higher" morality of Zeus articulated in the proem of the *Odyssey* and the anthropomorphic vindictiveness of Poseidon and Helios has long been regarded as one of the major obstacles to a coherent theology in the poem and one of its most serious compositional problems.[1] Analysts have claimed these discrepancies as evidence that the poem is a compilation of older and newer materials stitched together in a none too seamless fabric. I argue here for a radically unitarian position. The *Odyssey*'s literary design and theology, I believe, are both unified and interdependent; and the Poseidon and Helios episodes in books 5, 9, and 12, far from being anomalies or merely the residues of an Ur-*Odyssee,* are pivotal points in clarifying the poem's unified moral concerns.

There is little doubt that the *Odyssey* incorporates older strata of beliefs about the gods, just as it incorporates older strata of folklore in the creation of its hero.[2] But the evolution of an increasingly moral

[1] For discussion and bibliography (which must be exemplary rather than exhaustive), see Fenik (1974) 208n. 18 and 223ff. and Friedrich (1987) 384–85. For a typical analytic view, see Irmscher (1950) 56–64. In the milder variant of this approach advocated by Schadewaldt (1958) 15–32, especially 16, a later poet ("*Bearbeiter,*" "B") has grafted an ethical interpretation onto an earlier, ethically more primitive work, traces of which remain, however, in the figures of Poseidon and Helios. For a critique of the analytic approach, see Hölscher (1939) 81–82 and Bona (1966) 23ff. and 36ff. For the underlying unity of the conception of the gods in the poem, see Reinhardt (1948) 86ff.

[2] Whether the more self-consciously moralized theology of the *Odyssey* is the result of historical development or of different poets or of changing concerns, themes, or styles in

conception of the gods over many centuries need not exclude a coherent theology in the "monumental composition" of the poem's final phase. Viewed diachronically, nature divinities such as Helios, Proteus, or Circe may well represent a type of divinity older than Zeus or Athena. Synchronically, however, these differences among types of divinity form part of the poem's total vision of what gods might and should be.[3] In other words, Homer, as I shall argue, has brought together into an artistic and conceptual whole both older and more evolved notions of divinity and in this way grounds his epic in a self-consciously moral theology.[4]

I am especially concerned with two devices by which Homer achieves his moral effect: the juxtaposing of gods of different levels of moral sensitivity (such as Zeus and Poseidon) and the bracketing of the less moral, more "primitive" divine behavior in a well-demarcated section of the poem, the fabulous realm between Troy and Ithaca in books 5–13. Indeed, this bracketing process begins in the very opening lines of the poem, where Poseidon's wrath is firmly set apart from the pity of "all" the other gods:

θεοὶ δ' ἐλέαιρον ἅπαντες
νόσφι Ποσειδάωνος· ὁ δ' ἀσπερχὲς μενέαινεν
ἀντιθέῳ Ὀδυσῆϊ πάρος ἦν γαῖαν ἱκέσθαι.

(1.19–21)

And all the gods pitied him apart from Poseidon; but he raged unceasingly at godlike Odysseus until he reached his own land.

---

a single poet remains a matter of heated controversy: see, e.g., Post (1939) 158–90, especially 159ff., 188; Dodds (1951) 32–33; Kitto (1966) 143–44; Lesky (1967) 42–43; Lloyd-Jones (1971) 28–32, 37; Clay (1983) 215–39, with useful bibliography; and Hankey (1990) 94–95. For the folklore elements in the poem, see, e.g., Carpenter (1946) chapter 1, Page (1973) passim, Hölscher (1978) 52ff., Hölscher (1988) passim, Clay (1983) 68–74, and Calame (1986) 122ff.

[3] For a good statement of how diachronic and synchronic perspectives can be balanced and viewed as complementary, see Nagy (1990) 4–5.

[4] The poem's explicit concern with justice belongs to its "ethical" or "normative" quality, which stands in contrast to the tragic tone of the *Iliad*: see Aristotle, *Poetics* 24.1459b12ff. Not every divine action, of course, fits into a neat moral scheme, and even generalizations about moral behavior and divine justice have to be understood in context, as part of the flow of action and the interplay of character. A typical example is *Od.* 17.485–87, where a suitor's comment on the gods' moral watchfulness follows Odysseus' invocation of "the gods and Erinyes of beggars" when Antinous throws a footstool at him. There is a further irony in putting such a moral in the mouth of one of "the overweening young men" who share in Antinous' *hubris* and thus in his doom. Cf. also the sequence of prayers and omens in 15.523–48, especially after Athena's appearance to Telemachus in 15.9ff., which is parallel to her appearance to Nausicaa in 6.21ff.: see Hölscher (1939) 85.

Isolated from the other gods, Poseidon is cast at once into the role of the "other," the blocking force or obstacle to Odysseus' return and to Zeus' will.[5]

As the *Odyssey* is a poem about change, the theology, too, is intimately bound up with the shifting experience and widening understanding of the hero. Odysseus has "seen and come to know the mind of many men" (1.4), but he has also seen and come to know many forms of the mind of gods. Even though our extended view of him over many years is condensed into the relatively brief span of days in the foreground, we follow an entire lifetime, from birth to death, as it is stamped with the presence or absence of divine justice. We also see the lingering traces of the amoral, unscrupulous trickster.[6]

On the human level the superimposition of Odysseus' past on the present shows us how a moral consciousness is shaped over the course of a lifetime of suffering and witnessing divinity's workings among mortals. Analogously, on the divine level, Zeus' program for retributive justice at the beginning is not an accomplished fact of the world order but appears as work in progress. Hence he states his theodicy in the form of a complaint, uses present and future tenses (1.32–41), and brings us into the present with the phrase "as even now" (ὡς καὶ νῦν) in 1.35. Before the end of the first book, in fact, we see a mortal making just the accusation that Zeus has tried to refute, namely, that the god is responsible for the ills of humankind. Defending Phemius' right to sing his song of the ill-fated Returns of the Achaeans, Telemachus argues that "the singers are not responsible [*aitioi*], but Zeus is somehow responsible, who gives to men who earn their bread to each as he wills" (1.347–49; cf. 11.558–60).[7]

Odysseus, too, in the early state of moral awareness that we see in him during his wanderings at sea, adheres to a similar view. When he meets the shade of Ajax in Hades, he tries to exculpate himself with the excuse that "no one else is responsible (*aitios*), but Zeus hated the army of the Danaan spearmen exceptionally, and he placed upon you your portion of doom" (11.558–60). The blaming of Zeus gets a characteristically lighter turn in Demodocus' song of Ares and Aphrodite,

---

[5] This is the only time in the poem that *nosphi* (apart from) occurs first in the line and with a proper name, a stylistic detail that adds to the isolation of Poseidon.

[6] See Rutherford (1986) 160–61.

[7] In the *Iliad* the attribution of "responsibility" to the gods or to Zeus is fairly common: see 3.164f. and 19.86–89, 270–74, 409f. One may even wonder whether the *Odyssey* proem has in mind that of the *Iliad*, where the poet asks "which of the gods" threw Agamemnon and Achilles together in strife (1.8).

where Hephaestus directs his charge of divine "responsibility" to Zeus himself. Aphrodite, he complains, preferred the handsome Ares to himself because of his own lameness, a fact for which "no one else is responsible, but my parents are, who I wish had not given me birth" (8.310f.). The shift of "responsibility" presumably forestalls any countercharges from the adulterers and increases his right to reparations; but the blaming of his parents and his abrupt, petulant wish dissolve the issue of justice into burlesque domestic quarreling.

In the world of mortals, however, Zeus' "responsibility" is more serious. In the course of Telemachus' travels on the Greek mainland, we hear of Zeus' justice at work, through the agency of Athena, in the shipwreck of some of the Trojan heroes because "not all were perceptive or just" (3.133f.). Locrian Ajax's foolish boast that he could escape the sea even against the gods' will (4.503–5) fatally incurs Poseidon's wrath (4.499–511). These instances of divine justice, though glimpsed only fleetingly, prefigure the realization of Zeus' justice in the main line of the action as we follow the principal hero in the great crisis of his life.[8]

Although the Odyssey seems more advanced morally than is the Iliad, it nevertheless resembles it in making the omniscient narrator's increasing clarification of Zeus' will accompany the hero's gradual understanding of that will. Achilles, overreaching, transgressive hero that he often is, initially identifies his goals with the will of Zeus and only too late recognizes the suffering implied in that identification.[9] Odysseus, whose life is defined by restraint, moderation, and continuity, can use his moral understanding as a way of achieving his goals.

The Odysseus who arrives on Ithaca in book 13 has performed the narrative act of recollecting his many years of travel.[10] In addition to this integrative work of bringing past experience into his present time of life, in book 13 he has the benefit of planning his future moves with Athena. She puts him once again in contact with the basic traits of his character by reaffirming them to his face (291–99, 330–38). At the same time, she permits him a privileged (if abbreviated) account of divine arrangements beyond his mortal knowledge. "I knew in my heart," she says, "that you would return after the loss of all your companions, but I

---

[8] See Clay (1983) 47ff.

[9] Cf. especially Il. 18.74–93, where Achilles acknowledges the disastrous results of his request of Zeus, and 24.525–51, where he expounds human suffering in the parable of Zeus' two jars. On Achilles' tragic recognition at the end of the Iliad, see Whitman (1958) 202ff. and Mueller (1984) 56–59.

[10] See above, Chapter 2.

did not want to fight with Poseidon, brother of my father, who put anger in his heart in wrath because you blinded his own son" (13.340–43). This recognition of Athena's concern also changes Odysseus' understanding of the gods' ways. The Odysseus of the second half of the poem, defending his house on Ithaca, is surer of divine help and more prudent and self-controlled than the Odysseus who defended his own and his men's lives against the Cyclops.

His first instructions to his son consist in sharing his special knowledge of the gods' help for righteous vengeance. When Telemachus first appeared in the poem, he complained to Athena, disguised as Mentes, about the gods' "evil devising" of his father's woes (1.234–45; cf. also 1.348). But, many books later, as Odysseus reveals himself to his son, he uses his own example to correct Telemachus and teach him about Athena's power and concern. As he explains how the goddess could change his appearance, his hymnic phrasing resembles Hesiod's invocation of Zeus' might in the proem of *Works and Days:*

> αὐτάρ τοι τόδε ἔργον 'Αθηναίης ἀγελείης,
> ἥ τέ με τοῖον ἔθηκεν ὅπως ἐθέλει, δύναται γάρ,
> ἄλλοτε μὲν πτωχῷ ἐναλίγκιον, ἄλλοτε δ' αὖτε
> ἀνδρὶ νέῳ καὶ καλὰ περὶ χροΐ εἵματ' ἔχοντι.
> ῥηΐδιον δὲ θεοῖσι, τοὶ οὐρανὸν εὐρὺν ἔχουσιν,
> ἠμὲν κυδῆναι θνητὸν βροτὸν ἠδὲ κακῶσαι.
>
> (*Od.* 16.207–12)

This is the work of Athena, driver of the spoils, who makes me just as she wishes—for she has the power—sometimes like a beggar and sometimes like a young man who clothes his form in lovely raiment. Easy it is for the gods who hold the broad heavens either to glorify a mortal man or to abase him.

> ῥέα μὲν γὰρ βριάει, ῥέα δὲ βριάοντα χαλέπτει,
> ῥεῖα δ' ἀρίζηλον μινύθει καὶ ἄδηλον ἀέξει,
> ῥεῖα δέ τ' ἰθύνει σκολιὸν καὶ ἀγήνορα κάρφει
> Ζεὺς ὑψιβρεμέτης, ὃς ὑπέρτατα δώματα ναίει.
>
> (*Works and Days* 5–8; cf. *Theog.* 447)

Easily does Zeus of the lofty thunder who dwells in the highest abode give strength but bear hard on him who is strong; and easily does he diminish the conspicuous man and strengthen the obscure, and easily does he set straight the crooked and wither the manly.

Shortly afterward, Odysseus counters Telemachus' dismay at the odds against them by assuring him of the help of "Athena along with Father Zeus" (16.260). In the removal of the arms from the great hall, the miraculous glow from Athena's golden lamp gives him another opportunity to instruct his son in "the ways of the gods" (*dikē theōn,* 19.43). The gods can work a "great wonder" or "marvel" (*mega thauma*) for a mortal whom they wish to aid, as Telemachus says here (19.36); and we are reminded of Odysseus' first words to his son in book 16, as he begins his paternal task of initiating him into the gods' ways and tells him not to "wonder" (*thaumazein*) too much (201–12, especially 203).

In his other relations on Ithaca, too, Odysseus displays a moral awareness deeper than that of most of those around him. In a famous reflection on the feebleness of humans and the ephemerality and uncertainty of human life, he warns Amphinomus of the doom awaiting those who "devise deeds of overweening violence" (*atasthala mēchanoōntas,* 18.143).[11] In his first address to Penelope in his disguise as a beggar, he gives a definition of kingship that stresses piety, fair judgment, and concern for the people (19.108–114; cf. Hesiod *Works and Days* 225–37). His disguise also provides several occasions for revealing mistaken assumptions about the gods. Both Eurycleia and the cowherd Philoetius blame Zeus for their master's failed return when Odysseus in fact is standing before them (19.363–69, 20.201–10).[12] His advantage over the suitors lies in his moral superiority as much as in his cunning (*mētis*).[13] The pattern is already established, embryonically, in his first

[11] See Nagy (1979), who notes that *atasthaliai* "are conventionally associated in Homeric diction with acts denoted by the word *hubris* and its derivatives" (163). Human suffering because of men's own *atasthaliai* is a recurrent theme, although it is not unique to the *Odyssey*: cf. *Il.* 4.409 and 22.104. See Post (1939) 164; also Schadewaldt (1958) 31, with note 13; Andersen (1973) 12–14; and Clay (1983) 34–38. It is interesting for Odysseus' identification with the moral aims of Zeus that his generalization on the feebleness of human life in *Od.* 18.130f. closely resembles Zeus' remark in *Il.* 17.446f. With Odysseus' warning to Amphinomus, we may also compare his monitory tale to Antinous about how *hubris* results in disaster, 17.431–44.

[12] Dimock (1989) 330 suggests that this despair about Zeus' justice is answered by Laertes in 24.351ff. This is perhaps too programmatic, but this darkness about justice doubtless serves as the foil to the light that comes at the end. Fenik (1974) 223–24 seems to me to exaggerate the contradiction between Athena's urging on the suitors (18.346ff. and 20.284) and, in the proem, Zeus' dissuading the evildoers. The two actions belong to different stages of human crime; and the contrast, in fact, strengthens the divine justice. The gods' justice receives independent confirmation from an area removed from the main events of the poem: Zeus and Artemis work together in punishing the maidservant who kidnapped Eumaeus as a child (15.475–81, especially 477f.).

[13] On the poem's concern with the moral basis of Odysseus' victory over the suitors, see the careful study of Saïd (1977) 9–49, especially 28, with the further literature there cited.

major victory by cunning that we meet in the poem, his encounter with
the Cyclops, Polyphemus.

Near the end of this episode, Odysseus reads the Cyclops a moral
lesson: the evil deeds were bound to recoil back upon him because he
did not revere the laws of guest friendship. Zeus and the other gods,
therefore, have punished him:

> καὶ λίην σέ γ' ἔμελλε κιχήσεσθαι κακὰ ἔργα,
> σχέτλι', ἐπεὶ ξείνους οὐχ ἅζεο σῷ ἐνὶ οἴκῳ
> ἐσθέμεναι· τῷ σε Ζεὺς τείσατο καὶ θεοὶ ἄλλοι.
>
> (9.477–79)

> Very much indeed were your evil deeds going to find you, wretch, since
> you had not the reverence to forbear eating your guests in your house;
> therefore did Zeus and the other gods requite you.

This reflection on retribution from Zeus, which the god himself had
introduced in the proem (*tisis*, 1.40), offers a moral interpretation of
Odysseus' own action: he succeeds because he identifies his purposes
with the gods' ways of justice and vengeance. He comes to grief because
he cannot resist the temptation to gloat over his victory and make sure
that his enemy knows the identity of his vanquisher (9.491–505).[14]

The Cyclops episode, however, raises serious problems for divine
justice. On the one hand, the Cyclopes "trust to the immortal gods,"
who in fact seem to look after them, for their untilled and unplowed
land bears grain and grapes (9.109–11), and "Zeus's rain makes increase
for them" (111). On the other hand, they are overweening and without
laws (9.106). If the gods are the guardians of righteous behavior, why
do they shower such abundance on these "arrogantly behaving Cyclopes," ἀνδρῶν ὑπερηνορεόντων, as the poet calls them at the beginning of the Phaeacian episode (6.5)?[15] The narrative of Polyphemus
explores this contradiction and at least partially resolves it by showing
that the Cyclopes' trust in the gods is misplaced, at least in the case of the
signal example of Cyclopean *hubris*, Polyphemus.

---

[14] The folly of Odysseus' Iliadic boasting over Polyphemus has often been pointed
out: see Hogan (1976) 202, Austin (1981) 41–42, and Clay (1983) 121ff. On the avoidance
of gloating as a higher ethical behavior, see Blundell (1989) 56 and 62ff., apropos of
Sophocles' *Ajax*.

[15] The oxymoron of the phrase perhaps suggests the outlandishness of regarding the
Cyclopes as "men."

Phaeacians and Cyclopes, Zeus and Poseidon

As Geoffrey Kirk and Pierre Vidal-Naquet have pointed out, the Cyclopes make their appearance in an unstable conjunction of opposites. They occupy both a golden age paradise where, "trusting to the gods," they receive the earth's fruits without toil, and a subhuman condition of dwelling in mountain caves with only a rudimentary social organization and isolated nuclear families (9.106–15).[16] Odysseus' arrival brings out the negative side of their primitive society, for just this "lack of concern for one another" prevents them from coming to Polyphemus' aid (οὐδ' ἀλλήλων ἀλέγουσι, 115; cf. 399–412). Eager to get back to sleep in their individual caves (401–4), they readily accept his statement about "Nobody" as an excuse to dismiss his complaint.

Polyphemus, in other words, crystallizes the savage side of the Cyclopes' precivilized world; and with this savagery he brings into the narrative a more primitive, less morally evolved notion of divinity. Through his encounter with Odysseus, he moves, unwittingly, toward a world where higher moral norms come into play. Whether he acknowledges Zeus or not (9.275–78), he eventually gets judged and punished according to a world order defined by the justice of Zeus rather than the wrath of Poseidon.[17]

Odysseus' Phaeacian hosts are almost the exact opposite of the Cyclopes, from whose proximity they once fled (6.4–8). Taken together, the Phaeacians and the Cyclopes embody the two poles of a privileged closeness to the gods. The Phaeacians are above, the Cyclopes are below the usual human norm of relations with the divine among humankind. The difference is analogous to that between the golden age and the silver age in Hesiod (*Works and Days* 115–19, 133–39), except that the Phaeacians also have traits of a fully human, Iron Age world of cities, sea

[16] See Kirk (1970) 162–71, Vidal-Naquet (1986) 21–22, and Rawson (1984) 1160–63. More recently, O'Sullivan (1990) 16–17 has rightly criticized Kirk's view of the Cyclopes' "superculture," but he goes too far in the opposite direction, paying too little attention to their ambiguous place between savagery and the golden age. Mondi (1983) 22ff. argues that the contradiction in the Cyclopes reflects Homer's conflation of two traditions, a folktale tradition of a man-eating ogre and an old Greek myth, reflected in Hesiod *Theog.* 139–46, of smith-gods who forge Zeus' thunderbolt and are rewarded for their aid against the Titans with the Elysium-like paradise reflected in *Od.* 9.107–15. This explanation is attractive for the origins of the Homeric Cyclopes but still does not account for the use to which Homer puts his composite version (if such it is) in the poem.

[17] Polyphemus' description of his fellow Cyclopes as "not being concerned" (*ou . . . alegousi*, 9.275) with Zeus is perhaps an ironic echo of their lack of "concern for one another" (*ou . . . alegousi*, 9.115).

travel, and complex social organization. Despite this contrast, however, the Phaeacians and the Cyclopes share a certain unpredictability in their responses to guest-host situations, one of poem's most important codes of behavior for defining "normally" civilized humans, that is, Greeks.[18] Supercivilized though they in some ways are, the Phaeacians shift mysteriously from the lack of response to Odysseus' request for hospitality in Alcinous' long, embarrassing silence (7.153–66) to the extravagant generosity of transporting him home and giving him lavish gifts.

In his formal welcome of Odysseus, Alcinous can point to a time not long in the past when the gods used to visit them and participate in their sacrifices, "since we are near to them, as are also the Cyclopes and the savage races of Giants" (7.199–206; cf. 5.35, 19.279). The three races—Phaeacians, Cyclopes, and Giants—enjoy this privilege because of common descent from or close connection with Poseidon (cf. 7.56ff., 13.130); but that genealogical relationship, as we shall see, points to other affinities. Each of the three belongs to a stage of moral behavior before that of the ordinary mortal world; each is a remnant of a more archaic past. Even the Phaeacians, as we have observed, have something of the Cyclopes' isolation and hostility to strangers.

Several additional features of the narrative contribute to the association of the Cyclopes with an older world. In their combination of agricultural abundance and asocial violence they resemble the two earliest of Hesiod's five ages, the Golden and Silver Races. Like the Phaeacians (7.114–21), they resemble the Golden Race in the spontaneous agricultural richness of their land (9.107–11; cf. 9.123f.; Works and Days 117f.).[19] Unlike the Phaeacians, they are close to the Silver Race in their rudimentary social organization, their aggressive violence, and their lack of respect for the gods (9.106, 112; Works and Days 134–37).[20]

By associating the Cyclopes and the Phaeacians with the Giants (7.59 and 206), Homer makes the two former peoples seem part of a more distant time, for the Giants generally belong to an older order.[21] In

[18] See G. Rose (1969) 389–93.

[19] It is an important difference between the Cyclopes and Phaeacians, however, that the abundant produce of Alcinous' orchard belongs to a landscape that has been bounded, contained, and ordered by walls, rows, drying places, etc. (7.112f., 123f., 127) and adjoins an elaborate architectural complex that in turn reflects a high degree of social and political organization (7.130ff.).

[20] See also Slatkin (1986a) 264–66. It is interesting that the Odyssey never describes Polyphemus' behavior explicitly in terms of hubris or atasthaliai, perhaps because his world is still ignorant of a standard of action that opposes dikē and hubris.

[21] On the problem of the chronological placement of Homer's Giants, see Heubeck, West, and Hainsworth (1988) on 7.59. Odysseus refers to the Giants as a "savage race"

Hesiod's *Theogony,* for example, the Giants are born from Gaia and the severed genitals of Ouranos and are coeval with the Erinyes and the Meliai (185–87); and Hesiod's Cyclopes are the children of Gaia and Ouranos (139).[22]

Through his siring of Polyphemus and his association with the Giants (7.56–59), then, Poseidon is also displaced into an older world order. By making him the father of Polyphemus (though not necessarily of the whole race of Cyclopes), Homer virtually makes Poseidon one of the deities of primordial creation. His union with Thoōsa, a daughter of the ancient sea divinity Phorkys, to sire Polyphemus (1.72) reinforces this regressive pattern, for this otherwise unknown Thoōsa presumably belongs to the same generation as Phorcys' other children, the Graiai, the Gorgons, Echidna, and Typhon (cf. Hesiod *Theog.* 270–336). In his role as the father of Otus and Ephialtes, too, Poseidon acquires the same aura of pre-Olympian antiquity (11.305–20). These precocious and aggressive adolescents closely resemble Hesiod's Silver Race (cf. 9.317f. and *Works and Days* 132–36); but they also resemble the *Theogony*'s Titans or monsters such as Typhoeus in their attack on Olympus and also in their close connection with the earth (11.309).

The *Odyssey* as a whole tries to bring the polycentric, polytheistic world order under the unified morality of Zeus; and in so doing it tends to suppress or displace the cosmogonic strife that lies in the background of the *Iliad*.[23] The Odyssean Poseidon seems to move back into a pre-Olympian time of monsters, Titans, and Giants; but the poem subsumes this chronological or historical dimension of the world order into the here and now of Zeus' reign. By thus absorbing the struggles for cosmic sovereignty from the remote past into the present (or, in other terms, by projecting the diachronic on the synchronic axis of the narrative), the *Odyssey* establishes its Olympian, Zeus-governed present as

---

(*agria phula,* 7.206) and later likens the Laestrygonians to them (10.120). Indeed, these last are like slightly evolved Cyclopes: they are huge, violent, and anthropophagous, but they have an *agora* (market place, 10.114) and an *astu* (town) (10.118). Their capacity for cooperation, in fact, makes them far more dangerous than the Cyclopes. Whereas Polyphemus kills only six men, the Laestrygonians destroy all Odysseus' ships but one (10.121–32).

[22] For the differences between the Homeric and Hesiodic Cyclopes, see Mondi (1983) 18ff., 22ff. Like Homer, however, Hesiod introduces his Cyclopes with an epithet denoting their overweening violence (*huperbion ētor echontas, Theog.* 139; cf. *Od.* 6.5, 9.106), which may indicate that the two versions are not quite so separate as Mondi suggests.

[23] For example, *Il.* 1.401–6, 8.13–27, 8.477–83, 15.18–24. See Whitman (1970) 37–42 and Slatkin (1986) 10–14.

the only perspective from which an older order can be viewed. And in that perspective Poseidon appears as an archaic feature of the world, the representative of an obsolescent world order. Put differently, what is a diachronic process in Hesiod's *Theogony* and in the glimpses of cosmogonic narration in the *Iliad* has here become part of a contrast, in the present, between Zeus and Poseidon, in which the disruptive Poseidon is on the way out, as it were, and in fact disappears when the scene shifts fully to the narrative present on Ithaca.

In his contact with both Phaeacians and Cyclopes, Odysseus is the catalyst for pushing the residual old order into the new Zeus-governed world. Rejecting Calypso's offer of immortality (cf. 5.215–24), he refuses the possibility of a world, like that of the Phaeacians of long ago, where the barriers between god and mortal could be fluid (7.199–210). By injecting into the Phaeacians' world the sharp separation between mortality and divinity that he carries with him from the Calypso episode, he radically alters their relation to their most important god, Poseidon. Just as the Phaeacian island is the point of Odysseus' own return from the moribund ease of Calypso's island to the "real" world of work, suffering, and justice on Ithaca, so the Phaeacians' contact with him introduces them to the harsher side of their divine ancestor (13.128–87).

Earlier in the Phaeacian episode, Demodocus' song of Ares and Aphrodite presents Poseidon as a dignified, effective peacemaker who conciliates conflicting positions through negotiation and the quasi-legal procedures of pledges and guarantees (8.343–58). But this image of a pacific Poseidon is bracketed by the frame of the song and thus separated from the Poseidon that Odysseus knows and will cause the Phaeacians to know (13.149–87). Demodocus' conciliatory Poseidon, spokesman of flexibility and forgiveness, is appropriate to his song's light, happy, sensual world of wit and laughter—the kind of world that the Phaeacians think of themselves as inhabiting (8.334–43; cf. 8.246–49). Appropriately, Demodocus' song suspends the seriousness of Zeus' moral order that dominates the rest of the poem. This is virtually the only episode in the *Odyssey* which depicts the frivolous side of the gods that is so abundant in the *Iliad*. Yet it is noteworthy that even the song allows Zeus himself no part of the frivolity; he is very much in the background (cf. 8.306).[24]

[24] See Burkert (1960) 143. The ancient commentators noted the absence of Zeus: see the scholion ad 8.344. Poseidon's attempt to end a quarrel here is very different from his eagerness to pick a fight with Apollo in the theomachy of the *Iliad* (*Il.* 21.435ff.).

Odysseus' anger at Euryalus' challenge has already revealed the differences between his world and the Phaeacians' (8.158–234); and his relation to Poseidon will soon take those differences to a more serious level. The imagined Poseidon of Demodocus differs from the Poseidon experienced by Odysseus, just as Demodocus' tale of the ultimately inconsequential punishment of Ares by Hephaestus differs from Odysseus' ruthless vengeance on his wife's suitors on Ithaca. In contrast to the wronged husband's acceptance of compensation from Poseidon in Demodocus' song, Odysseus categorically refuses any offer of compensation from the suitors (22.55–64).[25]

These differences are analogous to the contrast between Zeus' rosy view of helpful Phaeacians who will honor Odysseus "like a god" and send him home without harm and with rich gifts (5.36–40) and the dangerous Phaeacians about whom Athena gives Odysseus an early warning (7.32–36). Here, too, the Phaeacians' suspicion of strangers stands in suggestive proximity to their special favor from Poseidon (7.35).

These two views of the Phaeacians are an index of a "Jovian" and a "Neptunian" world order, respectively. Zeus, looking ahead to the fulfillment of the action in the broad perspective appropriate to his role in the poem (and his function as Zeus Teleios), defines the Phaeacians solely as the instruments of the return that he prophesies. But Athena, who executes those orders in the details of a mortal's experience and also embodies Odysseus' caution and suspicion, acquaints her charge with the other, Neptunian side. At the end of the episode, in book 13, the ominous side of the Phaeacians, again expressed through their relation with Poseidon, is turned against themselves (128ff.); but here, too, beyond their ken, Zeus is exercising some control over Poseidon (139–58), as he has done from the very beginning (1.68–79).[26] In book 1 Zeus intervened in Poseidon's wrathful persecution of Odysseus; in book 13 he tempers Poseidon's plan to smash the Phaeacian ship with the lighter punishment of metamorphosis into stone (cf. 150f. with 155f., 163f., and 168f.).[27]

---

[25] The parallelism between Hephaestus' situation in the song and Odysseus' situation on Ithaca was familiar to ancient readers: see Athenaeus 5.192 d–e and Burkert (1960) 140.

[26] Poseidon's punishment of Locrian Ajax in 4.503–11, however, suggests a morally concerned Poseidon who, like Zeus, reacts against boasting and the *atē* of defying the gods.

[27] Various attempts have been made, from Aristarchus on, to tone down Zeus' acquiescence in Poseidon's wrath; but the language of 13.158 need refer only to blocking

Both the Phaeacians and the Cyclopes are hosts who underestimate the consequences of entertaining their guest and as a result are themselves changed forever by a limitation or maiming of power. In both cases the loss is accompanied by the recognition of an ancient oracle (*palaiphata thesphata*, 9.507 = 13.172). The Phaeacians are superior to the Cyclops Polyphemus in remembering their oracle before its fulfillment (8.555–69). Yet the knowledge does them no good (cf. 8.562f.); and, like the Cyclopes, they trust too much in being "dear to the gods" (6.203; cf. 9.107). Thus King Alcinous dismisses the prophecy with an insouciance characteristic of Phaeacian complacency: "The god would accomplish these things, or they would be unfulfilled, as seemed dear to his heart" (8.570f). The Phaeacians' foreknowledge of the disaster connected with transporting a mortal such as Odysseus does not dissuade them from their promised escort. By contrast, Aeolus has a god's clear-sighted, distanced perspective on mortal life and refuses any further aid to Odysseus (10.72–75).

Polyphemus not only rejects Odysseus' claim to the rights of guests and strangers protected by Zeus (9.266–71) but also regards the Cyclopes as exempt from the rule of the gods. The Cyclopes, he explains, "pay no heed to Zeus who bears the aegis nor to the blessed gods, since we are much stronger" (*polu pherteroi*, 9.275f.). But Polyphemus is both impious and wrong.[28] The death of Locrian Ajax earlier (4.503–11) provided a warning about claiming independence from the divine will. The Poseidon of the Cyclopeia is not yet so morally developed.

The Cyclopes' absolute "trust in the gods" for their sustenance points to a less beneficent side of the divine gift, for the wine that makes Odysseus' revenge possible comes, ultimately, from "Zeus' increase" (9.111). The verse on this growth that "Zeus' rain" brings (111) has only one other occurrence in the poem, namely, in Polyphemus' mouth as he praises Odysseus' vintage and compares it to nectar and ambrosia.

> καὶ γὰρ Κυκλώπεσσι φέρει ζείδωρος ἄρουρα
> οἶνον ἐρισταφυλον, καί σφιν Διὸς ὄμβρος ἀέξει·
> ἀλλὰ τόδ' ἀμβροσίης καὶ νέκταρός ἐστιν ἀπορρώξ.
>
> (9.357–59)

---

the harbor, and in any case, Poseidon's threat seems not to have been carried out (cf. 13.179–83). For discussion see Friedrich (1989) 395–99.

[28] Contrast Homeric *Hymn to Demeter* 148, where one of the well-behaved and reverent princesses of Eleusis insists on how mortals must endure the gifts of the gods, "for they are much stronger" (*polu pherteroi*).

> For the Cyclopes also does the grain-giving earth bear wine from the full grape, *and Zeus' rain increases it;* but this is the pure stream of ambrosia and nectar.

The rain from Zeus that gives the Cyclopes their easy life has also provided Odysseus with the means of vengeance.

Polyphemus' comparison of the wine to nectar and ambrosia (9.359) also points up the extreme distance between this cave-dwelling herdsman/cannibal and the gods on Olympus. Polyphemus calls the wine "ambrosial" and "nectareous" (359) when its purpose is to avenge his raw-eating cannibalism (344, 347). The *vin ordinaire* that the Cyclopes know, moreover, is a gift of Zeus that grows without sowing or plowing (109). It thus stands in the ambiguous relation of the rest of Cyclopean life to civilization and "culture" in general. The *grand cru* that Odysseus enlists against Polyphemus, on the other hand, is hypercivilized: it is a gift of Maron, priest of Apollo, bestowed because Odysseus and his men protected the priest and his family (196–201).[29]

It is right, morally and artistically, then, for this wine to stand at the furthest possible distance from Polyphemus' life and behavior. Maron gave it to Odysseus, along with other "radiant gifts" (9.201), as a reward for "revering" the gods (ἀζόμενοι, 200) and for preventing possible violence. Its presence among Odysseus' stores is itself the result of a civilized exchange between men: respect for the gods, the inhibition of violence, and the giving of guest-gifts.

In every way Maron's life is the antithesis of that of the Cyclops. Whereas Polyphemus inhabits a cave on the mountain with his sheep and without gods, Maron, a priest of Apollo, lives in a grove of the god (9.200f.) with his small but complete human household, including wife, child, and servants (206f.).[30] The gifts that accompany his wine include gold and silver vessels and also other civilized foodstuffs, the "provisions" (ἥα) that Odysseus loads on his ship.[31] His wine is a "divine drink," of sweet and godlike bouquet, to be mixed in the proportion twenty to one (205–11). But the Cyclops, though he calls it a draught of nectar and ambrosia, drinks it unmixed and then belches it out along with gobbets of raw human flesh.

[29] See Austin (1983) 20–21.

[30] The fact that Maron keeps the knowledge of this wine from all the servants except the housekeeper (9.205f.) of course shows its preciousness, but it may also prefigure the guile with which Odysseus uses it against Polyphemus.

[31] In 2.289f. such "provisions" are described as including "wine and grain, marrow of men" and so imply the food of a fully civilized diet, not the milk and raw (human) meat of the Cyclops.

ἦ, καὶ ἀνακλινθεὶς πέσεν ὕπτιος, αὐτὰρ ἔπειτα
κεῖτ' ἀποδοχμώσας παχὺν αὐχένα, κὰδ δέ μιν ὕπνος
ἥρει πανδαμάτωρ· φάρυγος δ' ἐξέσσυτο οἶνος
ψωμοί τ' ἀνδρόμεοι· ὁ δ' ἐρεύγετο οἰνοβαρείων.

(371–74)

So he spoke, and reclining backward he fell on his back and then lay there
leaning his thick neck to one side; and sleep conqueror of all seized him;
and from his gullet there gushed forth wine and gobbets of human flesh,
and drunken with wine he belched.

In fact, he merely substitutes the new drink of wine for the milk that he
drank "unmixed" with his equally grisly meal earlier.

αὐτὰρ ἐπεὶ Κύκλωψ μεγάλην ἐμπλήσατο νηδὺν
ἀνδρόμεα κρέ' ἔδων καὶ ἐπ' ἄκρητον γάλα πίνων,
κεῖτ' ἔντοσθ' ἄντροιο τανυσσάμενος διὰ μήλων.

(296–98)

But when the Cyclops filled his big belly eating human flesh and drinking
after it unmixed milk, he lay there within his cave stretching himself out
among his sheep.

This "unmixed milk" (akrēton gala, 297) thus prepares for the disparity
that emerges between the civilized origins of the wine and its monstrous
drinker and is not, as Denys Page claimed, "a very small but very
characteristic oversight."[32]

The wine, so perverted from its original use in civilized behavior,
proves to be the appropriate exchange with the Cyclops after all. Odysseus gives it to him in place of the guest rights that Polyphemus refused
to honor, and it completes the negative reciprocity of Cyclopean hospitality. All the guest-gifts of this land are harmful, and the wine enables
Odysseus to rob Polyphemus of his sight as the pendant to the Cyclops'
gift of eating Odysseus last.

The Cyclopes are taken in by Odysseus' trick of "No-Man" (Outis/
Mētis), because, as they tell Polyphemus, "if no man is doing you
violence, alone as you are, there is no way to avoid sickness from great Zeus,
but do you pray to your father Lord Poseidon" (9.410–12). Polyphemus, then, was even duller than his fellow Cyclopes, for in respect to
both life (111) and possible death (411), the Cyclopes are in fact depen-

---

[32] Page (1955) 7.

dent on and weaker than the gods.[33] Later, Polyphemus will take their advice and pray to Poseidon, but only when it is too late (526ff.).

In one further respect the Cyclops has little justification for boasting of superiority to the gods, for his own life is hedged about by a prophecy of disaster (9.507–14). He lacks the wit to see that such oracles, though communicated by a *mantis anēr*, (prophet, 508), nevertheless derive from Zeus and the will of Zeus. Although he knows that for the life of Odysseus there is a destined portion (*moira*, 532) over which he has no control, he cannot perceive any moral pattern or larger purpose behind these future events. Odysseus, by contrast, in his first address to Polyphemus, had attributed his landing on the Cyclopes' island to the counsel or *mētis* of Zeus (262).[34]

When Polyphemus answers Odysseus' boast with his own claim to be the son of Poseidon, he raises the possibility that his divine father "will heal me if he wishes, he *and not anyone else of the blessed gods* or of mortal men" (520f.).[35] By so vehemently separating Poseidon from the other gods, Polyphemus projects on Olympus something of his own isolation among the Cyclopes. He betrays a total lack of understanding about the divine order, wherein Poseidon's "will" (αἴ κ' ἐθέλῃσι, 520) is subordinate to that of Zeus. The poem's very first scene had shown Zeus already countermanding Poseidon's will (1.78f.); and in book 5 Zeus reiterates that Odysseus' return is part of his "unerring plan" (*nēmertea boulēn*, 30). When that plan is fulfilled in book 13, Poseidon even repeats Zeus' words (13.136–38 = 5.38–40) and has to content himself with punishing the Phaeacians (cf. 13.131–33).

Polyphemus' emphatic exclusion of "anyone else of the other blessed gods" in 520, then, is a serious blunder, and it reflects a mode of behavior consistent with what we have seen of him hitherto. He has unjustifiably presumed on Poseidon's "will" and power. His fellow countrymen might have given him better advice, for they know that

---

[33] The ancient commentators noted the contradiction between Polyphemus' claim in 9.275 and this statement in 9.411 and attributed it to his bad character and his isolation from the other Cyclopes: see the scholion ad 9.411.

[34] Zeus' "unerring plan" (earlier in the work but later in the chronology of Odysseus' return) had already set forth another part of the hero's *moira*, namely, that he will "see his dear ones and come to his high-roofed house and his own native land" (5.41f.). Zeus' statement is not inconsistent with the Cyclops' curse, for Zeus also knows that the return is not *apēmon*, "without pain" (5.40); but here, where he addresses Odysseus' divine sponsor, he emphasizes the gains rather than the losses. Cf. Alcinous' confidence that there is "no fear for [his ships] to be harmed" (*pēmanthēnai*, 8.563), because "we are the pain-free escorters of all" (*pompoi apēmones*, 8.566).

[35] This confidence in Poseidon's potential helpfulness forms a pendant to Alcinous' facile dismissal of the prophesied threat from Poseidon in 8.570f.

diseases come from Zeus and are not to be avoided (9.411), even though they suggest that he also pray to Poseidon (412).

It is an inconsistency worthy of Polyphemus' moral obtuseness that although he boasts that Poseidon himself "will heal me if he wishes," he in fact prays only for revenge. He asks for the blockage of Odysseus' return, not for the healing of his eye. The other Cyclopes had advised him differently: "One cannot avoid sickness [that comes] from great Zeus; but do you pray to your father Lord Poseidon" (9.411f.). Their counsel had made such a prayer for healing a real possibility;[36] but Polyphemus' own brutishness condemns him to continue his suffering. The Cyclops is left blind in more than one sense.

Another feature of the prophecy reveals the same brutishness and ignorance. Polyphemus can understand it only in his own terms, that is, brute force and conquest (9.513–16): he expected a big, strong attacker, but instead only some small, puny fellow "subdued me with wine" (516).[37] Nor does he make any connection between this prophecy and his behavior toward Odysseus or his flouting of Zeus Xenios (272–78). Despite his curse on Odysseus, he is an unregenerate believer in brute force. Paradoxically, however, he succeeds despite himself; and the means that he uses only as a last resort proves to be the right one. His last missile fails to reach Odysseus' ship, but his curse eventually does hit its mark (536–40). The spoken word of the prayer, the invisible and distant fulfillment, is, after all, the more effective instrument of revenge.

Polyphemus would also repeat his earlier outrage in his ironical offering of "guest-gifts" (ἵνα τοι πὰρ ξείνια θείω, "that I may set guest-gifts beside you," 9.517f.; cf. 356, ἵνα τοι δῶ ξείνιον, "that I may give you a guest-gift"). Yet the parallelism between his gesture of stretching forth his hands in prayer to Poseidon (527) and Odysseus' prayerful gesture to Zeus Xenios (294) confirms Odysseus' interpretation of his revenge as an act of just punishment, or tisis, sponsored by the gods (τῶ σε Ζεὺς τείσατο καὶ θεοὶ ἄλλοι, "therefore did Zeus and the other gods requite you," 479; cf. 270, 275–78). Indeed Odysseus' claiming of "Zeus and the other gods" as avengers in 479 may be an ironical reminder of Polyphemus' own scorn of "Zeus and the blessed gods" in 275–76.

Even in the depths of Polyphemus' cave, Odysseus had expected

---

[36] The phrasing of 9.412 suggests that Polyphemus might expect help from Poseidon for his eye because the god is his father.

[37] Dimock (1989) 113 seems to me to read the Cyclops' response far too optimistically. For the Cyclops' acceptance of the power of the gods, except in the narrowest sense of his prayer to Poseidon, there is no evidence in the text.

divine help, in this case from Athena, for the act of *tisis* (εἴ πως τεισαί-μην, δοίη δέ μοι εὖχος Ἀθήνη, "if I might somehow pay you requital and Athena grant me the boast," 9.316f.). At that point he and his men were in the grip of *amēchaniē*, "despairing helplessness" before the Cyclops' "cruel deeds" (295). But the tables are turned when the Cyclops' only recourse is prayer to the god—a tacit acknowledgment, to us, though not to himself, of that inferiority to the gods that he had so strongly abjured in his first act of violence (275ff.). This moral ignorance of the Cyclops supports, on the contrary, the view of the gods stated in the proem. Polyphemus' *atasthaliai* include both the cruel acts themselves and the false assumptions about the gods on which his behavior rests (275–77).

Odysseus at this stage still has much to learn about the gods, as his own narrative enables us to discern. He invoked Zeus' justice in his first boast (9.478–80), but he soon takes the dangerous step of presuming what Poseidon will do: "Would that I could deprive you of life and send you down to Hades, since not even the Earth-shaker will heal your eye" (525).[38] It is at this point of Odysseus' gratuitous verbal aggression that Polyphemus utters his curse (526–35). Only then does Odysseus glimpse the possible power of the prayer and therefore (implicitly) his own folly: "So he [Polyphemus] spoke in prayer, and the god of the dark hair heard him" (536). When Odysseus sacrifices the Cyclops' great ram to Zeus "who rules over all," he recognizes that Zeus "did not lay hold of the sacrifices but was deliberating how all the well-oared ships should perish and all my goodly companions" (552–55). Viewed only as narrative information, these lines show the limited knowledge of a mortal, one who is immersed in the stream of events. But they may also indicate the retrospective knowledge of the man who is telling this tale many years later and from this distance can discern a pattern of divine intervention that he could not see before.

We should not assume that Odysseus' comment in 9.553–55 proves the moral arbitrariness of Zeus or is the result of the sloppy fitting together of different versions. Homer is careful to separate his narratorial omniscience from Odysseus' ignorance of divine interventions, even when they are on his behalf.[39] We the audience know Zeus' design

---

[38] See the scholion ad 9.525 for the folly of Odysseus' assumption.

[39] *Od.* 12.389f. is the clearest instance. Cf. also 6.325f., where Odysseus does not know that Athena is in fact beside him now, in disguise, to help him; and in 7.263, in summarizing his travels to Arete, he does not know whether Calypso let him go "because of Zeus' message or whether her mind was changed." On Homer's care to keep mortal and divine knowledge distinct, see Jörgensen (1904) 366ff.

only by the poem's fiction of the omniscient narrator who can tell us what the gods say on Olympus (cf. 1.65–79 and 5.30–42).[40] The connection between the Cyclops' curse and the will of Zeus is made only in the third-person account of the omniscient narrator in a scene on Olympus to which Odysseus cannot, of course, be privy (13.125–45; cf. 1.68–75). In contrast to the direct, material, and anthropomorphic intervention of Poseidon in his affairs, this negative sign from Zeus in 9.552 is remote, mysterious, and hard for Odysseus to explain or interpret.

On Polyphemus' island the hero is drawn toward resemblance with his antagonist. For both the hero and the monster, in different ways, hatred and anger threaten to override their own good. If Poseidon's wrath is an extension of the primitive brutishness of the son who calls it forth, Odysseus sinks to a similar level of impulsive anger and vengefulness: he addresses the Cyclops "with wrathful spirit" (κεκοτηότι θυμῷ, 9.501)[41] and makes his disastrous boast (501–5). Yet, unlike the Cyclops, Odysseus eventually recognizes the consequences of his behavior, for he is, of course, telling this tale of his own errors. He lets us see his own retrospective recognition of his folly when he tells how he refused to heed his companions' "gentle words" (492f., 500).

The closest that Polyphemus comes to any such opportunity for reflection is his address to his ram, a dumb beast who is carrying his enemy to safety.

> Dear ram, why have you now come forth last from the cave? [. . .] Do you long for the eye of your lord, the eye that No-Man put out with his evil companions, subduing my wits by wine? I think that he has not yet escaped destruction. Would that you could be of the same mind [homophroneois] and be able to speak and say where he avoids my might. (9.477f., 452–57)

Many centuries later Theocritus and Ovid exploited the touch of pathos that for a moment humanizes the monster; but even his best attempt to

---

[40] The inconsistency, if such it is, between what Odysseus says of Zeus in 9.553–55 and what Zeus says in books 1 and 5 can most simply be explained by Odysseus' assumption that human affairs generally are governed in some way or another by Zeus (so too, e.g., Nausicaa at 6.188f.) and that Poseidon's agency will, however remotely, have the approval of Zeus: see notes 42 and 43 below.

[41] This phrase, "with wrathful spirit," recurs only twice more in the poem, both in situations of extreme anger: Odysseus' address to the impudent maid Melantho in 19.71 and the mutilation of Melanthius in 22.477. It is akin obviously to the kotos (wrath) of Poseidon himself (11.102 = 13.342).

reach out in sympathy to another living creature is bound to failure. Cyclopean "like-mindedness" or fellow-feeling (*homophrosunē, homophroneois*, 456) is very different from the civilized *homophrosunē* to which Odysseus can appeal in his tactful address to Nausicaa (6.181–85); it is only a wish addressed to a dumb creature that is in fact rescuing his hated enemy. On the level of plot, then, as well as of language, Polyphemus can only reiterate the means of his deception ("No-Man," in 9.455, 460). And he can only reiterate his own outrageous violence of dashing out the brains of his victims as the brief moment of sympathetic calm gives way to thoughts of revenge: "So would his brain be dashed against the ground all over my cave as he is beaten every which way, and my heart would find rest from the woes that no-good No-Man gave me" (9.458–60; cf. 9.289f.).

In the Cyclops episode, however, Odysseus is still partially blind to the will of Zeus. Despite his foreboding at the sacrifice of Polyphemus' ram (9.553–55), he never makes the explicit connection between Poseidon's anger and Zeus' complicity in the hardness and losses of his return. In his retrospective comment on the sacrifice, he mentions neither the Cyclops nor Poseidon.[42] He learns of Poseidon's wrath, at first hand, only when he has escaped from it to Ithaca (13.342f.). Strictly speaking, he is incorrect in asserting that Zeus "was deliberating how all the well-oared ships should perish and my goodly companions" (9.554f.), for we never hear of Zeus planning in exactly this way. His "unerring plan" aims in quite the contrary direction, toward the "return of Odysseus" (5.30). Early in the poem he explicitly says that Poseidon's anger at the blinding of his son and not any plan of his own is the cause of Odysseus' delay (1.68–70).

The nature of divine justice appears differently when Odysseus gets beyond the morally primitive realm of the Cyclops. When he describes the culminating disaster of his travels, the shipwreck off Thrinacia, he attributes both destructiveness and helpfulness to Zeus: Zeus destroys the ship by lightning (12.415f.; cf. 7.250), and Zeus prevents Scylla's

---

[42] Even Teiresias' prophecy does not seem to open his eyes (11.102f.). When Ino-Leucothea asks Odysseus why Poseidon hates him so (5.339–41), she naturally assumes that a shipwrecked man has incurred the sea god's wrath: see 4.505ff. In 5.423, 5.446, and 6.326 Odysseus knows of or assumes Poseidon's wrath; but even though he has had the prophecy of Teiresias, he says nothing of the Cyclops. When Odysseus does get a brief glimpse of divine dealings, thanks to Calypso, it is of the wrath of Helios, not Poseidon (12.374–90). Some of the difficulty of 9.553–55 may be due to Homer's attempt to combine a straightforward narration of the past with the first-person retrospection.

reappearance (12.445f.).[43] In noting this helpful intervention, Odysseus here gives Zeus the paternal epithet "father of gods and men" (12.445). This shipwreck, unlike that of book 5, is under the sign of Zeus, not Poseidon, for it is not merely the result of a specific god's personal animosity but has a claim to justice. Odysseus' explicit mention of Zeus at this point may reflect his recognition of the justice of his companions' doom. He had recently learned from Calypso, shortly after Hermes' visit to her island (12.389f.), that the agent of destruction is Zeus, but he also knows that Zeus has taken over from Helios the task of punishing a human transgression against divine prerogatives (cf. 12.374–88). When he makes his men swear a solemn oath on Thrinacia "that no one by his evil recklessness [*atasthaliai kakai*] kill any cow or sheep" (12.300f.), he echoes the poet's own words in the proem on their fatal *atasthaliai* (1.6–9) and so, presumably, is moving closer to the truthful knowledge embodied in that narratorial omniscience.

Helios and Thrinacia

Although the Cyclops includes "losing all the companions" in his curse (9.534), it is not the curse itself that produces this part of his revenge. It results from the men's own transgression of a divine command, the taboo on eating the cattle of Helios.[44] The pattern validates Zeus' theology in the proem, which we now see through Odysseus' eyes, and also introduces an important change in the conception of divinity. Helios' revenge, unlike Poseidon's, develops from a series of carefully demarcated stages that reveal the companions' responsibility at nearly every point.[45]

[43] There is no necessary contradiction between Zeus' role here and his "unerring plan" to effect the "return of Odysseus" in 5.30f., as the latter passage is spoken seven years after Odysseus has lost men and ships off Thrinacia (12.415f.).

[44] On the religious and ritual violations involved in the eating of Helios' cattle, see Vernant (1979) 243–48. Before Thrinacia, Odysseus does not know that his men are doomed. Teiresias had pointed out that even the Cyclops' curse would not necessarily lead to the companions' annihilation, for Poseidon would only make the return "hard" (*argaleon*, 11.101). Circe then repeats Teiresias' words verbatim (12.137–41 = 11.110–14).

[45] Schadewaldt (1960) 865–66 gives a good account of the gradual, step-by-step process of the companions' doom but overstates the importance of Odysseus' oath, which he regards as a moralizing addition to fit the episode into the theology of the proem (867–68). The oath is, in fact, not mentioned again after the landing on Thrinacia (12.298–304). See also Bona (1966) 10ff. and Andersen (1973) 12–14.

In the first stage, repeating the warnings of Teiresias and Circe, Odysseus urges them to bypass Thrinacia (12.271–76). Led by the factious Eurylochus, the men refuse, complaining of exhaustion (278–93). Odysseus gives in on the condition that they swear not to harm the cattle, and the men so swear (303f.). When they do land, Odysseus repeats the warning yet again (320–23).

With the second stage, a month passes, and they are becalmed and short of food (12.325–32). Odysseus withdraws to pray to all the gods of Olympus, but they answer his prayer by "pouring sweet sleep on [his] lids" (337f.). In his absence, Eurylochus "began his evil plan" (339) and makes a second speech, rousing the companions to disobey. They can, he suggests, make reparation with offerings if they reach Ithaca; in any case a swift death at sea is preferable to slow starvation on the island (340–51).

Odysseus awakens in the third stage, discovers what the men have done, and complains to Zeus and the other gods for having "brought [him] to disastrous folly [atē] through pitiless sleep," during which the others "devised their enormous deed" (12.371–73). This complaint to "Zeus and the other gods" illustrates just the accusation that Zeus leveled against humankind in the proem (1.32ff.). The underlying cause of the catastrophe is the men's own folly, not the gods' malevolence. The gods merely make use of the weakness of mortal flesh (Odysseus' somnolence) to give the companions the space and freedom in which to destroy themselves.[46] In contrast to the Cyclops episode, this moral causation is kept prominently in view.

And in the final stage, Helios learns of the slaughter of his cattle and at once addresses Zeus, threatening to withhold his light from the world unless he receives tisis, "retribution" (12.378, 382). Meanwhile, the men sacrifice and eat the forbidden cattle, after which Zeus, in due course,

---

[46] The gods' role in sending sleep is arguably ambiguous. The sleep seems to come as an ironic answer to Odysseus' prayer of 12.337f. The contrast between the generic epithets of the "sweet sleep" (glukus hupnos, 338; nēdumos hupnos, 366) that frames this motif and the "pitiless sleep" (nēleēs hupnos) with which the gods have allegedly lulled him into "infatuation" (atē) in his outcry on awakening in 12.372 may also suggest that Odysseus is blaming the gods for the normal mortal weaknesses of the flesh. Compare the role of sleep in proving the weaknesses of mortality in the Gilgamesh Epic (tablet 11.197–228). The thematically related sleep in the Aeolus episode (Od. 10.31ff.) is naturalistically motivated by Odysseus' ten days at the rudder all alone (10.31–33). The unmotivated sleep of the Helios episode is possibly the result of a deeper weariness and of increasing loss of control. For the problem and review of previous literature, see Bona (1966) 21–23.

lures them again to the open sea, where he destroys the ship. Only Odysseus survives (397ff.).

The gods, to be sure, do not go out of their way to help the straitened Greeks; and the "sweet sleep" that they send to Odysseus precipitates the disaster. We feel sympathy for the doomed companions; their fault, given the circumstances, might seem pardonable and in any case not deserving of such severe punishment. Yet it involves the serious transgression of the boundaries between human and divine, and Odysseus' narrative emphasizes the men's responsibility rather than divine malevolence. Although Zeus sends the winds that drive the Greeks to moor their ships in a hollow cave (12.312–17), this happens only *after* Eurylochus has "forced" Odysseus to make the Thrinacian landing in the first place (297). It is significant that no divine agency is mentioned for the month-long south wind that strands them on the island. Homer says only, "For the whole month the south wind blew unceasingly" (325). Like Aegisthus in the proem and like the suitors later, the companions are fully warned. They also yield to "reckless folly" (*atasthaliai*), despite having alternative courses of action. When they decide to sacrifice Helios' cattle, they are not actually starving: they are living on fish, birds, and other game (330–32). This diet may not be to their taste, but it is enough to keep them alive.

In terms of the common Homeric device of double determination, the gods' intervention is the visible expression of the companions' loss of morale, discipline, and good judgment. At the moment when Odysseus accedes to Eurylochus' request to land, he recognizes that "a god was plotting evils" (καὶ τότε δὴ γίνωσκον ὃ δὴ κακὰ μήδετο δαίμων, 12.295). This divine "devising" has its visible, human equivalent when Eurylochus "began his evil counsel to the companions" immediately after the gods send sleep to Odysseus (339). Odysseus himself presciently interprets his men's initial disobedience as "evil recklessness," *atasthaliai kakai* (300), thereby bringing their act into line with Zeus' warnings in the proem and the punishment of the suitors.

Even this brief analysis shows how carefully motivated is Helios' anger and how different it is from the circumstances and execution of Poseidon's wrath.[47] To this extent, therefore, Odysseus' explanation for his and his men's suffering progresses from a model of wrathful retaliation to one of personal responsibility and to an at least partially defined moral causality.

Poseidon never mentions justice. He is motivated solely by anthropomorphic, personal animosity. Odysseus had committed no crime in punishing the Cyclops, and the god is merely holding a bitter grudge. When Zeus sanctions Poseidon's reprisal against the innocent (13.128–58), he is acceding to a pattern of behavior which, as we have noted, is bracketed as remote or obsolete through the association of Cyclopes, Phaeacians, and Poseidon with an older golden age/silver age world. It is as if a remnant of the Phaeacians' ancient proximity to the Giants and Cyclopes still clings to them (cf. 6.4–6, 7.59ff.). Even so, Zeus tempers Poseidon's violence, so that the sea god does not "smash" the ship but only turns it to stone (13.151 and 163f.; cf. 13.177f.).[48] Poseidon now goes off "apart" (nosphi, 13.164), resuming the situation where we found him at the opening of the epic (1.20).

From Vendetta to Justice

Poseidon's anger is pure wrath (kotos, cholos) in a narrowly personal vendetta. Homer's contemporaries, of course, would recognize the right of a family member to exact vengeance. Odysseus implies a story of just such a family vendetta in his first lie on Ithaca (13.258–73). A little later Telemachus learns of a similar story from the prophet Theoclymenus (15.224, 272–78). And the poem will end with the attempt by Antinous' father to take vengeance for the killing of his son (24.433–37). Yet Zeus' opening paradigm of family vengeance, the story of Orestes, embeds such vendettas in a clearly moral structure of the overstepping of limits, the lack of good sense, and retribution (huper moron, agatha phronein, and tisis, 1.35–43).

The motif of brutal divine anger drops out of the poem when Odysseus escapes from Poseidon's realm in book 13.[49] Once outside the god's

[47] Such considerations also show the inadequacy of the analysts' view of Helios as a mere doublet of Poseidon: see the review of scholarship in Schadewaldt (1960) 861, with note 1. Equally mistaken, I believe, is the view put forth by Fenik (1974) that the Helios episode is "a hasty attempt to harmonize the Helios story with the ethical norms set forth by Zeus in his first speech, an attempt that is simply abandoned within the wrath-tale itself" (225–26). The problem arose, Fenik argues, because the poet did not want to change "the old adventure stories of the Apologoi" when he incorporated them into his epic (226). But we should distinguish between possible origins and the final effect or, in other words, between the diachronic and synchronic perspectives.

[48] For Zeus and Poseidon here, see above, note 27.

[49] For the blinding of Polyphemus and the anger of Poseidon, see, for instance, in addition to book 9, 1.68–79, 5.339–41, 5.446, 6.328–31, 11.101–3, 13.125ff., and 13.339–43. In Demodocus' song of Ares and Aphrodite, however, it is, ironically, Poseidon who points the way to a peaceful, nonviolent solution: see note 24 above.

reach, he establishes a new relation with divinity, beginning with his face-to-face meeting with his patron goddess, Athena, for the first time since he left Troy (cf. 13.314–23).[50] This relation is at once more personal and more focused on moral behavior than what has preceded. The Cyclopes' and Phaeacians' respective relationships with their gods are based on genealogy; Odysseus' relation with Athena, as she indicates, is based on an affinity of natures.[51] The shift, in other terms, is from a metonymic to a metaphoric principle, from contiguity (by blood) to affinity (by nature).[52] Zeus, who is the most detached of all the gods, is also the fullest embodiment of this relation by principle rather than by kinship. After he appeases his brother Poseidon's wrath against Odysseus and the Phaeacians, he becomes almost wholly a remote Olympian guardian of justice and retribution.

The Helios episode prepares for this progression, for it embodies a shift from the narrow, personal motivation of a particular god (Poseidon against Odysseus) to a universal god concerned with the preservation of world order (Zeus keeping Helios in the heavens). Even Helios' wrath has a moral structure, for the slaughter and eating of the forbidden cattle violates the sacrificial code that keeps the proper distance between god and man.[53] The grouping of both these movements at the poem's major geographical transition in book 13 brings together the two developments of divinity: the change from paternal loyalty to affinity of character and the change from purely anthropomorphic wrath to the administration of justice.

By the end of the epic, Odysseus comes close to realizing Zeus' Olympian plan on earth (albeit with some important qualifications, as

---

[50] On the importance of this scene as a transitional moment in Odysseus' situation, see Rutherford (1986) 157–59, with the bibliography in his note 63.

[51] For example, *Od.* 13.296–99, 330–32. See above, Chapter 3; also Clay (1983) 42–43, 198–99. Cf. *Od.* 5.5–20 and Pucci (1987) 20–23. Note too that Athena's emphasis on her skill in *pasi doloisi* (all wiles) in her identification of herself to odds in 13.298f. echoes the same terms in Odysseus' self-revelation to the Phaeacians in 9.19f.: see Pucci (1982) 52.

[52] One should be careful not to moralize this meeting excessively; and Rutherford (1986) 148 rightly raises the point that Athena's delight in their affinity rests on trickery rather than moral behavior. But morality is not entirely excluded. To be sure, Athena stresses cleverness rather than morality as their common bond; yet the quality of good sense or firmness of mind (*echephrōn*) in 13.332 has a moral application: cf. 22.411–16. She appreciates Odysseus' moral qualities, moreover, at the very beginning, when she praises his piety in 1.60–62, and Zeus had agreed. In their meeting in book 13, she obviously cannot talk of *sharing* the quality of piety with him because she is speaking as a god, and Homer would not call a god "pious."

[53] See above, note 44.

we shall see) and answering the god's complaint, made in the proem, about mortals. He echoes Zeus' words as he stands over the bodies of the suitors: "Therefore by their recklessness did they meet their ugly doom" (22.416; cf. 1.34). Later, Laertes recognizes his son and his deed in similar terms, the requital of the suitors' "reckless insulting" (*atasthalon hubrin eteisan*, 24.351f.).[54] Even Penelope, skeptical as she is about Odysseus' return, has no doubts about the mechanism of divine justice: "Some one of the immortals killed them, looking angrily at their outrage that pains the heart and their evil deeds. . . . Therefore did they suffer woe because of their reckless folly" (23.63–68). The slain suitors, on the other hand, remain totally blind to the moral pattern behind their death. Amphimedon, explaining their demise to Agamemnon in Hades, sees behind Odysseus' return only some vague "evil divinity" (*kakos daimōn*, 24.149). He dimly discerns "the mind of Zeus" (ἀλλ' ὅτε δή μιν ἔγειρε Διὸς νόος αἰγιόχοιο, "but when the mind of aegis-bearing Zeus awakened him [Odysseus]," 24.164), but only as the agent that "arouses Odysseus" from his tolerance of blows and insults, not as a moral intelligence behind the return as a whole. Like the Cyclops, he never mentions "retribution" or "justice" (*tisis, dikē*).

The Complexities of Justice

The account of the Cyclops' curse in book 9 shows Odysseus' life story in a triple refraction: he hears his destined portion (*moira*) foretold (1) in the words of an enemy in a tale (2) which he is now telling to the Phaeacians and (3) which we now hear as a tale-within-a-tale. That he reports his own failings, particularly with editorial comments such as "it would have been much better" (9.228), shows the narrator's own perspective of greater understanding of his past. He even reports the charge that his own "reckless folly" caused the Cyclops' destruction of his men (10.435–37). At that point Odysseus was not prepared to credit this view of his moral responsibility, and he would have drawn his sword to strike off the speaker's head (10.438–41). To be sure, he attenuated the men's accusation by his unflattering account of the accuser's character and situation: Eurylochus has been traumatized by witnessing Circe's magic (10.431–34). Nevertheless, Odysseus does not

---

[54] On this passage see Dimock (1989) 330. Note too the prophet Halitherses' remark on the death of the suitors because of their own "evil folly" (*atasthaliēsi kakēsi*, 24.458); and he is heeded by the suitors' kin no more than he was by the suitors themselves when he interpreted the omen of the eagles in the assembly of book 2.

suppress the accusation, nor his own violent reaction to it (10.438–42).[55] It is, of course, possible that his intention is also to display himself to the Phaeacians as a man who has learned better; but were his aim only to please his guests, he might have kept wholly silent about these unfavorable details.

This retrospective technique expresses one of the *Odyssey*'s underlying messages, namely, that human life is always in process: to live as a mortal is to suffer and to change and to keep learning about both humans and gods (1.3). Even when Odysseus has reached his goal of reunion with Penelope, there is more toil ahead, which he unfolds as he relates Teiresias' prophecy (23.248ff.).[56] Even when he is safe among the Phaeacians and tells them of the Cyclops' prayer, he has learned that an ultimately happy *nostos* (return) can be robbed of its joy by the losses and sufferings that attend it (9.532–34).

By the end of the poem, Odysseus does seem to have learned from his mistakes. When he has killed the last of the suitors, Eurycleia would raise the cry of triumph, but Odysseus "restrained her and held her back, eager though she was" (κατέρυκε καὶ ἔσχεθεν ἱεμένην περ, 22.409). The hero who years before could not restrain his own boasting can now check his servant in a situation where boasting might indeed be safe and appropriate.[57] Yet even in that earlier episode his capacity for such restraint saved his life, for he resisted his initial impulse to kill Polyphemus in his cave (ἕτερος δέ με θυμὸς ἔρυκεν, "a different impulse held me back," 9.302). It is "not piety to boast over dead men," he tells Eurycleia now, for it is the "portion from the gods," their own "harsh deeds," and their own "overweening insolence" that brought about their doom (22.412–16). The last word in 416 brings us back to Zeus' warnings about men's *atasthaliai* in the proem (1.33f.; cf. 1.7), but it is now Odysseus himself who puts this moral construction on the events.[58]

Just before this gesture of moral restraint, Odysseus himself moral-

[55] Gill (1990) 10–11 rightly stresses the ethical accountability and accessibility of Odysseus' account of his past; yet the situation becomes far more complex when one also considers the multiple refractions of the embedded narrative form.

[56] See above, Chapter 9.

[57] The scholion ad 22.412 cites the occasion of a boast by Odysseus over a fallen enemy in the *Iliad* (11.450) but rather oddly says nothing of the far more relevant boast to Polyphemus in the *Odyssey*. See also above, note 14.

[58] *Schetlia erga* (harsh deeds) here in 22.413 was also Odysseus' phrase for the Cyclops' first outrage in 9.295. The phrase occurs only one other time in the *Odyssey*, when Eumaeus, criticizing the suitors, generalizes about the morality enforced by the gods: "The blessed gods do not love harsh deeds, but they pay back retributive justice and the rightful deeds of men" (14.83f.).

izes the meaning of his victory as he heeds Telemachus' request to "hold
back" from killing the bard and the herald (22.356, 367). "Take courage," Odysseus tells the herald, Medon, "since [Telemachus] rescued
and saved you, so that you may know in your heart and tell another man
too that doing good is far better than doing evil" (372–74). As herald
and bard are so closely associated in this scene, Odysseus' pronounce-
ment can apply to the bardic as well as to the heraldic voice: this
message is what the two professional communicators will henceforth
announce to mortals (ἀτὰρ εἴπῃσθα καὶ ἄλλῳ, "so that you may tell
another one too," 373). This moral message also has the authority of
"great Zeus," at whose altar both bard and herald now find refuge (379).
The poem's last scene continues this grouping of bard and herald for a
moral function as they awaken just in time to explain the gods' ways to
the suitors' angry kinsmen. The herald's last task, again in close association with the "divine singer," Phemius (24.439–40), is to warn these
men that Odysseus acted with the gods' aid (24.438–49).

In preparing Odysseus for the bloody deed of revenge at his arrival
on Ithaca, even Athena had taken pleasure in envisaging "some one
of the suitors splattering the ground with his blood and his brains"
(13.395f.). Her contemplated revenge is strikingly similar to the Cyclops' murderous feasting (cf. 9.289f. and 9.458–60). Her expectation
seems to be realized when we do in fact hear of Odysseus, in third-
person narration, as "splattered with the blood and gore" of the suitors,
though to the relief of the modern reader, Homer leaves out the brains
(22.402). Here, too, Odysseus, like the Cyclops, is compared to a
ravening lion (22.402–5 and 9.292; cf. also 4.335ff.). Yet, as we have
noted, he immediately restrains himself and his servant with a concern
for "piety" (22.411–16), and he orders the purification of the chamber
soon after (22.480f.). In this way he separates himself from the brutality
of his more "primitive" Cyclopean stage and comes closer to the broad
perspective of Zeus found in the proem.

Odysseus' house on Ithaca now realizes the positive paradigm of
Zeus' justice, of which the negative paradigm was the house of Agamemnon. In Odysseus' house both Penelope and Laertes respond to the
deed of vengeance with a moral interpretation similar to that of Odysseus (and of Zeus): the suitors have suffered for their wanton outrage,
evil deeds, recklessness, and reckless outrage (hubris, kaka erga, atasthaliai, atasthalos hubris, 23.64–67, 24.351f.).

No situation or perception in the Odyssey remains static for very
long, and the poem ends neither with the hero's exemplary moral

restraint nor with his close kin's moral justification but with the continuation of the hero's rashness and impulsiveness. In the closing scene, Odysseus does not heed Athena's first call to "hold back from battle" (ἴσχεσθε πτολέμου, 24.531; cf. 22.409), despite the "pale green fear" that grips everyone else (24.531–36). To stop him requires a thunderbolt from Zeus himself and then a second admonition from Athena to "hold back" directed specifically at him (ἴσχεο, 543). Athena's warning to "hold back" also repeats Odysseus' own command to Eurycleia of restraint just after the suitors' deaths (ἴσχεο, 22.411) and earlier to Telemachus (ἴσχανε, 19.42; cf. also 22.356, 367). Athena thus uses Odysseus' own admonition against him. It is not just the Cyclops and the suitors who refuse to "heed the gods" and who fall prey to their moral blindness. Yet Odysseus soon does "obey" the goddess (*epeitheto*, 24.545), as he did not obey his men in the Cyclops episode (9.228 and 500).

The little scene with Athena reflects one of the underlying themes of the epic. Mortal life is always subject to time and change and to the uncontrollable contingencies that these hold. And humans are always subject to fits of rashness, anger, and destructive folly. Hence there is always need of Odysseus' virtues of adaptability, moderation, and the awareness of possible retribution from the gods. As we see him in this closing episode of the poem, Odysseus, despite (and even because of) his successes and victories, still needs the restraint, foresight, and prudence associated with his goddess Athena.

This danger of slipping back to careless self-importance may explain a curious omission near the end of the poem. Despite all the suffering that Polyphemus' curse has cost him, when he comes to tell this portion of his adventures to Penelope in their joyful night of reunion, Odysseus speaks only of having punished the Cyclops and says nothing of his responsibility for having provoked the curse that so delayed his return (23.312f.). The habit of self-presentation in the Iliadic mold dies hard. Or perhaps Odysseus assumes that his wife will be more interested in hearing about his cleverness than about his folly and its cost.

At the end, however, Odysseus is not allowed to become the kind of hero who seeks the unlimited extension of his will and his passion, as did Achilles in *Iliad* 18–22.[59] Athena, so closely identified with his most

---

[59] In *Iliad* 24 the gods also intervene and impose limits (e.g., 24.112–19), but only after the hero has crossed, or threatened to cross, these limits and thus stands in a position of tragic excess and violation.

"Odyssean" characteristics (cf. 13.330–38), calls him back at the end to being truly Odysseus. As in the proem, she and Zeus work together; they collaboratively insist that this is not the world of the *Iliad* nor the place for the *Iliad*'s unchecked surge of warlike violence and bloodlust (24.526–47).

In the *Iliad*, the attempts early in the action to "end strife" prove ineffectual or partial.[60] In the *Odyssey*, divine fiat imposes the cessation of the "strife" (*neikos*, 24.543) that divides the social order. These gods, like Zeus in the last book of the *Iliad*, hold out to humans the hope that they may attain (or regain) the more orderly society that we glimpse fleetingly in the assembly of book 2, in aspects of the Phaeacian kingdom and in Odysseus' almost Hesiodic praise of good kingship to Penelope in book 19 (108–14; cf. *Works and Days* 225–37). In this world, as in the *Iliad*, violence is not to be the final solution; and the poem ends not with battle but with the conciliatory and civilizing act of oaths on both sides (24.546).[61]

Conclusion: Fantasy and Realism

Odysseus' last Iliadic battle faces both backward and forward. It is a renewal of the vigor of his father, who, thanks to Athena, actually makes the kill, like a warrior of the *Iliad* (*Od.* 24.516–25). And it assures the future of his line in his son's proof of valor and Laertes' joy in the presence of three generations fighting together (24.504–15). As we know, however, Odysseus' last triumph is not the end of his story. His life requires some further, unknown effort beyond the immediate satisfaction—an effort that is characteristically Odyssean in its motifs of travel, ambiguous words, and encounters with unfamiliar people and customs (cf. 1.3f.). And here he will have to draw on strengths outside himself, in this case the "hope" that Penelope opposes to his foreboding (23.286f.; cf. 23.248–50).[62]

In the proem Athena asks Zeus, in a striking phrase, why he has so

---

[60] Cf. *Il.* 1.210, 1.319, 2.221–24, 2.243, 2.277. On *neikos* (quarrel) and *eris* (strife) in relation to the social order envisaged by epic, see Nagy (1979) 226–27, 311ff.

[61] With the *Odyssey*'s closing act of reconciliation we may compare the great scene of reconciliation between Achilles and Priam in *Iliad* 24 or the gods' demand for the return of Hector's body at the beginning of that book; but the *Iliad*'s reconciliation is more firmly grounded in the action and holds a more profoundly tragic sense.

[62] Penelope's expression of "hope" to Odysseus in a moment of discouragement also recalls Athena's similar "hope" to encourage Telemachus in 2.280.

hated Odysseus (τί νύ οἱ τόσον ὠδύσαο, Ζεῦ, 1.62). Zeus' disclaimer at once imposes a moral structure on the tale: he recognizes Odysseus' piety and gives assurance of his safe return (1.63–67). Yet this same speech also opens a gap between Zeus' moral concerns (the respect for piety) and another kind of divinity, the purely anthropomorphic vengefulness of Poseidon for Odysseus' blinding of his son (1.68–75).

Viewed narratologically, Zeus can be regarded as an authorial function: the sign of the poet's intention to redefine the inherited material of his tale and stamp it with a moral meaning. This moral redefinition of the story stands out all the more sharply against Zeus' allusion to Poseidon's unceasing wrath immediately after his praise of Odysseus (1.68–79). Homer could easily have accommodated the motif of Poseidon's wrath to the moral interpretation of Odysseus' sufferings, for he might have traced its cause to Odysseus' own *atasthaliai,* on the analogy of Zeus' example of Aegisthus (1.32–43). The Cyclops episode, however, avoids this model, for Odysseus, not Zeus, is its narrator, and he never refers to his provocation of Polyphemus as reckless violence. Yet the proem, by the very fact of allowing the moralized interpretation of the whole poem to become visible in Zeus' explicit blaming of Poseidon, also reveals the other possibility, namely, that the poet might have sung a tale of divine wrath, cruelty, injustice, and nonrationalized and nonmoralized misfortune and that in fact the poem we are hearing exists as the negation of such a tale.

This "other" in the narrative—the possibility of a surd, malevolent, and amoral blocking force or of uncontrollable violence—never fully disappears, even after Poseidon's effective exit from the action in book 13. We glimpse it through the chinks in the moralized tale that we have already noted: the doom of the companions in the Thrinacian episode and our sympathy for them, Odysseus' ruthless determination to extirpate all the suitors, his vengeance on the maidservants, and his bloodthirstiness in the last battle. Interpreters have sometimes regarded these morally recalcitrant elements as part of the poem's myth of "nature's" refusal to assimilate to "culture" or as the clash between the centripetally organized "high" mythic structure and the "lower" centrifugal material of folktale.[63] However we conceptualize it, the tension remains as a disturbing but also dynamic force in the poem. It becomes visible particularly when the Zeus narrative and the Poseidon narrative meet, as they do in Zeus' explanation of Odysseus' suffering in the proem, in

[63] See Peradotto (1990) 75–93, especially 82–83.

the final and suspended fate of the Phaeacians, and (in displaced form) in the wrath of Helios.

Zeus' thunderbolt that commands restraint at the end (24.539) marks the establishment of his order among humans. The narrative progression to this ending is comparable with the movement toward the sovereignty of Zeus in Hesiod's *Theogony*. What is explicitly evolutionary in Hesiod, however, is here enacted paradigmatically in the purely human events and in the "realistic" space and time of Ithaca. Despite the divine intervention and the fabulous events in Odysseus' travels, the *Odyssey* returns emphatically to the human plane and even more than the *Iliad* keeps this human plane in the foreground. Like the *Iliad,* too, emphasizing personal choice and responsibility, it prepares the way for Attic tragedy.

Ending with the authority of Zeus and Athena together repeats the strategy of the proem, momentarily uncovering and then rejecting irrational violence. It also reaffirms the moral order enunciated by Zeus in the proem, once again in combination with Athena (1.32–67). Indeed, the ending seems to look back directly to the proem with Athena's warning, in the last verse of direct speech in the poem, that Odysseus' disobedience will incur Zeus' wrath (24.544). His disobedience would turn him into that object of Zeus' "hatred" that Zeus himself abjured there (1.62–67).[64] Odysseus' hesitation to obey re-creates the proem's chink or gap in the smoothness of a completely rationalized, morally ordered narrative in which the hero is rewarded for following the justice of Zeus. In like manner we are reminded of the continuing wrath of Poseidon, in the domestic side of the return, as Odysseus tells Penelope of Teiresias' prophecy and his future inland journey with the oar (23.248–53, 265–84).

Both the poem's movements toward closure—the domestic in book 23 and the martial in 24—therefore still leave a gap between fulfillment and suspension, one analogous to the closure of the *nostos* narrative with the anxious Phaeacians in book 13. Although husband and wife are reunited, there is the threat of future separation and "measureless suffering" (23.249). Although the hero has defeated the enemies of his house and has won back his kingdom, there remain his closing recalcitrance to peace and the abruptness of a divinely imposed ending.

All of which is to say that the *Odyssey* is poetry, not moral philosophy. The model of a god's personal wrath as a blocking force is never

---

[64] On the echo between these passages, see Peradotto (1990) 166–67.

entirely forgotten (cf. 23.276–79, 352f.), so that Zeus' justice emerges not as a flat certainty but often as a distant and precarious goal. The world implied in Zeus' speech in the proem of book 1, a world governed ultimately by divine justice, has the status of a vision, a kind of hypothesis set forth in the quasi-authorial voice of the ruler of gods and mortals; but it is vision still open to the other, harder, and more painful visions of how mortals and gods may behave. For all its exuberant fantasy and imagination, the *Odyssey*, like the *Iliad*, has a profound realism in its exploration of why misery, violence, and suffering still continue to define the human condition.

References

Abrahamson, Ernst. 1960. *The Adventures of Odysseus*. St. Louis.

Allen, T. W., ed. 1912. *Homeri Opera*. Vol. 5. Oxford Classical Texts. Oxford.

Amory, Anne. 1963. "The Reunion of Odysseus and Penelope." In Charles H. Taylor, Jr., ed. *Essays on the "Odyssey."* Bloomington. 100–21.

Andersen, Øivind. 1973. "Der Untergang der Gefährten in der Odyssee." *Symbolae Osloenses* 49:7–27.

———. 1992. "Agamemnon's Singer (*Od.* 3.262–272)." *Symbolae Osloenses* 67:5–26.

Armstrong, James I. 1958. "The Arming Motif in the *Iliad*." *American Journal of Philology*. 79:337–54.

Arthur, Marylin B. 1982. "Cultural Strategies in Hesiod's *Theogony*: Law, Family, Society." *Arethusa* 15:63–82.

Auerbach, Erich. 1957. *Mimesis: The Representation of Reality in Western Literature*. Trans. Willard Trask. New York.

Austin, Norman. 1972. "Name Magic in the *Odyssey*." *California Studies in Classical Antiquity* 5:1–19.

———. 1975. *Archery at the Dark of the Moon: Poetic Problems in Homer's "Odyssey."* Berkeley and Los Angeles.

———. 1981. "Odysseus Polytropos: Man of Many Minds." *Arche* 6:40–52.

———. 1983. "Odysseus and the Cyclops: Who Is Who." In Rubino and Shelmerdine, eds., 3–37.

———. 1991. "The Wedding Text in Homer's *Odyssey*." *Arion*, 3d series, 1, no. 2:227–43.

Autrain, Charles. 1938. *Homère et les origines sacerdotales de l'épopée grecque*. 3 vols. Paris.

Bassett, S. E. 1938. *The Poetry of Homer*. Sather Classical Lectures 15. Berkeley.

Baudouin, Charles. 1957. *Le triomphe du héros*. Paris.

Benveniste, Emile. 1969. *Le vocabulaire des institutions indo-européennes*. 2 vols. Paris.

Bergren, Ann. 1981. "Helen's 'Good Drug': *Odyssey* IV 1–305." In Stephan Kresic, ed. *Contemporary Literary Hermeneutics and Interpretation of Classical Texts*. Ottawa. 200–214.

Bertolini, Francesco. 1988. "Odisseo Aedo, Omero carpentiere: *Odissea* 17.384–85." *Lexis* 2:145–64.

———. 1989. "Dal folclore all' epica: Esempi di trasformazione e adattamento." In Diego Lanza and Oddone Longo, eds. *Il meraviglioso e il verosimile tra antichità e medioevo*. Florence. 131–52.

Blake, William. 1914. *The Marriage of Heaven and Hell*. Ed. John Sampson. Oxford.

Block, Elizabeth. 1985. "Clothing Makes the Man: A Pattern in the *Odyssey*." *Transactions of the American Philological Association* 115:1–11.

Blundell, Mary Whitlock. 1989. *Helping Friends and Harming Enemies: A Study in Sophocles and Greek Ethics*. Cambridge.

Bona, Giacomo. 1966. *Studi sull' "Odissea."* Turin. = Università di Torino, Facoltà di Lettere e Filosofia, Filologia Classica e Glottologia 1.

Bradley, Edward M. 1975. "On King Amphidamas' Funeral and Hesiod's Muses." *La Parola del Passato* 163:285–88.

———. 1976. " 'The Greatness of His Nature': Fire and Justice in the *Odyssey*." *Ramus* 5:137–48.

Brillante, Carlo. 1993. "Il cantore e la Musa nell' epica greca arcaica." *Rudiae: Ricerche sul Mondo Classico* 4:7–37.

Brown, Calvin S. 1966. "Odysseus and Polyphemus: The Name and the Curse." *Comparative Literature* 18:193–202.

Buffière, Felix. 1956. *Les mythes d'Homère*. Paris.

Burkert, Walter. 1960. "Das Lied von Ares und Aphrodite." *Rheinisches Museum für Philologie* 103:130–44.

———. 1985. *Greek Religion* (1972). Trans. John Raffan. Cambridge, Mass.

Calame, Claude. 1977. *Les chœurs de jeunes filles en Grèce archaïque*. 2 vols. Rome.

———. 1986. *Le récit en Grèce ancienne*. Paris.

Calhoun, G. M. 1933. "Homeric Repetitions." *University of California Publications in Classical Philology* 12, no. 1:1–25.

Carpenter, Rhys. 1946. *Folk Tale, Fiction, and Saga in the Homeric Epics*. Sather Classical Lectures 20. Berkeley and Los Angeles.

Caswell, Caroline P. 1990. *A Study of Thumos in Early Greek Epic*. Mnemosyne Supplement 114. Leiden.

Clarke, H. W. 1962. "Fire Imagery in the *Odyssey*." *Classical Journal* 57:358–60.

Clay, Jenny Strauss. 1983. *The Wrath of Athena*. Princeton.

Cook, Erwin. 1992. "Ferrymen of Elysium and the Homeric Phaeacians." *Journal of Indo-European Studies* 20:239–67.

Crane, Gregory. 1988. *Calypso: Backgrounds and Conventions in the "Odyssey."* Beiträge zur klassische Philologie 191. Frankfurt.

Detienne, Marcel. 1973. *Les maîtres de vérité dans la Grèce archaïque*. 2d ed. Paris.

Dimock, George E. 1956. "The Name of Odysseus." *Hudson Review* 9:52–70.

———. 1989. *The Unity of the "Odyssey."* Amherst, Mass.

Dodds, E. R. 1951. *The Greeks and the Irrational*. Sather Classical Lectures 25. Berkeley and Los Angeles.

Dorson, Richard M. 1964. *Buying the Wind: Regional Folklore in the United States.* Chicago.

Dougherty, Carol. 1991. "Phemius' Last Stand: The Impact of Occasion on Tradition in the *Odyssey.*" *Oral Tradition* 6:93–103.

Durante, Marcello. 1960. "La terminologia relativa alla creazione poetica." *Rendiconti dell' Accademia Nazionale dei Lincei* 15:244–49. = Schmitt, ed., 1968. 283–90. In German translation.

Edwards, Anthony T. 1985. *Odysseus against Achilles: The Role of Allusion in the Homeric Epic.* Beiträge zur klassische Philologie 171. Meisenheim/Glan.

Eitrem, Sam. 1938. "Phaiaken." In *Real-Encyclopädie der classischen Altertumswissenschaft.* Vol. 38. 1518–34.

Elderkin, G. W. 1940. "The Homeric Cave on Ithaca." *Classical Philology* 35:52–54.

Else, G. F. 1965. *Homer and the Homeric Problem.* Lectures in Memory of Louise Taft Semple. First Series. Cincinnati.

Falkner, Thomas M. 1989. "Ἐπὶ γήραος οὐδῷ: Homeric Heroism, Old Age, and the End of the *Odyssey.*" In T. M. Falkner and Judith de Luce, eds. *Old Age in Greek and Latin Literature.* Albany. 21–67.

Farron, S. G. 1979–80. "The Odyssey as Anti-Aristocratic Statement." *Studies in Antiquity* 1:59–101.

Fenik, Bernard. 1974. *Studies in the "Odyssey."* Hermes Einzelschriften 30. Wiesbaden.

Finley, John H., Jr. 1978. *Homer's "Odyssey."* Cambridge, Mass.

Finley, Moses. 1965. *The World of Odysseus.* Revised ed. New York.

Fitzgerald, Robert, trans. 1963. *The Odyssey.* New York.

Foley, Helene P. 1978. "'Reverse Similes' and Sex Roles in the *Odyssey.*" *Arethusa* 11:7–26.

Ford, Andrew. 1992. *Homer: The Poetry of the Past.* Ithaca, N.Y.

Frame, Douglas. 1978. *The Myth of Return in Early Greek Epic.* New Haven.

Francis, E. D. 1983. "Virtue, Folly, and Greek Etymology." In Rubino and Shelmerdine, eds., 74–121.

Fränkel, Hermann. 1962. *Dichtung und Philosophie des frühen Griechentum.* 2d ed. Munich.

Freud, Sigmund. 1922. *Group Psychology and the Analysis of the Ego.* Trans. James Strachey. London.

———. 1955. *Totem and Taboo* (1913). In *The Standard Edition of the Complete Psychological Works of Sigmund Freud.* Ed. and trans. James Strachey et al. Vol. 13. London.

Friedrich, Rainer. 1987. "Thrinakia and Zeus' Ways to Men in the *Odyssey.*" *Greek, Roman, and Byzantine Studies* 28:375–400.

———. 1989. "Zeus and the Phaeacians: Odyssey 13.158." *American Journal of Philology* 110:395–99.

Frontisi-Ducroux, Françoise. 1986. *La cithare d'Achille.* Rome.

Frye, Northrop. 1957. *Anatomy of Criticism.* Princeton.

Gennep, Arnold van. 1960. *The Rites of Passage* (1908). Chicago.

Germain, Gabriel. 1954. *Genèse de "l'Odyssée."* Paris.

Gernet, Louis. 1968. "La notion mythique de la valeur en Grèce." In *Anthropologie de la Grèce antique.* Paris. 93–137.

Gill, Christopher. 1990. "The Character-Personality Distinction." In Christopher Pelling, ed. *Characterization and Individuality in Greek Literature.* Oxford. 1–31.

Glenn, Justin. 1971. "The Polyphemus Folktale and Homer's Kyklopeia." *Transactions of the American Philological Association* 102:133–81.

——. 1978. "The Polyphemus Myth: Its Origin and Interpretation." *Greece and Rome* 25:141–55.

Goldhill, Simon. 1988. "Reading Differences: The *Odyssey* and Juxtaposition." *Ramus* 17:1–31.

Haft, Adele. 1983–84. "Odysseus, Idomeneus, and Meriones: The Cretan Lies of *Odyssey* 13–19." *Classical Journal* 79:289–306.

Hague, Rebecca. 1983. "Ancient Greek Wedding Songs: The Tradition of Praise." *Journal of Folklore Research* 20:131–43.

Hankey, Robin. 1990. "'Evil' in the *Odyssey*." In Elizabeth Craik, ed. *Owls to Athens: Essays on Classical Subjects for Sir Kenneth Dover.* Oxford. 88–95.

Hansen, William F. 1976. "The Story of the Sailor Who Went Inland." In Linda Dégh, Henry Glassie, and Felix Oinas, eds. *Folklore Today: A Festschrift for Richard M. Dorson.* Bloomington. 221–30.

——. 1977. "Odysseus' Last Journey." *Quaderni Urbinati di Cultura Classica* 24:27–48.

——. 1990. "Odysseus and the Oar: A Folkloric Approach." In Lowell Edmunds, ed. *Approaches to Greek Myth.* Baltimore. 241–72.

Harsh, Philip W. 1950. "Penelope and Odysseus in *Odyssey* XIX." *American Journal of Philology* 71:1–21.

Hart, W. M. 1943. "High Comedy in the *Odyssey*." *University of California Publications in Classical Philology* 12, no. 14:263–78.

Havelock, Eric A. 1963. *Preface to Plato.* Cambridge, Mass.

——. 1982. *The Literate Revolution in Greece and Its Consequences.* Princeton.

Herington, C. J. 1985. *Poetry into Drama.* Sather Classical Lectures 49. Berkeley and Los Angeles.

Heubeck, Alfred, and Arie Hoekstra, eds. 1989. *A Commentary on Homer's "Odyssey."* Vol. 2, bks. 9–16. Oxford.

Heubeck, Alfred, Stephanie West, and J. B. Hainsworth, eds. 1988. *A Commentary on Homer's "Odyssey."* Vol. 1, bks. 1–8. Oxford.

Hoekstra, Arie. 1965. *Homeric Modifications of Formulaic Prototypes.* Amsterdam.

Hogan, James C. 1976. "The Temptation of Odysseus." *Transactions of the American Philological Association* 106:187–210.

Hölscher, Uvo. 1939. *Untersuchungen zur Form der "Odyssee."* Hermes Einzelschriften 6. Berlin.

——. 1978. "The Transformation from Folk-Tale to Epic." In Bernard C. Fenik, ed. *Homer: Tradition and Invention.* Leiden. 51–67.

——. 1988. *Die "Odyssee": Epos zwischen Märchen und Roman.* Munich.

Irmscher, Johannes. 1950. *Götterzorn bei Homer.* Leipzig.

Jörgensen, Øve. 1904. "Das Auftreten der Götter in den Bücher ι—μ der *Odyssee.*" *Hermes* 39:357–82.

Katz, Marylin Arthur. 1991. *Penelope's Renown: Meaning and Indeterminacy in the "Odyssey."* Princeton.

Kirk, G. S. 1970. *Myth: Its Meaning and Function in Ancient and Other Cultures.* Sather Classical Lectures 40. Berkeley and Los Angeles.

Kitto, H. D. F. 1966. *Poiesis: Structure and Thought.* Sather Classical Lectures, vol. 36. Berkeley and Los Angeles.

Knight, W. F. Jackson. 1936. *Cumaean Gates.* Oxford.

Kurke, Leslie. 1991. *The Traffic in Praise: Pindar and the Poetics of Social Economy.* Ithaca, N.Y.

Lanata, Giuliana. 1963. *Poetica Preplatonica.* Florence.

Lattimore, Richmond, trans. 1967. *The Odyssey of Homer.* New York.

——. 1969. "Nausikaa's Suitors." In *Classical Studies Presented to Ben Edwin Perry.* Illinois Studies in Language and Literature 58:88–102.

Lefkowitz, Mary. 1981. *The Lives of the Greek Poets.* Baltimore.

Lesky, Albin. 1967. "Homeros." In *Real-Encyclopädie der classischen Altertumswissenschaft.* Supplementband 11. 687–846.

Levy, Gertrude R. 1948. *The Gate of Horn.* London.

——. 1953. *The Sword from the Rock.* London.

Lloyd-Jones, Hugh. 1971. *The Justice of Zeus.* Sather Classical Lectures 41. Berkeley and Los Angeles.

Lobel, Edgar, and Denys Page, eds. 1955. *Poetarum Lesbiorum Fragmenta.* Oxford.

Lord, Albert B. 1960. *The Singer of Tales.* Harvard Studies in Comparative Literature 24. Cambridge, Mass.

—— 1962. "Homer and Other Epic Poetry." In A. J. B. Wace and F. H. Stubbings, eds. *A Companion to Homer.* London. 179–214.

Marg, Walter. 1956. "Das erste Lied des Demodokos." In *Navicula Chiloniensis* (Festschrift Felix Jacoby). Leiden. 16–29.

——. 1971. *Homer über die Dichtung: Der Schild des Achilleus.* 2d ed. Münster.

Martin, Richard P. 1989. *The Language of Heroes: Speech and Performance in the "Iliad."* Ithaca, N.Y.

Merkelbach, Reinhold. 1952. "Bettelgedichte." *Rheinisches Museum für Philologie* 95:312–27.

Momigliano, Arnaldo. 1971. *The Development of Greek Biography.* Cambridge, Mass.

Mondi, Robert. 1983. "The Homeric Cyclops: Folktale, Tradition, and Theme." *Transactions of the American Philological Association* 113:17–38.

Monsacré, Hélène. 1984. *Les larmes d'Achille.* Paris.

Morris, Ian. 1986. "The Use and Abuse of Homer." *Classical Antiquity* 5:81–138.

Most, Glenn. 1989. "The Structure and Function of Odysseus' *Apologoi.*" *Transactions of the American Philological Association* 119:15–30.

Mueller, Martin. 1984. *The Iliad.* London.

Muellner, Leonard C. 1976. *The Meaning of Homeric EYXOMAI through Its Formulas.* Innsbrucker Beiträge zur Sprachwissenschaft 13. Innsbruck.

Murnaghan, Sheila. 1987. *Disguise and Recognition in the "Odyssey."* Princeton.

Nagy, Gregory. 1974. *Comparative Studies in Greek and Indic Meter.* Harvard Studies in Comparative Literature 33. Cambridge, Mass.

——. 1979. *The Best of the Achaeans.* Baltimore.

——. 1989. "Early Greek Views of Poets and Poetry." In George A. Kennedy, ed. *Cambridge History of Literary Criticism*. Vol. 1. Cambridge. 1–77.

——. 1990. *Pindar's Homer*. Baltimore.

Newton, Rick M. 1984. "The Rebirth of Odysseus." *Greek, Roman, and Byzantine Studies* 25:5–20.

——. 1987. "Odysseus and Hephaestus in the *Odyssey*." *Classical Journal* 83:12–20.

Olson, S. Douglas. 1989. "*Odyssey* 8: Guile, Force, and the Subversive Poetics of Desire." *Arethusa* 22:135–45.

Ong, Walter J. 1982. *Orality and Literacy*. London and New York.

O'Sullivan, James N. 1990. "Nature and Culture in the *Odyssey*." *Symbolae Osloenses* 55:7–17.

Page, D. L. 1955. *The Homeric Odyssey*. Oxford.

——, ed. 1962. *Poetae Melici Graeci*. Oxford.

——. 1973. *Folktales in Homer's "Odyssey."* Cambridge, Mass.

Pagliaro, Antonino. 1961. "Aedi e rapsodi." In *Saggi di critica semantica*. 2d ed. Messina-Florence. 3–62.

Pease, A. S. 1937. "Ölbaum." In *Real-Encyclopädie der classischen Altertumswissenschaft*. Vol. 34. 2020–22.

Peradotto, John. 1985. "Prophecy Degree Zero: Tiresias and the End of the Odyssey." In Bruno Gentili and Giuseppe Paioni, eds. *Oralità, Letteratura, Discorso: Atti del convegno internazionale*. Rome. 429–55.

——. 1990. *Man in the Middle Voice: Name and Narration in the "Odyssey."* Martin Classical Lectures, new series 1. Princeton.

Podlecki, A. J. 1961. "Guest Gifts and Nobodies in *Odyssey* 9." *Phoenix* 15:125–33.

Pollard, John. 1965. *Seers, Shrines, and Sirens*. New York and London.

Post, L. A. 1939. "The Moral Pattern in Homer." *Transactions of the American Philological Association* 70:158–90.

Pötscher, Walter. 1986. "Das Selbstverständis des Dichters in der Homerischen Poesie." *Literaturwissenschaftliches Jahrbuch*, Neue Folge, 27:9–22.

Pritchard, J. B., ed. 1955. *Ancient Near Eastern Texts Relating to the Old Testament*. 2d ed. Princeton.

Pucci, Pietro. 1977. *Hesiod and the Language of Poetry*. Baltimore.

——. 1979. "The Song of the Sirens." *Arethusa* 12:121–32.

——. 1982. "The Proem of the *Odyssey*." *Arethusa* 15:39–62.

——. 1987. *Odysseus Polutropos: Intertextual Readings in the "Odyssey" and "Iliad."* Cornell Studies in Classical Philology 46. Ithaca, N.Y.

Puelma, Mario. 1989. "Der Dichter und die Wahrheit in der griechischen Poetik von Homer bis Aristoteles." *Museum Helveticum* 46:65–100.

Raaflaub, Kurt. 1988. "Die Anfänge des politischen Denkens bei den Griechen." In Iring Fetscher and Herfried Münkler, eds. *Pipers Handbuch der Politischen Ideen*. Vol. 1. Munich and Zurich. 189–271.

Rawson, Claude. 1984. "Narrative and the Proscribed Act: Homer, Euripides, and the Literature of Cannibalism." In *Literary Theory and Criticism: Festschrift in Honor of René Wellek*. New York. 1159–87.

Redfield, James M. 1983. "The Economic Man." In Rubino and Shelmerdine, eds., 218–47.

Reinhardt, Karl. 1948. "Die Abenteuer der Odyssee." In *Von Werken und Formen*. Godesberg. 52–162.

Ritoók, Zs. 1975. "Stages in the Development of Greek Epic." *Antiqua Academiae Scientiarum Hungaricae* 23:127–40.

Roisman, Hanna M. 1990. "Eumaeus and Odysseus—Covert Recognition and Self-Revelation?" *Illinois Classical Studies* 15:215–38.

Rose, Gilbert P. 1969. "The Unfriendly Phaeacians." *Transactions of the American Philological Association* 100:387–406.

———. 1980. "The Swineherd and the Beggar." *Phoenix* 34:285–97.

Rose, Peter W. 1992. *Sons of the Gods, Children of Earth: Ideology and Literary Form in Ancient Greece*. Ithaca, N.Y.

Rubin, Nancy F., and William M. Sale. 1983. "Meleager and Odysseus: A Structural and Cultural Study of the Greek Hunting-Maturation Myth." *Arethusa* 16:137–71.

Rubino, Carl A., and Cynthia W. Shelmerdine, eds. 1983. *Approaches to Homer*. Austin, Tex.

Russo, Joseph A. 1982. "Interview and Aftermath: Dream, Fantasy, and Intuition in *Odyssey* 19 and 20." *American Journal of Philology* 103:4–18.

Russo, Joseph A., Manuel Fernández-Galiano, and Alfred Heubeck, eds. 1992. *A Commentary on Homer's "Odyssey."* Vol. 3, bks. 17–24. Oxford.

Russo, Joseph A., and Bennett Simon. 1968. "Homeric Psychology and the Oral Epic Tradition." *Journal of the History of Ideas* 29:483–98.

Rüter, Klaus. 1969. *Odysseeinterpretationen*, ed. K. Matthiessen. Hypomnemata 19. Göttingen.

Rutherford, R. B. 1986. "The Philosophy of the *Odyssey*." *Journal of Hellenic Studies* 106:145–62.

Saïd, Suzanne. 1977. "Les crimes des prétendants, la maison d'Ulysse, et les festins de l'*Odyssée*." In *Cahiers de l'Ecole Normale Supérieure*. 9–49.

Schadewaldt, Wolfgang. 1958. "Der Prolog der Odyssee." *Harvard Studies in Classical Philology* 63:15–32.

———. 1960. "Der Helioszorn in der *Odyssee*." In *Studi in onore di Luigi Castiglioni*. Vol. 2. Florence. 861–76.

———. 1965. "Die Gestalt des homerischen Sängers." In *Von Homers Welt und Werk*. 4th ed. Stuttgart. 54–87.

Schein, Seth L. 1970. "Odysseus and Polyphemus in the *Odyssey*." *Greek, Roman, and Byzantine Studies* 11:73–83.

Schmid, Wilhelm, and Otto Stählin, eds. 1929. *Geschichte der griechischen Literatur*. Vol. 1. Munich.

Schmitt, Rüdiger. 1967. *Dichtung und Dichtersprache in indogermanischer Zeit*. Wiesbaden.

———, ed. 1968. *Indogermanische Dichtersprache*. Wege der Forschung. Darmstadt.

Scott, J. A. 1939. "Odysseus and the Gifts from the Phaeacians." *Classical Journal* 34:102–3.

Scully, Stephen. 1981. "The Bard as Custodian of Homeric Society: *Odyssey* 3.263–72." *Quaderni Urbinati di Cultura Classica*, nuova serie, 8:67–83.

Seaford, Richard. 1989. "Homeric and Tragic Sacrifice." *Transactions of the American Philological Association* 119:87–95.

Segal, Charles. 1971. "Andromache's Anagnorisis: Formula and Artistry in *Iliad* 22.437–76." *Harvard Studies in Classical Philology* 75:33–57.

———. 1974. "Eros and Incantation: Sappho and Oral Poetry." *Arethusa* 8:139–60.

———. 1986. *Pindar's Mythmaking*. Princeton.

———. 1988. "Poetry, Performance, and Society in Early Greek Literature." *Lexis* 2:123–44.

———. 1988a. "Theater, Ritual, and Commemoration in Euripides' *Hippolytus*." *Ramus* 17:52–74.

———. 1989. "Song, Ritual, and Commemoration in Early Greek Poetry and Tragedy." *Oral Tradition* 4:330–59.

———. 1993. *Euripides and the Poetics of Sorrow: Art, Ritual, and Commemoration in "Alcestis," "Hippolytus," and "Hecuba."* Durham, N.C.

Seidensticker, Bernd. 1978. "Archilochus and Odysseus." *Greek, Roman, and Byzantine Studies* 19:5–22.

Sittig, Ernst. 1912. "Harpyien." *Real-Encyclopädie der classischen Altertumswissenschaft*. Vol. 14. 2417–31.

Slatkin, Laura. 1986. "The Wrath of Thetis." *Transactions of the American Philological Association* 116:1–24.

———. 1986a. "Genre and Generation in the *Odyssey*." *Metis* 1:259–68.

Snell, Bruno. 1953. *The Discovery of the Mind*. Trans. T. G. Rosenmeyer. Oxford.

Snell, Bruno, and Herwig Maehler, eds. 1975. *Pindari Carmina cum Fragmentis: Pars 2, Fragmenta*. Leipzig.

Snodgrass, Anthony. 1971. *The Dark Age of Greece*. Edinburgh.

———. 1980. *Archaic Greece: The Age of Experiment*. Berkeley and Los Angeles.

Stanford, W. B. 1952. "The Homeric Etymology of the Name Odysseus." *Classical Philology* 47:209–13.

———. 1954. *The Ulysses Theme*. Oxford.

———, ed. 1958–61. *The "Odyssey" of Homer*. 2d ed. 2 vols. London.

Stella, L. A. 1955. *Il poema d'Ulisse*. Florence.

Stewart, Douglas. 1976. *The Disguised Guest: Rank, Role, and Identity in the "Odyssey."* Lewisburg, Pa.

Svenbro, Jesper. 1976. *La parole et le marbre*. Lund.

Thalmann, William G. 1984. *Conventions of Form and Thought in Early Greek Epic Poetry*. Baltimore.

———. 1992. *The "Odyssey": Poem of Return*. New York.

Trahman, C. R. 1952. "Odysseus' Lies (*Odyssey* Books 13–19)." *Phoenix* 6:31–43.

Van Leeuwen, Jan, and M. B. Mendes da Costa, eds. 1897. *Homeri Odysseae Carmina*. Leiden.

Vernant, Jean-Pierre. 1959. "Aspects mythiques de la mémoire et du temps." In *Mythe et pensée chez les grecs*. 3d ed. 1974. 2 vols. Paris.

———. 1979. "Manger aux pays du Soleil." In Marcel Detienne and J.-P. Vernant, eds. *La cuisine du sacrifice en pays grec*. Paris. 239–49.

———. 1986. "Feminine Figures of Death in Greece." *Diacritics* 16, no. 2:54–64.

——. 1989. "De la psychologie historique à une anthropologie de la Grèce ancienne." *Metis* 4:305–14.

——. 1990. *Myth and Society* (1974). Trans. Janet Lloyd. New York.

Vidal-Naquet, Pierre. 1986. "Land and Sacrifice in the *Odyssey:* A Study of Religious and Mythical Meanings." In *The Black Hunter.* Trans. Andrew Szegedy-Maszak. Baltimore. 15–38. Originally published as "Valeurs religieuses et mythiques de la terre et du sacrifice dans l'*Odyssée.*" *Annales, E. S. C.* 25 (1970): 1278–97.

Walsh, George. 1984. *The Varieties of Enchantment: Early Greek Views of the Nature and Function of Poetry.* Chapel Hill, N.C.

Wankel, Hermann. 1983. "Alle Menschen müssen sterben: Variationen eines Topos der griechischen Literatur." *Hermes* 111:129–54.

Wegner, Max. 1968. *Musik und Tanz: Archaeologia Homerica.* Vol. 3, chap. U. Göttingen.

West, Martin L., ed. 1971, 1992. *Iambi et Elegi Graeci.* 2 vols. Oxford.

Westermann, Anton, ed. 1843. *Mythographoi.* Brunschwig.

Whitman, Cedric H. 1958. *Homer and the Heroic Tradition.* Cambridge, Mass.

——. 1970. "Hera's Anvils." *Harvard Studies in Classical Philology* 74: 37–42.

Wilamowitz-Moellendorff, Ulrich von. 1884. *Homerische Untersuchungen.* Philologische Untersuchungen 8. Berlin.

——. 1959. *Der Glaube der Hellenen* (1931). 3d ed. 2 Vols. Darmstadt.

Woodhouse, W. J. 1930. *The Composition of Homer's "Odyssey."* Oxford.

Woolsey, R. B. 1941. "Repeated Narratives in the *Odyssey.*" *Classical Philology* 36:167–81.

Wyatt, William F., Jr. 1989. "The Intermezzo of *Odyssey* 11 and the Poets Homer and Odysseus." *Studi Micenei ed Egeo-Anatolici* 27:235–53.

Zumthor, Paul. 1984. *La poésie et la voix dans la civilisation médiévale.* Paris.

Zwicker, Johannes. 1927. "Sirenen." In *Real-Encyclopädie der classischen Altertumswissenschaft.* 2 Reihe. Vol. 3, pt. 1. 288–301.

Index

Breinigsville, PA USA
05 November 2010
248704BV00001B/1/P